Organizational Justice in Mergers and Acquisitions

Nicholas Jackson

Organizational Justice in Mergers and Acquisitions

Antecedents and Outcomes

palgrave
macmillan

Nicholas Jackson
Leeds University Business School
Leeds, West Yorkshire, UK

ISBN 978-3-030-06477-8 ISBN 978-3-319-92636-0 (eBook)
https://doi.org/10.1007/978-3-319-92636-0

This Palgrave Macmillan imprint is published by the registered company Springer Nature Switzerland AG
The registered company address is: Gewerbestrasse 11, 6330 Cham, Switzerland

Preface

Fair treatment of employees in the workplace is a much-debated subject, and any arguments are often formed around a very subjective and tenuous context. Scholars studying in this field tend to have focused their attention on the conditions that influence both the antecedents and outcomes of perceived fairness (e.g. see Bies & Moag, 1986; Folger, 1993; Greenberg & Wiethoff, 2001). An element of this research stream has focused on the increasing employee uncertainty to emerge from organizational change, and its effect on their perceived justice (fairness) amid interest of how this transpires into behavioral and attitudinal outcomes. One such example of corporate change that is often radical and can have disrupting consequences for the employee is that of mergers and acquisition (M&A).

During a period of increasing globalization over the past four decades, M&A has seen a significant proliferation in popularity as a form of developmental growth strategy, encouraged, in part, by a desire for increased competitive efficiency. Exponential growth of M&A, by both value and number of deals, occurred during the late 1990s and, following a dip around the turn of the millennium due to the early financial recession, growth returned to a similar resurgent pattern until the financial crisis of 2008. Since then, perhaps with some reflection of a more cautious outlook, the number of deals has fluctuated, peaking in 2015 at just under 40,000 and dipping to just under 37,000 in 2016. As an indication of their upsurge in popularity, the number of global deals has increased from just fewer than 3000 in 1983, and by value from US$84.9 billion in the same year to over US$3000 billion in 2016 (Thomson One Banker, 2017). Many motives present a compelling case for this method of integration, including: (i) access to global markets, (ii) diversification, (iii) the opportunity to achieve operational efficiencies, (iv) the opportunity to innovate through new capabilities and resources, and (v) benefits from increasing stability of the external environment through control of a supplier or competitor (see, for example, Hitt & Pisano, 2004; Horwitz et al., 2002; Worley & Cummings, 2001). Achieving strategic objectives such as these may present the organization with an opportunity to strengthen its resources and competences, perhaps providing the competitive advantage pursued through this form of developmental growth strategy.

There would seem to be a compelling case for this method of integration, which has lucrative offerings for an organization when compared to alternative strategies, such as organic growth or configurations of organizational alliance. The obvious benefit is the ability to grow the organization with an almost immediate effect. This may be the case but even so, despite the considerable increase in M&A over the past four decades, it is also acknowledged that, in a persistently high percentage of cases over this period, there has been a failure for many organizations to achieve their preacquisition strategic objectives. While attempts at problem-solving have engaged with central issues such as financial performance and resistance to change, it is evident that there is still a black hole when it comes to developing best practice for those organizations undertaking the process of integration. A consistency of underachievement is endemic.

In part, this persistently high rate of missed opportunity has been caused by a failure to understand the complexities of managing people through the transition of change. A widespread claim is that over half of all M&A that fail to meet their strategic objectives of integration do so because of difficulties originating from the attempted combination of employees from the integrating organizations. Full integration should result in the emergence of a new organization that assimilates the working practices and policies of the old organizations and a transformation for employees from previous organizational identities to a new organizational identity that encompasses a shared cultural meaning. However, barriers are often created through employee resistance to these changes. Two commonly cited examples are the difficulties encountered with employees experiencing cultural change and a transitioning of their identities into the newly formed organization and its environments. In a situation where they are often powerless to stop the progress of change, employees who experience difficulties adapting to these transitions will use forms of resistance, which in turn will become a barrier to integration. All too often the response by authorities is to drive through the necessary integration of operational functions without the full support of employees. Identifying and understanding the reasons why individuals resist the change to a new organization is therefore important if they are to be encouraged to transfer their identities and embrace the developing shared meaning of the new organizational culture.

One of the recognized levers of employee change resistance is whether they feel the changes being undertaken in the workplace have been fairly applied. Organizational justice is the psychological concept of fairness as perceived by the employee and broadly recognized to consist of three key elements or dimensions: (i) the distributions or outcomes (distributive justice), (ii) the procedures by which those distributions are determined (procedural justice), and (iii) the communication of both the distributions and how these have been determined (interactional justice). With the wealth of supporting evidence outlining the strength of association between perceived justice and workplace attitudes and behaviors there is a compelling argument to deepen our understanding of this concept within the context of M&A. Whereas organizational culture and identity have been recognized for their critical influence in the process of developing employee attitudes in a merger context and a substantial theoretical framework already exists, the frameworks surrounding organizational justice in the M&A process are less well established. Within the context of M&A, more clarity is needed about the mechanisms of fairness as they are perceived through the lens of the employee in relation to their outcomes and how these are determined and communicated.

Developed from both an academic and a practitioner perspective, this book aims to provide new insights into a strategically important area for organizations. The case study material that is developed within has been drawn from actual events involving corporate mergers. Along with the depth of research from previous studies in the field of organizational justice, this will provide an opportunity for both scholars and practitioners alike to develop a deeper understanding about the dynamics of this concept within the climate of a merger or acquisition. Several studies have highlighted the lack of empirical evidence relating to the cognitive process of perceived justice during and after a merger or acquisition. The focus for developing this text has, in part, been responsive toward the need to advance knowledge in this field and make use of an opportunity to bring together the different strands of research with newly developed material.

The text has been developed to improve clarity of understanding about the relationship between organizational justice and employee outcomes from the specific change process of a merger or acquisition. Other than a shortfall in current research, the requirement to further develop this area of study is based on concerns that perceived fairness in the workplace has potential to influence important attitudes and behaviors, such as job satisfaction, organizational citizenship behavior, and employee commitment to the organization.

The theoretical concepts and frameworks discussed in this book are considered in light of the author's own study conducted in two organizations that were able to share their own firsthand experiences of an organizational merger. One of the organizations was an established provider of higher education in the UK and the other formed from the outcome of a hospital trust merger. The study investigates the dynamics of perceived fairness within the specific change mechanisms of an organizational merger and considers the antecedents and outcomes of such a phenomenon. The use of a mixed methods design encompassed four separate phases, three of which were conducted within the recently merged university business school. In the first phase, a survey revealed that, when compared to social identity and organizational culture, perceived justice was a factor of greater importance in the employee evaluation process. Phase 2 consisted of a series of 25 staff interviews identifying and exploring the antecedents of organizational justice. In Phase 3, a second survey was introduced to test the significance of the key relationships to emerge from

Phase 2. The NHS Trust merger provided the setting for Phase 4 of the study where the second survey, initially introduced during Phase 3, was administered among 386 employees. It was established from this study that the main antecedents of organizational justice evolved from ineffective communication mechanisms, a distrust of authorities, and the merger procedures they implemented. The outcome of these perceived injustices was a belief that there had been a breach of psychological contract. The effect on behavioral and attitudinal outcomes from these perceived injustices was lower organizational citizenship behavior, lower affective commitment, and an increase in the intention to leave the organization in the near future.

With consideration to the reasons already discussed, the text was prompted by three specific and fundamentally decisive factors. First, it is evident that although a large body of knowledge has been developed through existing research within the broad context of organizational behavior in M&A, there is only a rudimentary understanding of how the process and the employees captured within it are affected by the concept of organizational justice. Second, it is evident that many of those organizations that set out on the journey of M&A with an idealistic perspective of their aims and integration objectives fail to understand the true cost of employee resistance and the factors that are most likely to encourage this. Organizational justice, its antecedents, and its outcomes may currently have a low profile but has a big impact. The opportunity to develop this text and draw from the cases included within has provided scope for a practical contribution, and I hope that practitioners will find this useful. Finally, an interest in the area derived from practical experience provides a context for the author's initial approach to the subject of M&A.

In developing this text there are a few people I feel the need to acknowledge for their various contributions, without which the book would remain incomplete. First, I would like to thank Gail Clarkson and Chris Allinson for their time and patience in supervising me as a PhD candidate at the University of Leeds. The text has been developed around ideas and outcomes from my PhD, and the support and guidance both Gail and Chris offered during this period was fundamental. I would like to thank both Liz and Lucy and the rest of the editorial team at Palgrave

Macmillan for their help and support while writing this text, particularly Lucy for keeping me on track with the timing of my submissions. Finally, I would like to thank my wife, Helen, for the patience, support, and interest she has demonstrated throughout the period. For this, I will be eternally grateful. I dedicate this book to Helen and my family.

Leeds, UK Nicholas Jackson

Contents

List of Figures

List of Tables

Part I

Mergers and Acquisitions

1

Introduction

1.1 Emerging Patterns and Trends

The popularity of mergers and acquisitions (M&A) as a development strategy has increased significantly over the past 25 years, due in part to an ongoing pressure for organizations and companies to continuously renew and change themselves in an attempt to remain competitive and innovative. When considering opportunities for growth, Johnson, Scholes, and Whittington (2011) define three forms of developmental strategy for organizations: internal development, acquisition, and alliances. In comparison to other developmental growth strategies, Horwitz et al. (2002) recognize that M&A can offer an enticing range of competitive advantages that organic growth cannot achieve. They cite as major advantages the acquisition of new capabilities and resources in addition to the potentially unrivaled opportunity for costcutting. Furthermore, they provide greater control than the alternative options of licensing or forming alliances (King, Dalton, Daily, & Covin, 2004). It is therefore recognized that this form of integration has potential to offer several benefits for organizations and when compared to alternative strategies, such as organic growth or an alliance, the ability to grow the organization with an almost immediate effect.

N. Jackson, *Organizational Justice in Mergers and Acquisitions*,
https://doi.org/10.1007/978-3-319-92636-0_1

If we consider merger trends over recent times, both the number of deals and financial value show the growth pattern which corresponds with a period of increasing economic globalization and significant rises in foreign direct investment. Within this context of globalization and subsequent intensification of competitiveness, M&A became the dominant mode of firm growth in the 1980s and 1990s for both European and U.S. firms (see Capron, 2004; Berggren, 2003; Hayward, 2002). In part recognition of this, there is a considerable body of research that examines M&A and their consequences. As Fig. 1.1 shows, there was a substantial increase during the period 1998–2000 and then an equally rapid decline during the years 2001–2003. This coincides with a period of considerable economic expansion and subsequent contraction in global markets and corporate valuations. The incline continued again in 2004 until 2007 when, due to the global financial crisis in the following year, there was a severe decline in corporate valuations. It is noticeable that even so, after an initial decline, the number of deals has continued in strength.

These periods of increased activity are not uncommon in M&A and are often referred to as "merger waves." Typically, a cyclical pattern emerges beginning with an intense period of activity and tailing off

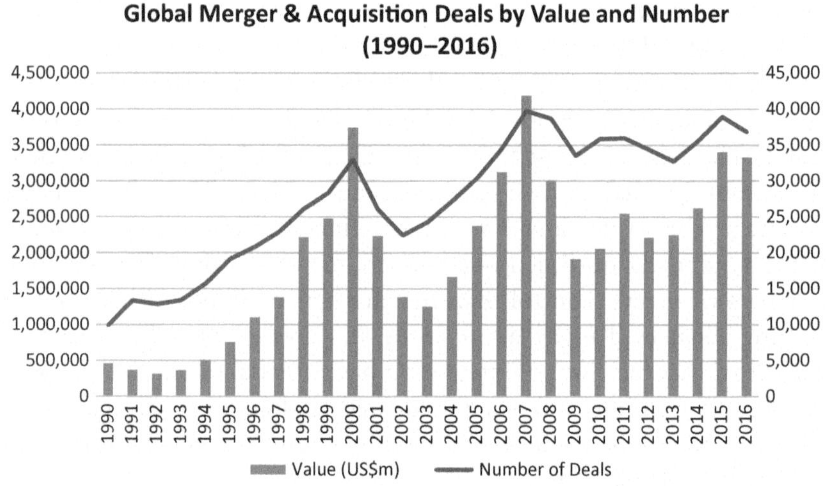

Fig. 1.1 Global merger and acquisition deals. (Note: Based on data presented by Thomson One Banker (2017))

eventually with much quieter and leaner spells in the intervening years. Going back to review activity from the early part of the twentieth century, there have been six merger waves recognized within the United States (globally acknowledged as trendsetters over this period). These consist of the periods 1893–1904, 1916–1929, 1965–1969, 1981–1989, plus the periods 1992–2000 and 2003–2007 (Vazirani, 2015), the latter two aligning with those periods presented in Fig. 1.1 and depicted as global M&A deals. Of interest are the most recent periods, identified as the age of the strategic mega-merger (1992–2000) and a period of intense corporate leverage (2003–2007). These two periods recorded incredible growth and culminated in unprecedented levels of merger activity by deal value and number of deals concluded (Vazirani, 2015).

Connecting with the interest M&A has received over these periods there has been a notable increase in the volume of research undertaken by both academics and practitioners encouraged in part, no doubt, by the wealth of interest in the effectiveness of integration compared to other forms of corporate expansion strategy. Often being the conduit for radical forms of change, M&A brings with it several challenges for organizations. While the data in Fig. 1.1 illustrate the considerable increase in the popularity of M&A, there is often a price to pay for the route to expansion that they offer. Even though these statistics bear out the fact that strategically they are often the preferred route for growing organizations, there are further data raising awareness to underachievement, underperformance, and stakeholder dissatisfaction. While research attempting to diagnose these issues has grown in abundance over this period, it is only of more recent times that attention has turned to the role of human behavior.

What many contributors to this topic often avoid doing with any clarity is defining what is meant by "failure" in terms of a merger or acquisition. When defining failure, we need to consider that it isn't necessarily referring to wholesale abandonment of the project but may be more reflective of the failure to achieve the strategic objectives that were outlined in the premerger prospectus. Researchers of M&A tend to dispute the key underlying causes of the failure (in whatever format) and tend to highlight both hard and soft factors, with little commonality of purpose. From a much broader perspective, it is evident there are several factors that are attributable to most of the failure rates, including paying the wrong price, buying at the wrong time, selecting the wrong partner, and buying for the wrong reasons. However, these tend to be easy opt-outs. For example, how do you define the wrong price if the deal turns into a massive success? It is only the wrong price if the merger isn't perceived as having achieved its objectives and therefore deemed to be a failure. However, upon closer scrutiny this may be for a variety of reasons including a failure to integrate staff and/or systems effectively, poor leadership, and failure to make available those with the necessary skills sets. Further analysis may then begin to get to the root-cause (i.e. what were the barriers impeding staff integration, what was needed from leaders, where were those with the necessary skill-sets, and why were they not readily available and in place at the right time?).

1.2 Methods, Typologies, and Objectives of Integration

The strategic direction of integration and the method of approach taken by either the merging entities or acquiring organization can also be categorized depending upon several criteria. These will have an important influence because the subtleties of each case will provide the employee with contrasting perceptions of the integration and have an influence on how they evaluate the changes being implemented. A relevant example is the power differential (acquirer relative to target) between the organizations involved, which may define whether the integration is deemed a merger or acquisition, as the former will consist of entities that are similar in size. The dispersal of power across the entities has also been recognized as a major influence on perceived equity and justice (Halvorsen, 1984) because of its effect on the decision-making process (Haspeslagh & Jemison, 1991; Mirvis, 1985; Olie, 1994). This potential domination effect may be significant toward how the new organization is developed as the dominating partner will have more opportunities to influence the structure and design (van Knippenberg, D., van Knippenberg, B., Monden, & de Lima, 2002).

1.2.1 Integration Method

Table 1.1 depicts the four recognized methods of integration and their characteristics including an acknowledgment of whether an acquisition is deemed to be either *hostile* or *friendly*. The difference between these two acquisition typologies is that a hostile bid is attempted without the approval of the target organization's board and a direct approach is made by the potential acquirer to the target organization's shareholders. A friendly bid will be offered to the target shareholders by the potential acquirer with the approval of their board. If these are considered in their extreme forms, then the contrast between the two is stark. For example, in a friendly acquisition with a low level of integration it is much more likely that the acquired organization will retain its own identity and most of its decision-making autonomy (Citera & Rentsch, 1993). However, in an environment of hostile acquisition with a high level of integration this is unlikely to be the case.

While the relative size of the integrating organizations may have significant influence, according to van Knippenberg et al. (2002) the difference between an actual merger and an acquisition is primarily, in practice, a legal matter. Even though during a merger the notion of equality is acknowledged, there will be a dominant partner due to their size,

Table 1.1 Forms of organizational integration

Method of integration	Characteristics
Merger	Entities are usually of a similar size. Transaction will consist of an exchange of shares with little or no cash
Acquisition	Friendly: Deal goes to shareholder vote *with* board of directors' approval (an agreed bid) Hostile: Deal goes to shareholder vote *without* board of directors' approval (a hostile bid)
Proxy contest	Attempt to gain control of target company's board of directors via a shareholder vote
Leveraged buyout	A purchase of shareholder equity by a group, often including incumbent management, and financed by debt, venture capital, or both

Note: Based on material presented in "*Acquisition strategy and implementation,*" by N. Hubbard, 2001. Basingstoke, UK: Palgrave profitability, power, and influence or even perhaps their viability in comparison to their intended partner (Rentsch & Schneider, 1991). In fact, it is acknowledged that, from a psychological perspective at least, most mergers are takeovers (Cartwright & Cooper, 1992). This led Hubbard & Purcell (2001) to avoid using the term "merger," and instead during research they used the term "acquisition" rather than "merger":

> Since the latter presupposes a marriage of equals which very rarely happens, even if the acquiring company's top management assert that this will be the case. Indeed, this promise may be the first act of many in setting up expectations which are subsequently not met. (p. 18)

From these inferences it is reasonable to accept that there will be a dominant partner in most cases and it may be prudent to measure relative dominance on a spectrum from minimal to extreme rather than presume there is a case of true equality.

It should also be noted that not only size of organization but power, influence, and even viability may determine which partner holds the dominating position in the relationship. It is also asserted that status may be an influencing factor. For instance, employees from the lower-status organization in a merger, or target organization in an acquisition, may feel the most threatened by the event (Terry & O'Brien, 2001). A typical impact of this situation would be that those employees then have a lower propensity to adapt and adjust to the merger (Terry, 2003). The resulting attitudinal and behavioral responses from employees of the lower-status or target organization are more likely to be negative than employees from a higher-status or acquiring organization (Covin, Kolenko, Sightler, & Tudor, 1997; Terry & O'Brien, 2001). For example, there may well be feelings of worthlessness and inferiority due to further loss of autonomy and status (Schweiger, Ivancevich, & Power, 1987). Hence, there is the challenge to overcome such negative affective reactions from this group of employees, reactions that positively influence behavioral resistance to change (Kavanagh & Ashkanasy, 2006). A common occurrence in mergers is for leaders to feel it is a simple process of needing to change the culture of the merging organizations to change the behavior of the respective employees. Such mind-sets exemplify the arguments pertaining to weak leadership and/or a leader's misreading of the situation. This is a consequence of failure by those at the helm to understand what motivates followers to change their behavior and the far more intricate processes involved. Subsequently, a result is often the resistance alluded to earlier.

1.2.2 Integration Typologies

According to Cartwright and Cooper (1992), there are four main strategic options for merging or acquiring organizations consisting of vertical, horizontal, conglomerate, and concentric integration. These are presented in Table 1.2.

An example of a vertical integration would be a customer acquiring or merging with a supplier or, indeed, the supplier acquiring the customer. The common requirement is that both organizations are from the same industry. A horizontal merger or acquisition is performed by two or more organizations at the same process level and from the same industry. This form tends to lead to the deepest level of integration, which may have consequences for the employee as processes are often duplicated. Both conglomerate and concentric integration generally involve organizations in less familiar fields and therefore a lower level of integration is often experienced.

The past 50 years has witnessed a radical change in the motives and objectives of integrating organizations. During the 1960s merger boom,

Table 1.2 Types of integration

Type of integration	Characteristics
Vertical	Two organizations from successive processes within the same industry
Horizontal	Two similar organizations in the same industry.
Conglomerate	Organizations in a completely unrelated field of business activity (e.g. footwear specialist acquiring a toy manufacturer)
Concentric	Organizations in an unfamiliar but related field (e.g. a brewer acquiring a snack foods manufacturer)

Note: Based on material presented in "*Mergers and acquisitions: The human factor,*" by S. Cartwright & C.L. Cooper, 1992. Oxford, UK: Butterworth-Heinmann Ltd.

the scale and geographical spread of integration was more constrained in comparison to the liberated and globalized markets organizations operate in today. During this earlier period most combinations were of a conglomerate type, whereas the merger booms in the 1980s, 1990s, and of more recent times have seen an increasing number of horizontal integrations involving partnerships of organizations from the same field of business (Cartwright & Cooper, 1995).

Unsurprisingly, acquisitions formed within a related area of industry tend to perform better and with more success than those originating from an unrelated area (e.g. see Cartwright & Cooper, 1992). This is largely due to the potential economic advantages generated by those organizations (e.g. economies of scale), but also other factors that are essential, such as an enhanced ability to transfer product knowledge and expertise. This trend toward the joining of related entities provides opportunity for deeper systems and human integration, and their success has subsequently become increasingly more dependent on wide-scale integration of their systems, procedures, practices, and cultures (Cartwright & Cooper, 1995). It may be the case that where an organization's primary objective includes creating efficiencies, employee reactions are less of an initial concern to them. Consequently, this may have very different repercussions from the employee's point of view (Hubbard & Purcell, 2001). There needs to be greater awareness of the important role that people play in the process of synergy realization following a merger. A problem with delivering synergies has been recognized in cross-border deals, in part, due to cultural and other human resource problems. A substantial number of merger failures can be traced to neglected human resource issues. These are classified by Schweiger et al. (1987), who suggest that how an individual perceives the effect of a merger and how it is managed will relate to its impact on the individual themselves. They propose that an individual will perceive their lot from one of the following scenarios:

- Irrelevant appraisal will lead to the individual being unaffected.
- Positive appraisal will create challenging opportunities for the individual.
- Negative appraisal will cause the individual to feel threatened and often to suffer harm or damage.

Where the integration is not identified as horizontal, an aim to take over the core competences of the acquired organization may be a key objective of the acquiring organization's senior management. Normally, in the case of a vertical, conglomerate, or concentric acquisition (see Table 1.2), there will be potential diversities within the integrating organizations' product or service market. In these cases, there may well be a renewed sense of purpose for the need to retain staff competences, due to their potential specialist and unique abilities, which could be paramount to successful implementation of acquisition objectives. This is not to diminish the role of the employee within a horizontally related acquisition because, for example, the target may have been acquired in respect of their superior experience, or their particular expertise in research and development. But in a situation of increasing dependence upon the target organization's capacity to offer unique capabilities, and perhaps the possession of superior core competences that are vital to the processes of that industry, the importance of retention and commitment of those key staff who can offer these will be vital (Johnson et al., 2011).

1.2.3 Strategic Objectives

Acquisitions, mergers, and change have been an ongoing part of the operational strategy of many organizations for years and have proven to be a significant and popular means for achieving corporate diversity, growth, and rationalization (Cartwright & Cooper, 1992). This strategy could provide the flexibility for organizations to grow quickly and meet objectives such as these which may be central to them being able to compete at an advantage.

Reviewing the list of possible primary motives or objectives for M&A presented in Table 1.3, it becomes evident that in many cases achieving these will be dependent on the retention of those employees who will remain an important factor in the formation of effective merger strategy. This will be especially the case for those who require specific market or technological expertise, and perhaps where they can make an important contribution from any tacit knowledge of the employee. On this basis, particularly where integration is deep and the changes to structure may be

Table 1.3 Motives for acquisitions and mergers

Motive	Characteristic
Adapting to a dynamic external environment	Offers the speed with which it allows the company to enter new product or market areas, particularly in a rapidly changing external environment
Access to new markets	Acquisition overcomes the creation of excess capacity and therefore the risk of competitive reaction is reduced
Increase market share Industry rationalization	Acquirer may seek competitor's order book to gain market share, or may seek industry rationalization by closing down their capacity
Deregulation of markets	Deregulation has been a major driving force behind merger and acquisition activity in many industries (e.g. utility companies)
Financial motives	For example, target company has a low price/earnings ratio, asset stripping, and so on
Acquisition of resources and competences	For example, R&D expertise, knowledge of production system, business processes, or market needs; international developments (market knowledge etc.)
Cost efficiencies/ rationalization	For example, target company further down experience curve and achieved efficiencies which would be difficult to match quickly by internal development; rationalization to cut out duplication or gain scale advantages
Expansion	Acquisitions may be a quick way to deliver growth but can also be destructive (e.g. "parent" does not have sufficient feel for acquired businesses and, accidentally, destroys value (diversification))
Stakeholder pressure	Stakeholder disparities—short- vs. long-term growth strategies

Note: Based on material presented in "*Exploring strategy* (9th ed.)," by G. Johnson, K. Scholes, & R. Whittington 2011. Harlow, UK: Prentice Hall

radical, potential employee contribution could seal their fate within the new organization, determining where or whether they are retained within the new structure. Where there is a duplication of skills and abilities and their specific contribution is limited, uncertainty for the employee is likely to proliferate. An example would be a horizontal form of integration which raises opportunities to take advantage from increased economies of scale and scope. It is often the case in these forms of M&A for a consolidation of processes to become one of the primary objectives. Consequently, the value of individuals within the new organization, and the scale of any adjustment they will endure, may be a decisive factor in shaping their attitudes toward the change. An extreme situation that might exemplify low levels of concern about the potential fallout from human integration would be where the prime objective is asset stripping or industry rationalization through the elimination of a competitor.

Of course, there has already been reference to the loss of personnel and the likely impact this may have on organizational effectiveness from a routine, day-to-day perspective and meeting the mid- to long-term objectives set from the merger. One area of concern with acquisitions is the loss of expertise through attrition of the strategy makers—the senior management. As is often the case, executives have embedded knowledge of their firm and, in addition to other critical contexts, such as industry experience and important relationships they may have developed with external stakeholders, this form of tacit knowledge is difficult to replicate quickly. Indeed, a widely held belief supports the notion that retaining executives in the acquired firm is a crucial aspect of any successful integration strategy (Krug, Wright, & Kroll, 2015).

However, retaining the acquired organization's senior managers in situ because of their previous experience is also deemed to offer potential limitations. These are the individuals who have previously had responsibility for the decision-making process, and if the organization is being acquired because it has underperformed then questions must be raised about those decision-makers who were responsible for past performance and underachievement. There are also a multitude of arguments that recognize that the change in process offers the opportunity for transformation and a chance to sweep clean the dusty corridors of recent times. In addition to the argument against retaining underachievers and poor decision-makers there are others that consider that these individuals may also be protagonists of resistance during and after the merger. Value is often created by the removal of such people at the top of an organization who are committed to their own goals, which may not align with those being pursued by the new organization. Situational factors will normally be critical here. This view is supported by agency theory, which purports that the failure of boards to correct poor functioning will lead to predator companies bidding for the rights to take them on and improve performance. This perspective was predominant during the early 1990s and for more than

25 years had been the dominant view of acquisitions providing justification for those supporting the removal of executives and a higher-than-normal attrition rate from the acquired organizations (Krug et al., 2015). Even so, executive turnover is generally recorded as high in organizations that have both good and bad performance records. This indicates that the acquirer's main interest is purely because the target will have something the acquirer values and that a high attrition rate for executives cannot simply be explained by aligning with poor performance.

Alternatively, an organization wishing to diversify, or perhaps enter a new product or geographic market, may be reliant upon retaining specialist knowledge, particularly within the target organization. Similarly, even within a related field, a target organization with greater experience or superior expertise in research and development may provide opportunities for an acquirer looking to progress within that field. Such core competences and unique capabilities of the existing workforce may be the prime motive behind the acquisition and provide the opportunity to achieve such objectives. The recognition of human resource as a core competence and its role in enabling the realization of strategic capabilities from a newly- integrated organization is, in part, due to a rapid increase in globalization and new technologies (Neef, 1999; Sullivan, 2000). Retaining this resource and maximizing its potential to sustain an achieved competitive advantage is then the challenge for integrating organizations.

Bresman, Birkinshaw, and Nobel (1999) acknowledge organizations that gain a competitive advantage over their rivals are doing so increasingly by "innovative recombination of knowledge" (p. 439). They maintain that this is often the key reason for acquisition. Galpin and Herndon (2007) discuss the importance of retaining knowledge during integration and the crucial role that this will play in overcoming mistakes made in the past. It is evident that for some acquiring organizations there is a premium value in resource acquisition, especially the unique resources that may be (i) vital to the acquirer if entering a new market (Barney, 1991) and (ii) the main target of the acquirer to enhance their current range of resources, provide core competences and, ultimately, to provide sustainable competitive advantage (Hitt & Pisano, 2004). Attaining knowledge may bring long-term benefits and revitalize the acquiring organization, encouraging its long-term survival. It may be the case however that there is no further capacity to take on new skills, an issue referred to by Cohen and Levinthal (1990) as the capability of *absorptive capacity*.

However, much of this information about potential synergies is unknown at the time of premerger, where a great deal of uncertainty still exists. It is often the case at this early stage for integrating partners to hire investment banks to collect vital information about potential gains, even though there is a lack of clarity about how much of this private information leads to an informed position about merger gains. Caution prevails because early stage enquiries will often not transform into a full-blown merger or acquisition, and if the companies decide in the end not to integrate they could draw on this information at some later stage to their own advantage when trading independently. Taking this into account, even though some information is readily available and accessible to both firms at an early stage, there is much more that remains private.

1.3 Common Features of Failure and Success

While the list of motives for M&A illustrated in Table 1.3 is certainly not exhaustive, it highlights the more common reasons that motivate the need to merge or acquire, and many of these are drawn by either the urgency for rapid expansion of the business or the objective of increasing efficiencies. For example, a dynamic and fluid external environment may not allow for time to expand or increase competencies organically or for the potential restrictions of an alliance with another organization. This is a very similar proposition for organizations wishing to access new markets, increase market share, or take advantage of a need to rationalize resources. Often, satisfying stakeholder pressure for short-term gain may be a key objective that drives the integration. Brueller, Carmelli, and Drori (2014) label the type of relatedness between the integrating partners as either *bolt-on acquisitions* (companies seeking either a product or market extension in a related field) or *new platform acquisitions* (interests in a new business space or activity).

1.3.1 The Negative Legacy

M&A provides the opportunity to speedily accomplish these aspirations. Although perhaps haste is of some significance to why over half of acquisitions fail to meet the objectives of the parties involved (Hubbard, 2001). This claim was also alluded to by Capron (1999) who stated that 50% of domestic acquisitions and 70% of cross-border deals fail to produce intended results. These claims are extended by Marks and Mirvis (2001) who state that three out of four M&A fail to meet their financial and strategic objectives, statistics that changed little over several decades of M&A. During the early 1970s, and based on managers' self-reports, failure rates of 46–50% were reported (Kitching, 1974), compared to studies by Rostand (1994) and Schoenberg (2006) reporting failure rates of 44–45%; figures that substantiate earlier claims (Hunt, Lees, Grumbar, & Vivian, 1987; Ravenscraft & Scherer, 1987). In a study of 540 organizations, only about one-third of the chief executive officers of acquiring companies were satisfied with the results (Erez-Rein, Erez, & Maital, 2004). Johnson et al. (2011) add that following an acquisition, shareholder returns of both organizations are lower than they were preintegration in as many as 70% of cases. Perhaps consistent with Wishard's (1985) early estimate that two hours of productivity per employee are lost per day during the early stages of a merger. These facts tend to lend support to the notion that in most cases M&A do not seem to lead to higher performance (Agarwal & Jaffe, 2000; King et al., 2004).

Tuch and O'Sullivan (2007) add, "In the short-run, acquisitions have at best an insignificant impact on shareholder wealth …. Long-run performance analysis reveals overwhelmingly negative returns" (p. 141). They purport that the most successful performers (or least negative) are the acquisition of hostile targets, those paid for in cash and acquisitions of larger targets. Previous empirical studies confirm findings that targets of hostile takeovers do not underperform targets of friendly acquisitions (Franks & Mayer, 1996; Kini, Kracaw, & Mian, 2004). This may not be surprising if, as is often reported, most hostile takeover targets have previously underperformed; their capacity for improvement from a low base may be reason for this.

1.3.2 Timing Is Everything

Successful integration may also be affected by other selection issues such as organizational reputation, performance, and timing of acquisition (Larsson, Brousseau, Driver, & Sweet, 2004). For instance, if a target for acquisition is a high performer, it is likely to cost the acquirer more. The acquirer may also encounter greater resistance from the workforce and management because they are more likely to have developed a high regard for both their own and their organization's potential. Conversely, staff from poor-performing organizations may welcome the opportunity to become part of a more successful regime. This may be particularly pertinent where employees hold the incumbent management responsible for the downturn and a change in leadership is perceived as a renaissance to revitalize the organization. It is acknowledged that takeover strategy is often motivated by a belief that the acquiring firm's management can manage the target's resources better (Gaughan, 2011).

The price paid by the acquirer may reflect the problems currently being encountered by the target organization, in which case any turnaround will be a relatively straightforward introduction of the acquirer's expertise or availability of new funding. Similarly, timing judgment of macroeconomic forces can be a contributor toward success or failure to meet target objectives. For instance, Larsson et al. (2004) comment: "Evidence suggests that corporate combinations made in late recessions have the advantages of lower prices, less organizational integration overload, and less employee resistance compared to those made during boom periods" (p. 16). It should be noted that in such cases the likelihood of all-round support and complicity of both workforce and management is considerably enhanced. Not all M&A are viewed as a threat, but in some cases as a potential opportunity. A prime example of an organization deploying a successful acquisition growth strategy is Cisco Systems, who, between 1990 and 2000, realized annual earnings per share growth of 59% and an annual average total return to investors of 73.4%. As established by Erez-Rein et al. (2004), Cisco achieved this rapid growth "using consummate skill in acquiring companies with the knowledge and human resources it needed" (p. 21).

1.3.3 The Acquisition of Knowledge and Capabilities

Considering evidence of this nature, it appears that there is scope for organizations to succeed in meeting their objectives from this form of integration. There are also success stories, and it is these that acquiring or merging organizations intend to aspire to. Because of the significant problems often encountered, it is too easy to dwell on the negative aspects of M&A and forget that they can also add value and can create significant opportunities for both organization and individual alike to fulfill unmet needs (Marks & Cutcliffe, 1988). There is an opportunity to learn new knowledge and capabilities (Barkema, Bell, & Pennings, 1996; Barkema & Vermeulen, 1998), and this is an example of how acquisitions can "revitalize acquiring firms and thereby foster their long-term survival" (Hitt & Pisano, 2004, p. 47).

The utilization of both tacit and explicit knowledge within an organization is an illustration of how effective the event of new corporate partnerships can be in this process of revitalization. Repeated use of an organization's knowledge base may lead toward a tendency to become rigid and narrow (Miller, 1993), but corporate acquisitions tend to revitalize the acquiring firm and encourage their long-term survival. A combination of existing forms of knowledge can encourage new knowledge to evolve (Kogut & Zander, 1992). When, over time, an alternative response is required, such rigidity means they will have little scope to adapt to new circumstances, and this may ultimately impinge on their very survival (Hannan & Freeman, 1984); a phenomenon Levitt and March (1988) called the *competency trap*. Vermeulen and Barkema (2001) continue this argument by asserting that acquisitions can "revitalize a firm and enhance its ability to react adequately to changing circumstances" (p. 458). Their argument proposes that cultural clashes and tensions arising at implementation are at least partly, if not fully, compensated by breaking the acquiring firm's rigidities and enhancing their knowledge bases. Potentially, this may not be true in an unrelated acquisition because mechanisms are not in place to absorb the new knowledge, therefore affecting the acquiring firm's ability to absorb new practices (Cohen & Levinthal, 1990; Lane & Lubatkin, 1998).

The next chapter investigates some of the key challenges faced by organizations and the factors they need to consider when moving people through the cycle of change instigated by the process of M&A.

References

Agarwal, A., & Jaffe, J. F. (2000). The post-merger performance puzzle. In C. Cooper & A. Gregory (Eds.), *Advances in mergers and acquisitions* (Vol. 1, pp. 7–14). New York: Elsevier Science.

Barkema, H. G., Bell, J. H. J., & Pennings, J. M. (1996). Foreign entry, cultural barriers and learning. *Strategic Management Journal, 17*, 151–166.

Barkema, H. G., & Vermeulen, F. (1998). International expansion through start-up or acquisition: A learning perspective. *Academy of Management Journal, 41*, 7–26.

Barney, J. B. (1991). Firm resources and sustained competitive advantage. *Journal of Management, 17*, 99–120.

Berggren, C. (2003). Mergers, MNES and innovation—The need for new research approaches. *Scandinavian Journal of Management, 19*, 173–193.

Bresman, H., Birkinshaw, J., & Nobel, R. (1999). Knowledge transfer in international acquisitions. *Journal of International Business Studies, 30*, 439–462.

Brueller, N. N., Carmeli, A., & Drori, I. (2014). How do different types of mergers and acquisitions facilitate strategic agility. *California Management Review, 56*(3), 39–57.

Capron, L. (1999). The long-term performance of horizontal acquisitions. *Strategic Management Journal, 20*, 987–1018.

Capron, L. (2004). The long-term performance of horizontal acquisitions. *Strategic Management Journal, 20*, 987–1018.

Cartwright, S., & Cooper, C. L. (1992). *Mergers and acquisitions: The human factor*. Oxford, UK: Butterworth-Heinmann Ltd.

Cartwright, S., & Cooper, C. L. (1995). Organizational marriage: "hard" versus "soft" issues? *Personnel Review, 24*(3), 32–43.

Citera, M., & Rentsch, J. R. (1993). Is there justice in organizational acquisitions? The role of distributive and procedural fairness in corporate acquisitions. In R. Cropanzano (Ed.), *Justice in the workplace: Approaching fairness in human resource management* (pp. 211–230). Hilsdale, NJ: Erlbaum.

Cohen, W. M., & Levinthal, D. A. (1990). Absorptive capacity: A new perspective on learning and innovation. *Administrative Science Quarterly, 35*, 128–152.

Covin, T., Kolenko, T. A., Sightler, K. W., & Tudor, R. K. (1997). Leadership style and post-merger satisfaction. *The Journal of Management Development, 16*(1), 22–34.

Erez-Rein, N., Erez, M., & Maital, S. (2004). Mind the gap: Key success factors in cross-border acquisitions. In A. L. Pablo & M. Javidan (Eds.), *Mergers and acquisitions: Creating integrative knowledge*. Oxford, UK: Blackwell Publishing.

Franks, J. R., & Mayer, C. (1996). Hostile takeovers and correction of managerial failure. *Journal of Financial Economics, 40*, 163–181.

Galpin, T. J., & Herndon, M. (2007). *The complete guide to mergers and acquisitions: Process tools to support M&A integration at every level* (2nd ed.). San Francisco: Jossey-Bass.

Gaughan, P. A. (2011). *Mergers, acquisitions, and corporate restructurings* (5th ed.). Hoboken, NJ: Wiley.

Halvorsen, K. (1984). Mergers creating inequalities. *Journal for Contemporary Research, 25*, 389–414.

Hannan, M. T., & Freeman, J. (1984). Structural inertia and organizational change. *American Sociological Review, 49*, 149–164.

Haspeslagh, P., & Jemison, D. B. (1991). *Managing acquisitions: Creating value through corporate renewal*. New York: Free Press.

Hayward, M. L. A. (2002). When do firms learn from their acquisitions experience? Evidence from 1990–1995. *Strategic Management Journal, 23*, 21–39.

Hitt, M., & Pisano, V. (2004). Cross-border mergers and acquisitions: Challenges and opportunities. In A. L. Pablo & M. Javidan (Eds.), *Mergers and acquisitions: Creating integrative knowledge*. Oxford, UK: Blackwell Publishing.

Horwitz, F. M., Anderssen, K., Bezuidenhout, A., Cohen, S., Kirsten, F., Mosoeunyane, K., et al. (2002). Due diligence neglected: Managing human resources and organizational culture in mergers and acquisitions. *South African Journal of Business Management, 33*(1), 1–10.

Hubbard, N. (2001). *Acquisition strategy and implementation*. Basingstoke, UK: Palgrave.

Hubbard, N., & Purcell, J. (2001). Managing employee expectations during acquisitions. *Human Resource Management Journal, 11*(2), 17–33.

Hunt, J. W., Lees, S., Grumbar, J., & Vivian, P. D. (1987). *Acquisitions: The human factor*. London: London Business School/Egon Zehnder International.

Johnson, G., Scholes, K., & Whittington, R. (2011). *Exploring strategy: Text & cases* (9th ed.). Harlow, UK: Prentice Hall.

Kavanagh, M. H., & Ashkanasy, N. M. (2006). The impact of leadership and change management strategy on organizational culture and individual acceptance of change during a merger. *British Journal of Management, 17*(March Suppl), S81–S103.

King, D. R., Dalton, D. R., Daily, C. M., & Covin, J. G. (2004). Meta-analyses of post-acquisition performance: Indications of unidentified moderators. *Strategic Management Journal, 25*, 187–200.

Kini, O., Kracaw, W., & Mian, S. (2004). The nature of discipline by corporate takeovers. *Journal of Finance, 59*, 1511–1552.

Kitching, J. (1974). Winning and losing with European acquisitions. *Harvard Business Review, 52*(2), 124–136.

Kogut, B., & Zander, U. (1992). Knowledge of the firm, combinative capabilities, and the replication of technology. *Organization Science, 3*, 388–397.

Krug, J. A., Wright, P., & Kroll, M. J. (2015). Top management turnover following mergers & acquisitions: Solid research to date but still much to be learned. *The Academy of Management Perspectives, 3015*(1), 30–46.

Lane, P. J., & Lubatkin, M. (1998). Relative absorptive capacity and interorganizational learning. *Strategic Management Journal, 19*, 461–478.

Larsson, R., Brousseau, K. R., Driver, M. J., & Sweet, P. L. (2004). The secrets of merger and acquisition success: A co-competence and motivational approach to synergy realization. In A. L. Pablo & M. Javidan (Eds.), *Mergers and acquisitions: Creating integrative knowledge*. Oxford, UK: Blackwell Publishing.

Levitt, B., & March, J. G. (1988). Organizational learning. In W. R. Scott (Ed.), *Annual review of sociology* (Vol. 14, pp. 319–340). Palo Alto, CA: Annual Reviews.

Marks, M. L., & Cutcliffe, J. G. (1988). Making mergers work. *Training and Development Journal, 42*(4), 30–36.

Marks, M. L., & Mirvis, P. H. (2001). Making mergers and acquisitions work: Strategic and psychological preparation. *Academy of Management Executive, 15*, 80–92.

Miller, D. (1993). The architecture of simplicity. *Academy of Management Review, 18*, 116–138.

Mirvis, P. H. (1985). Negotiations after the sale: The roots and ramifications of conflict in an acquisition. *Journal of Occupational Behavior, 6*(1), 65–84.

Neef, D. (1999). Making the case for knowledge management: The bigger picture. *Management Decision, 37*(1), 72–85.

Olie, R. (1994). Shades of culture and institutions in international mergers. *Organization Studies, 15*, 381–405.

Ravenscraft, D., & Scherer, F. M. (1987). *Mergers, sell-offs and economic efficiency*. Washington, DC: Brookings Institution.
Rentsch, J. R., & Schneider, B. (1991). Expectations for postcombination organizational life: A study of responses to merger and acquisition scenarios. *Journal of Applied Social Psychology, 21*, 233–252.
Rostand, A. (1994). *Optimizing managerial decisions during the acquisition integration process*. Paper presented to 14th Annual Strategic Management Society International Conference, Paris.
Schoenberg, R. (2006). Measuring the performance of corporate acquisitions: An empirical comparison of alternative metrics. *British Journal of Management, 17*, 361–370.
Schweiger, D. M., Ivancevich, J. M., & Power, F. R. (1987). Executive actions for managing human resources before and after acquisitions. *Academy of Management Executive, 1*, 127–137.
Sullivan, D. P. (2000). Cultural cognition in international business research. *Management International Review, 40*, 269–298.
Terry, D. J. (2003). Social identity and diversity in organizations. *Asia Pacific Journal of Human Resources, 41*, 25–35.
Terry, D. J., & O'Brien, A. T. (2001). Status, legitimacy, and ingroup bias in the context of an organizational merger. *Group Processes and Intergroup Relations, 4*, 271–289.
Thomson One Banker. (2017). *M&A Financial Advisory Q4 2016* [online]. Retrieved October 20, 2017, from http://www.banker.thomsonib.com
Tuch, C., & O'Sullivan, N. (2007). The impact of acquisitions on firm performance: A review of the evidence. *International Journal of Management Reviews, 9*(2), 141–170.
van Knippenberg, D., van Knippenberg, B., Monden, L., & de Lima, F. (2002). Organizational identification after a merger: A social identity perspective. *British Journal of Social Psychology, 41*, 233–252.
Vazirani, N. (2015). A literature review on mergers and acquisitions waves and theories. *SIES Journal of Management, 11*(1), 3–9.
Vermeulen, F., & Barkema, H. G. (2001). Learning through acquisitions. *Academy of Management Journal, 44*, 457–476.
Wishard, B. J. (1985). Merger human dimension. *The Magazine Bank Administration, 61*(6), 74–79.

2

Human Influence

2.1 Behavior Management

The potential for merger success is often exacerbated by factors working against it, including attrition of key managers, conflict, and struggles for power by those who remain, resulting in a general lethargy toward commitment, loyalty, and satisfaction at all levels (Piekkari, Vaara, Tienari, & Santii, 2005). According to Mirvis (1985), a common feature of mergers and acquisitions (M&A) is for employees to experience a phenomenon the two scholars recognize as *merger syndrome*. This is where there is a tendency for increased self-interest, as employees become preoccupied with what the integration means for themselves, their incomes, and their careers. Organization members begin to develop a sense of loss as they enter the merger that is reminiscent of the phases experienced of losing a loved one. This is often treated as a personal crisis, which may manifest itself as listlessness, apathy, a preoccupation with the past, lack of commitment to the new culture, fear, and/or active resistance to the new system (Cartwright & Cooper, 1992; Marks & Mirvis, 1998). There is little surprise that this leads on to a display of negative attitudes and behaviors, which could be realized through decreased job satisfaction, organizational commitment, loyalty, and productivity. Inevitably, outcomes may include

N. Jackson, *Organizational Justice in Mergers and Acquisitions*,
https://doi.org/10.1007/978-3-319-92636-0_2

an impact on the quality of work produced, leading to an increase in defective products, mistakes, and withdrawal behaviors.

Forces within the organization social system will automatically use resistance in their attempt to neutralize any efforts toward implementing change strategies (Kavanagh & Ashkanasy, 2006). For example, the significant impact from merging cultures is often one of the major obstacles to the successful integration of organizations, and therefore a clear understanding of the day-to-day functioning of its operators is vital. Schein (1992) refers to organizational culture being underpinned by deep assumptions that are patterned and shared and the influence this has upon how change occurs. A changing of minds as well as behavior needs to be invoked as part of the corporate plan designed around the merger, and leaders will need to engage in considered planning of such fundamental soft issues. If leaders do not understand how to motivate behavior change, this will result in the increased likelihood of resistance to the very proposal of change (Valikangas & Okumara, 1997).

There is recognition that effective management during a merger has a significant impact on ensuring that the organization is implementing the change in accordance with their plan, hence reducing the levels of ambiguity and stressfulness associated with the merger. Because of their inherent links with change, mergers have been associated with other stressful life events that provoke feelings of tension and anxieties through loss and stress (Cartwright, Tytherleigh, & Robertson, 2007). It is accepted that because of the wholesale nature of change, its speed of impact, and the subsequent uncertainties that evolve, being part of a merger can be a particularly stressful activity (Amiot, Terry, Jimmieson, & Callan, 2006). Consider, for example, the complexity of managing the multilevel stakeholder relationships involved at implementation, which will be context-specific and case-specific. Among other factors of influence, the characteristics of such relationships will be dependent on the level of diversification, the M&A type being performed, the level of integration (specific to degree of overlap between merging entities), and the strategic fit and geographical scope of the merging entities (Parvinen & Tikkanen, 2007).

2.1.1 The Role of Communication

Even though there are expectations of change, employees will still be searching for some clarity regarding a direction from their leaders and early closure after the announcement of merger (Tetenbaum, 1999). The relationship between managers and their employees becomes more critical during times of instability, regarding anxieties about job security, role stability, and social support (Marks & Mirvis, 1998; Rousseau, 2001). The priorities of leaders during this period of change need to be the conveyance of a clear vision about the nature and destiny of the merged organization. Of consideration here will be the level of attentiveness toward the concerns of employees, and one of the most critical factors will be the clarity of communication. Throughout the process there needs to be clear information that informs members how the change will be managed and honest communication of how this will impact their environment, at least in the short- to medium- term. This will be an important item to manage if interpersonal relationship concerns, such as trust, can be protected or developed. Uncertainty surrounding reporting lines and changes to organization structure, particularly how these will affect routes and patterns of communication, should be prominent concerns for managers during these times. One of the priorities of change leaders at this stage should be quality communication with employees at all levels, particularly in relation to the crucial role they play in disseminating information to the lower levels of the organization. Making those connections is imperative to maintain and, indeed, enhance the leader-member relationship, and trust will play a big part in this. Indeed, employee trust (discussed at length in Chap. 8) is affected by the quality of communication at key points throughout the change process, but also before and after the change has been announced and implemented. This will affect the state of employee relations, which is also paramount to the development of trusting relationships between employees and the management (Nikandrou, Papalexandris, & Dimitris, 2000).

Regular communication is essential if leaders are to demonstrate a level of control and show that objectives are being implemented as proposed. If these messages are communicated openly and without hesitation from the outset, then they will not only keep organization members informed as developments occur, but they encourage an atmosphere where they are more likely to regard the adjustment period as less traumatic (Appelbaum, Gandell, Shapiro, Belisle, & Hoeven, 2000). Clear and continuous communication means that employees can develop a sense of prediction about future events that will help them cultivate a deeper understanding of why such action is necessary at all. It is one of the key functions for the leaders of change to ensure mechanisms are in place to disseminate information among its workforce (Richardson & Denton, 1996). The evidence suggests that reporting at key stages of the process is fundamental if feelings of uncertainty associated with the situation are to be reduced and employees feel less threatened, as this encourages stability through enhanced predictability. It is not necessarily the change per se that is the cause of such grief and anxiety, but the uncertainty connected with the perceived change to routines.

2.1.2 Frontline Managers

The role of the middle manager is a primary function that is complex and exacerbated by an impending conflict of interest. As reported by Bligh and Carsten (2005), a potentially conflictual role for managers during times of organization restructuring (e.g. organizational mergers) is highlighted by the multifaceted nature of the psychological contract. The acceptance of varying expectations, in part dependent on the challenges of the role between the different levels of an organization's hierarchical structure, will offer a better chance for developing more nuanced solutions to dealing with the fallout rather than those applied through perceiving this as a unidimensional, one-size-fits-all situation. The diversity of relationships and contractual obligations will impact expectations on a more multilevel scale. This situation presents a janus model of manager who on the one hand has a duty to their seniors while at the same time needs to be seen on the side of the employee or subordinate. Managers hold multiple contracts with various members of the organization and how they prioritize these multifoci relationships in the new postmerger era is important. This is particularly so because of a recognition that understanding organizational change is critically influenced by our awareness of the impact from employee psychological contracts (Bligh & Carsten, 2005; Hubbard & Purcell, 2001). This multifaceted role of the frontline managers (FLMs) or supervisors will mean they are obligated on two fronts, needing to form and maintain contracts mutually as agents of the organization from one perspective and employees on the other. If all three levels are working cogently and coherently, then this task is simplified. However, if mistrust of senior personnel is developed by those at lower levels in the organization, then the task of those responsible for implementing change strategies becomes more problematic. A need to juggle conflicting priorities can lead to a risk of losing any trust developed in the relationship with their subordinates.

Among the complexities of this relationship are the judgments made by those same managers to make important decisions, such as the amount, timing, and quality of the information they disseminate. In relation to the quality, the level of detail and accuracy will be a key concern for them when they must absorb, interpret, and consider the implications arising from the volume of information they are given from senior ranks and others in the position of articulating the strategy and outcomes from change. Employees may depend on the relationship with their immediate supervisor to interpret the change (i.e. gain knowledge and understanding of the change), its consequences, and its impact on their environment. These relationships, which rely on the basic tenets of social exchange theory, are critical to the way change is perceived and whether it will be accepted or, ultimately, resisted. It is therefore evident that the role of the middle manager or change agent is an exceptional one that is likely to play a pivotal role in determining outcomes, such as the level of resistance demonstrated by the workforce or, indeed, more change-friendly behaviors. In a merger situation, FLMs will play a key role in trying to persuade their workforce that any perceived expectations they developed throughout the merger process have been adhered to, and where this is not the case, legitimation of this is offered through reasoned evidence. This legitimate reasoning is of primary importance where events begin to move offtrack and perceived promises are not being met. Involvement of the workforce through periods of change has been found to temper feelings where it is perceived that expectations are not being met (e.g. see Shield, Thorpe, & Nelson, 2002). Indeed, their study found support for the influential role of the manager and that managers who used what was perceived to be honest, believable, and fair communication were successful in reducing employee concerns about job instability. Empowerment and job enrichment during restructuring has also been found to positively affect the employee, maintaining trust and loyalty to the organization through such times (Niehoff, Moorman, Blackley, & Fuller, 2001). On a more negative tone, decreased satisfaction and commitment to the organization have both been identified as the result of incompetent management during the restructuring exercise (Pate, Martin, & Staines, 2000).

Prolonged delays pertaining to the process of integration raise the prospect of eroding morale and extending the uncertainty, which can also be exacerbated by other factors, such as organizational size and the complexity and nature of the change that is required (Horwitz et al., 2002). For example, as opposed to domestic partnerships, consider the additional challenges posed by cross-border alliances where there is the complexity associated with multilevel integration of cultures at both national and organizational level. This is recognized by Barkema, Bell, and Pennings (1996) as "double-layered acculturation," deepening and extending the layers of consciousness, extending the barriers to change, and subsequent resistance by organizational members. The challenge of effective interorganizational communication may be exacerbated by additional diversity factors such as those of a linguistic and cultural nature taking the goal of establishing shared assumptions and values to another level.

The significance on this scale of planning to manage employees through the process is essential to note because mergers are often associated with high turnover and reductions in innovation (Hitt, Hoskisson, Ireland, & Harrison, 1991). Historically, there has been a lack of attention received from behavioral issues in the postmerger implementation process, and it is only in more recent times that important relationships between human behavior and performance have been critically assessed. The integration of companies often involves turning the lives of people inside out, and this affects them not only in material ways, but also beyond the auspices of the paycheck and the basic issue of job security. Essentially, mergers are often dramatic events of reform that upset the organizational lives of people within.

2.2 Employee Reactions

The discussion so far has largely focused on how the dynamic forces of integration may lead to feelings of negativity in the employee and its subsequent effect on behavior within the organization. Cartwright and Schoenberg (2006) refer to the "emotional and behavioural response of the employees involved" (p. S3) and discuss previous research that highlights underperformance because of the "cumulative dysfunctional impact that the event itself, its associated uncertainty and the subsequent process of integration have on individual organizational members." In a study of senior managers transiting through a takeover of their own organizations, Vince (2006) identified several common-factor emotional reactions including shame, powerlessness, and purposelessness. Such emotional reactions can only encourage attrition of senior members who see loss of managerial authority as a violation of their psychological contracts with the organization. This at a time when developing a shared sense of purpose that permeates throughout and across both organizations is critical to retaining core staff members who will be key to rebuilding organizational capabilities (Horwitz et al., 2002).

In addition to managing morale, encouraging key players to remain onside and gaining their support for new initiatives is essential for building a successful new organization. The reaction of members can vary considerably and will be dependent on a series of factors, including their personality type and ability to cope with stress. The uncertainty and insecurity spreads fear and stress and these are prone to exaggeration while others may perceive such events as a challenge or an opportunity for personal improvement. Coping strategies during a merger are bound with attempts to manage the change affecting their work and employment relationships. This relates to how people cope with change in relation to the attitudes and behaviors they develop, particularly in situations where there have been announcements leading to uncertainties, such as layoffs or restructuring.

The response outlined earlier will, in part, have been encouraged by members' self-belief, which has its origins in the theory of self-efficacy. Evidence here suggests that those who are more capable of engaging with a high value of the self will also demonstrate a greater preparedness for change and are more likely to display tendencies of being able to adjust toward their new context, avoiding disillusionment and feelings of betrayal relating to expectations of their new deal. Along with a notion that the change is less likely to have made an impact on the terms of their employment relationship, self-efficacy in relation to coping with changes is linked with job satisfaction, reducing the significance of any intentions to leave and decreased work irritation. With the issue of resistance to change in its various workplace formats, these are desirable behaviors and attitudes to try and develop. As already discussed, inherent to the development of psychological coping in these situations is the quality and level of communication directed by those managers responsible for designing and implementing the change. Once again, emphasizing how critical the quality of communication will be during these periods.

Disruption to employee security and routines can often be identified as an instigator to resistance of post-M&A integration plans and the amount of quality information shared with employees during this period will impact these processes. As Yoo, Lyytinen, and Heo (2007) recognize, merger activity is renowned for disrupting the usual knowledge sharing processes that are enjoyed on an intra- and interorganization basis. Skepticism among employees is often related to perceived information withheld by managers in relation to possible restructuring plans, particularly in the target company where there is little incentive for those with responsibility to reveal rationalization plans, given the likelihood of lay-offs among staff (Conyon, Girma, Thompson, & Wright, 2001, 2002). A systems view of knowledge sharing proposes that this will take place at differing levels in the organization; on the one hand between managers and on the other between employees (Nonaka, 1994). Any reconfigurations or rationalization planning will essentially be confined to a level of management within the organization unless specific channels of communication are installed to develop this on more explicit terms.

However, there is a need to understand the nature of interaction that will develop not only between the different levels of hierarchy during a merger (if indeed they take place at all), but also with stakeholders external to the organization. These are exacerbated in a merger due to the potential impact the disruption will have on communication systems, disrupting the flow of knowledge and information sharing across multilevels on an inter- and intra-organization basis. Equally, at both inter- and intra-organization level, knowledge and information sharing will be reliant on the quality of relationship building, which will be dependent on the development of trust in those interactions. Where managers are central to postintegration restructuring and rationalization plans, there is more likely to be mistrust within the manager-employee relationship. An immediate threat evolves from the prospects of downsizing, which may be perceived as having a greater impact on operatives rather than those managers involved in the planning process. In these circumstances, a combination of being more "at risk" and tending to be more risk averse will increase the potential for employees to resist change (Vaara, 2002).

Nonetheless, it also needs to be stressed that integration can provide the openings and opportunities to prosper and change for the better. Clarke and Salleh (2011) identify the need to understand change resulting from the context of a merger rather than merely focusing on how to manage its outcomes. Perhaps a more optimistic perspective of surviving change is necessary. For example, taking a view that identifies the motivators and aspirations of those who have successfully managed the process should become the focus, as opposed to addressing the perspective of how to avoid resistance. For example, Huy (2002) recognizes that while employees seek out predictable and dependable relationships that lead to consistency in behavior and ways of thinking, they are also, simultaneously, seeking out opportunities for new stimulation and personal development. Once again, this emphasizes a point that the dynamic forces of change in the context of integration can reinvigorate the relationship between organization and employee, reinforcing the intrinsic values that motivate and encourage productive behaviors. This may be particularly pertinent in a working environment that has become uncertain and dysfunctional due to poor leadership and ambiguous objectives. In these circumstances, change may offer the opportunity to move on from previous failings.

2.3 Influential Factors

Factors particular to a situation of transformational change can be identified for their influence as catalysts in the relationship with employee attitudes and behaviors and their potential to prompt reactions. Two of the most influential forces both recognized and discussed within the framework of M&A are organizational culture and identity (e.g. see Badrtalei & Bates, 2007; Horwitz et al., 2002; Teerikangas & Very, 2006; Ullrich, Wieseke, & van Dick, 2005; van Knippenberg, D., van Knippenberg, B., Monden, & de Lima, 2002; van Leeuwen, van Knippenberg, & Ellemers, 2003). Two other factors that form a prominent role in these discussions are organizational justice and the psychological contract (PC) (e.g. Bellou, 2007; Bligh & Carsten, 2005; Klendauer & Deller, 2009; Restubog, Bordia, & Bordia, 2009). All four factors are considered in greater depth with an emphasis on the role they play in the formation of employee behavior and attitudes at individual and group level.

2.3.1 Culture

Research in the field provides us with some insight toward how individuals respond to conditions that arise from an integration of varying cultures (Hofstede, 2001) including an effect on levels of experienced uncertainty and any subsequent impact on their emotional reaction (Sorrentino et al., 2008). Drawing on these considerations it is clear that strategy-makers who are developing change on this level need to be aware of human barriers that may well emerge from an incorporation of cultures. The depth of integration will increase levels of uncertainty and a uniting of cultures in such circumstances is likely to influence pockets of resistance and a 'them-and-us' attitude across both organizations. Where there is a duplication of systems and technical skills then there is more opportunity for efficiencies to be a central target of the merger, provoking an environment that is rife with suspicion and uncertainty. These considerations become less of a concern for strategy-makers where a more autocratic approach to integration may be taken. Examples include significant disparities in the comparative size or status between the acquirer and the acquired. Where this differential of power exists, there is more scope for the acquirer to impose their own policies and operational procedures at speed. It may also be more appropriate where the merged entity needs to quickly embed integrated processes (e.g. the organization operates within a dynamic external environment where a more laboured approach to integration would jeopardize a successful outcome). In comparison, this approach is unlikely to be effective where there is a merger of equals, in consideration of both organization size and their premerger status.

2.3.2 Identity

In relation to the previous section, it is worth noting that the intensity of in-group loyalty and its influence on a collectivistic culture may have severe implications for the move toward a unified culture across the employees of both organizations. A strong in-group mentality has the potential to encourage the persistence of a subgroup temperament and has been found to undermine the goals of collaboration and cooperation across the newly-formed teams and departments (Clarke & Salleh, 2011). Those organizational members who can demonstrate a stronger sense of organizational identification tend to experience more pro-social attitudes in the workplace, such as organizational citizenship behavior, and lower levels of conflict, leading to higher levels of motivation and job satisfaction (Van Dick, Ullrich, & Tissington, 2006). These are critical factors upon which either the success or failure of the integration will be dependent. In these circumstances, faith and religious beliefs should not be underestimated also for their impact. The transfer of an individual's identity from the old organization to a newly-integrated organization will therefore influence the level of resistance to culture change, and, subsequently, this will have important implications toward any support for new initiatives.

The process of identity after a merger is complex, and if we consult the social identity theory (SIT) literature there are some very specific nuances that need to be considered in the situation where organizations are attempting to integrate their workforces. Where there are two or more groups, bias toward the in-group is often prevalent (intergroup bias), but this is not necessarily due to anti-out-group behavior. The majority of perceived in-group bias is more akin to pro-in-group behavior. However, this situation changes where there are perceived status differences between groups. In these circumstances, status can be defined as the general prestige in which a group is held, and SIT theory recognizes that those who perceive that they belong to two distinct groups (e.g. via the process of M&A) will be affected by the mechanisms of in-group bias and intergroup discrimination (Tajfel & Turner, 1979; Turner, Hogg, Oakes, Reicher, & Wetherell, 1987). The combining of two or more organizations (e.g. joint venture and M&A) orchestrates a unique set of circumstances where such intergroup status differences become accentuated.

The emphasis on in-groups and out-groups has a foundation in social categorization theory, which is an antecedent of perceived status differences between groups and a common cause of intergroup conflict (Haunschild, Moreland, & Murrell, 1994). Under conditions where intergroup status differences exist, typically intra-group conflict for the high-status group is low, and these individuals are more likely to find a seamless and low-stress process of integrating and identifying with the newly-formed organization (Amiot, Terry, & Callan, 2007). For this group, there is a better chance of successful integration into postmerger structures. For the low-status group, there is often a common perception that the merger process was unfair, and the integration and identification process for these individuals is more of a strain and more likely to lead to resistance to change. Where status leads to the problems of intergroup conflict, difficulties arise in situations of joint-brand M&A (i.e. where the distinction between two or more brands originating from the premerger organizational status is retained) because there is a tendency for perceptions of any difference between intergroup status to continue unchallenged, leading to further conflict and the development of a "them-and-us" attitude.

This intergroup discrimination and favoring of one's own social group is much more likely for those from the high-status group. There is little perceived benefit from leaving their own group and joining forces with the out-group, and indeed there will be benefits from preserving their positive social identity by discriminating against or excluding those from the low-status group. Conversely, those from the low-status group may hold aspirations to join with those from the high-status group and take advantage of entering a new relationship that offers to provide members with positive social identification (Terry, Carey, & Callan, 2001). These perceptions of low social identification with their premerger group may be a new development for those employees due to their new circumstances.

To combat this reduced status identification, those individuals will either attempt to disassociate from their original group (and affirm their identity to the new group) or collectively act to enhance the status of their pre-merger group (Tajfel & Turner, 1979). However, due to feelings of loyalty toward their own group, or any barriers to joining the high-status group, there may be an increased prospect for those individuals to resist the change and demonstrate withdrawal behaviors.

2.3.3 Organizational Justice

While culture and identity are recognized as having a major influence on the process of individuals perceiving and reacting to change, a third component, organizational justice, is also discussed. Recognized also in some earlier literatures as relative deprivation theory (see Lee, Kim, Kim, Kwon, & Cho, 2013; Tropp & Wright, 1999; Walker & Pettigrew, 1984), typical antecedents upon which fairness will be judged include impeding potential progressions in career path (Larsson, Driver Holmqvist, & Sweet, 2001), unwelcome job changes or transfers (Buunk & Janssen, 1992), and adverse changes to the reward or incentive systems (Citera & Rentsch, 1993). This judgment about whether there has been a transgression of fair dealing will involve a process of comparison that encapsulates the enactment of reflection encountered when considering the fairness of an outcome or distribution (distributive justice). Dependent on evaluating a ratio of contributions made and rewards received (Adams, 1965), the process of determining distributive justice will be compared to other similar points of reference. This "referent other" may relate to several similar criteria, including (i) another person (ii), a generalized other (e.g. an occupational group), (iii) comparison to own previous input/output ratios, and (iv) input/output ratio specified for the situation (Adams, 1965). Therefore, in a merger situation it is likely that employees will perceive their circumstances as unfair if they consider their own position to be disadvantaged in comparison to others going through the change. The sincerity of those responsible for designing and implementing the change processes involved in a merger will be scrutinized and evaluated by organizational members for the degree that their own interests are being considered.

Hubbard and Purcell (2001) acknowledge that during the change implementation process, properly managed employee expectations will lead to less employee uncertainty and ambiguity. They assert:

> If, however, there is a mismatch in expectations, and employee perceptions of trust in management and the 'fairness of the deal' are thwarted, the outcome can be expected to be undesirable for both the individual's sense of well-being and organizational performance. (p. 18)

Here there is deemed to be a relationship between employee commitment to the organization, perceptions of trust in management, and fairness of outcomes from the decision-making process. There is also reference to the relationship between an employee's perception of fairness, its affect upon the employee, and recognition that this may influence organizational performance. However, if it can be shown that the procedures and processes employed to determine an outcome are genuinely fair, even if those outcomes are undesirable to the employee, then this action is likely to moderate the impact of negative reactions (Thornhill & Saunders, 2003). This method of building trust in the relationship and increasing the probability of employees accepting the outcomes, even when those outcomes are adverse, has been termed the *fair-process effect* (Folger & Cropanzano, 1998; Folger, Rosenfield, Grove, & Cochran, 1979).

According to Serpa, in a merger there is an ethical challenge to ensure that all employees are treated equitably within the new organization. Serpa (1988) maintains, "Without equity, the chances of success for the new corporation are markedly reduced since the more qualified employees may not be retained" (p. 359). This links neatly to the incidence of high turnover in M&A, which has long been acknowledged (see Cartwright & Cooper, 1993; Lipponen, Olkkonen, & Moilanen, 2004). This is one of the key outcomes of generating a potentially unstable environment, leading to uncertainty and a subsequent lowering of commitment toward the organization (Galpin & Herndon, 2007). A study in the United States revealed senior executive turnover rates of almost 50% within the first year of the deal and rising to almost 75% by the end of three years (Unger, 1986), statistics confirmed in further studies (see Krug & Hegarty, 1997). Taking these statistics into account it is hardly surprising that so many collaborations fail to meet their targets, considering that often one of the primary objectives of contemporary acquisition strategy is to benefit from the knowledge and skill being acquired.

The evidence is clear that individuals will develop withdrawal strategies if they experience inequitable outcomes and will more readily accept change if they perceive their own treatment as being just and fair (Cordery, Sevastos, Mueller, & Parker, 1993; Kirkman, Shapiro, Novelli, & Brett, 1996; Konovsky & Cropanzano, 1991). Group cohesion is assisted by a perception of fair distribution of rewards, which also contributes toward cooperation to reduce situations of conflict (Deutsch, 1985; Lind & Tyler, 1988; Sitkin & Bies, 1993). In addition, it has been found that individuals are more likely to engage in *organizational citizenship behaviors* (Moorman, 1991), an employee act of unrewarded extra-role behavior. It is also acknowledged that organizational citizenship behavior is influenced by *procedural justice* (perceived fairness in the process of setting procedures) with perceived organizational support acting as a mediating variable (Kaufman, Stamper, & Tesluk, 2001; Moorman, Blakeley, & Niehoff, 1998; Rhoades & Eisenberger, 2002). Such actions may be particularly favorable during integration when achieving primary objectives will be dependent upon maximizing cooperation from the workforce.

The discussion referred to earlier and led by Hubbard and Purcell (2001) relating to expectations of trust in management and employee perceptions of fairness in the process is an example of their PC with the organization. The significance of this relationship is discussed in more detail.

2.3.4 Psychological Contract

A PC emerges when one party believes that a promise of future returns has been made, a contribution has been given, and, therefore, an obligation to provide future benefits has been created (Rousseau, 1989). It is based on the specific job, exists purely between the company and its employee (Robinson, 1996), and includes expectation of what is the employee's role, and the behavior that is expected and rewarded in fulfilling that role (Hubbard, 2001). This framework has been advanced to distinguish between two types of contract: (i) *transactional*, which is based on the principles of economic exchange (e.g. pay and benefits), and (ii) *relational*, which is based on the principles of social exchange and more akin to facets of the job such as communication and social support. The transactional contract, based on the economic exchange relationship, is relatively short-term in contrast to the relational contract, which is more long-term (Bligh & Carsten, 2005). Typically, the transactional contract is held by employees who have temporary contracts and few commitments to the organization, whereas the relational contract is inextricably bound in organizational loyalty and support.

It has been reported that employees will periodically tend to reassess their PC relationship with the organization and consider any changes that have taken place (Rousseau & McLean Parks, 1993). In a case of organizational restructuring it has been proposed that the existing PC is replaced by a new one (Baruch & Hind, 1999), and similarly in the event of a merger the initial contract formation ceases to exist (Bellou, 2007). There is evidence that from the perspective of the employee a simple termination and replacement of the PC is rather more difficult in practice and that a more complex relationship will endure. For instance, change will alter the contract (Morrison, 1994), so during the change process typically encountered in an M&A employees will be vigilant to ensure that there is no breach of the organization's expected contribution. The new expectations are not created through pronouncements of what is expected from future exchanges; it is rather the case that employees seem to detect changes in the new setting and make comparisons with the previous ones (Louis, 1980).

Breach and Its Outcomes

PC breach takes place when one party in a relationship perceives that the other party has neglected to fulfill what has been committed or promised (Rousseau, 1995). By their nature they are enveloped within the social and economic exchange relationships experienced between the employee and organization, whereby it is expected that contributions from one party will be reciprocated with the other party providing some contribution in return. Therefore, the norms of reciprocity (Gouldner, 1960) are particularly relevant to this relationship. Possible impacts on the individual and organization of perceived contract breach have been identified as having potentially negative consequences on organizational outcomes. For instance, significant relationships have been found with job performance and citizenship behavior (Restubog & Bordia, 2006; Restubog, Bordia, & Tang, 2006; Robinson & Morrison, 1995; Turnley, Bolino, Lester, & Bloodgood, 2003) and important workplace attitudes such as commitment, satisfaction, and turnover intentions (Kickul & Lester, 2001; Restubog & Bordia, 2006; Restubog et al., 2006; Turnley & Feldman, 1999).

Cartwright and Cooper (1992) add that the period following a merger announcement or rumor is one of personal risk analysis and self-appraisal when the employee will decide whether they wish to form another contract with their new employer. Alternatively, they may decide that they do not wish to form part of the new organization and leave the company altogether. These situations are likely to be moderated by factors such as alternative employment prospects, financial considerations, social support, and the effect of demographic variables (i.e. age, education, geographical mobility, etc.). Again, consistent communication is important during these stages of the merger or acquisition process if employee uncertainty is to be addressed.

As the period of integration begins, employees are often expected to become familiar with a new setting, accept its principles and values, and adjust their attitudes and behavior accordingly (Chao, O'Leary-Kelly, Wolf, Klein, & Gardner, 1994). This need for them to enter a process resembling organizational socialization often aggravates employee uncertainties (Schweiger & DeNisi, 1991). Hubbard (2001) discusses renegotiation of the PC needing two main elements: trust (depending heavily on trust that neither party will take advantage of the other) and effective communication. The new PC will be developed out of the new socialization process, which is more likely if there has been a smooth route of implementation supported by effective two-way communication for the individual. The study by Schweiger and DeNisi similarly emphasizes the importance of honest and direct communication with employees following a merger. Because of their disruptive nature, mergers tend to have a negative impact on employees, and how they cope with the changing organizational environment will be directly affected by the effectiveness of the organizational communication. In this, senior managers will play an important role.

2.4 Justice and Its Relationships with Culture, Identity, and the Psychological Contract

A change of culture following a merger or acquisition need not carry the negative connotations this often presents and, indeed, may be a desirable outcome for the organization, particularly in a situation of high-level integration. Artifacts and symbols such as the company name and logo can have a psychological impact on how individuals in the acquired organization perceive fairness (Citera & Rentsch, 1993). Importantly, such apparently trivial matters can play a significant part in forging expectations of future decision outcomes. Similarly, in hostile takeovers acquired employees are more likely to form a defense of their organization, and become invested in its preservation. As this occurs, their identification with the cultural symbols of the old organization will remain strong at a time when management will be attempting to transfer their identity to the newly-integrated organization, leading to a circumstance where they may feel a sense of lost identity (Citera and Rentsch).

Mayer, Greenbaum, Kuenz, and Shteynberg (2009) discuss the relationship between personal and social identity and an individual's perception of fairness. Their research investigated the thesis that when objectively fair procedures are used in determining a decision, they will have a weaker influence on an individual's justice perceptions if the outcome of that decision violates their personal or social identity. Even when that individual was allowed a level of control in the process, when the outcome violated their identity, they tended to doubt that their opinions had been considered. This is something exemplified in the *value protection model* (VPM). Skitka (2002) defines individuals with moral convictions of ethical behavior, which she termed *moral mandates*. A moral mandate is described as "a selective self-expressive stand, on a specific issue, not a generalized orientation toward the world" (p. 589), referring to it as a property of the person, and a facet of personal identity. Such convictions, if challenged by perceived unethical behavior, cannot be overcome by fair procedures or allocations, and such a belief plays a critical role in how individuals reason about fairness. Through the framework of the VPM, it becomes evident how personal identity, in the guise of the moral mandate effect, appears to have a bound relationship with an individual's perception of fairness.

Further evidence of the identity-justice relationship is provided by the link established with social identity, defined as an individual's will to gain status, desire to feel accepted, and fundamental need to belong (Baumeister & Leary, 1995). The *group value model* offered by Lind and Tyler (1988) proposed that fair procedures are important because they help an individual feel like a valued group member helping to instill them with group procedural justice values and beliefs during the socialization process. Subsequently, if an individual who is insecure about their status within the group experiences perceived procedural injustice, they are likely to suffer a strong negative reaction. Similarly, if the individual perceives procedures affirming their status in the group as being fair, they will display a strong positive reaction. There is evidence that typical behavior from resentment caused by a perceived injustice is likely to result in negative behaviors such as lower cooperation, lower productivity, lower work quality, and the withdrawal behavior of stealing (Shapiro & Kirkman, 1999). This is particularly apt because at a time when managers need to keep everyone on board and focused on achieving the strategic objectives of the merger, a situation needs to be avoided where employees feel resentment to the change.

Part of an individual's depersonalization process in the transfer from personal to social identity is assisted in a realization and acceptance of group norms (Terry & Hogg, 1996). This socialization process is discussed by Salancik and Pfeffer (1978) in a framework evolved from their *social information processing theory*, which supports the argument that individuals form judgments about organizational practices, values, and norms based on information gathered from others in their direct social contexts. Within this process, socially constructed common perceptions are formed from shared information. The theory professes that within the confines of a social group setting, this information exchange will lead to relatively homogenous justice perceptions in the work group. This has also been labeled *contagious justice* (Liao & Rupp, 2005) and can be considered in light of evidence that judgments formed around procedural justice are consistent across members of the same culture and that this will influence the individual during their period of socialization with the group. It is important to understand that individuals also form attitudes toward injustice imposed on groups and organizations that they identify with (Mayer et al., 2009).

Again, we can see that this relationship between identity and justice becomes visible and is reflected through the lens of the *group engagement model* offered by Tyler and Blader (2003). The level of procedural fairness experienced by an individual within a group context determines the quality of their relationship with that group by indicating the level of respect they command with other members. This goes on to help promote pride in group membership, further developing the relationship between identity and perceived fairness and influencing organizational identification with the newly-merged group (Amiot et al., 2006; Lipponen et al., 2004; Meyer, 2001). It is proposed within this framework that procedural justice judgments are used by individuals during times of uncertainty and change, such as mergers and similar reorganizations, to understand their identity-relevant implications (Tyler & De Cremer, 2005).

It is also clear that the significance of this reciprocal relationship between identity and fairness is rooted within the fundamental premises of the PC, which is characterized by organization loyalty and support (Bligh & Carsten, 2005). There is further support that the perceived justice of the merger implementation is positively related to the postmerger organizational identification and perceptions of common in-group identity (Lipponen et al., 2004). This proposition of shared identity with the group is offered by Thompson and Bunderson (2003) as an additional third dimension to the traditional perspective of psychological contracts being either relational or transactional. Their collectivistic notion of an ideological PC is based on the employee sharing a common overarching purpose with their organization (Brickson, 2005).

In addition to the four influential characteristics of culture, identity, justice, and the PC, the nature of change can also have a purposeful influence on the employee's interpretations and reactions. While this may depend on the scale of change, it will also be influenced by the organization's strategic intentions and the model of change adapted to these circumstances.

2.5 An Interrelated Process

The complexity of integration is evident, and it has been asserted that the failure to meet an objective may also impact the attainment of other objectives within the organization. As Kavanagh and Ashkanasy (2006) assert, "Mergers are highly complex events with a seemingly infinite number of factors that can lead to success or failure" (S82). They refer to the social systems view of organizations and propose that a more holistic perspective is required to understand the impact from an organization level as well as each factor's subsequent interrelation with each other. This view is supported by Sudarsanam (2003), who recognizes the need to perceive the process of integration as a series of dynamic interrelated events. There is a need to consider mergers from a more joined-up and interrelated perspective, avoiding a temptation to see different stages of M&A through a lens that depicts these as fragmented and isolated, resulting in each being the sole determinant of failure or success.

An expansion on this theme is offered through an empirical study carried out by the accountancy firm, and management consultants, KPMG, who surveyed 110 of the largest cross-border deals during the late 1990s. Their findings supported the principle that the likelihood of successful integration is significantly enhanced if both *hard* (e.g. financial performance) and *soft* (e.g. communication, culture, and team selection) issues are considered in preimplementation planning of a deal. Support for the proposition that the reasons for failure are highly interrelated was one of the main issues to emerge from the research (KPMG, 1999).

2.5.1 Integration Management

Birkinshaw, Bresman, and Hakanson (2000) delineate the two processes quite succinctly in their framework for integration management, which is displayed in Fig. 2.1. The key point being made within their framework is that for acquisition success to be achieved, both dimensions, task and human integration, need to be realized, and a situation where one is achieved at the expense of the other has the potential to impede the route to what they acknowledge as acquisition success. While they engage with the notion that task and human integration are conceptually distinct, in practice they are not independent of one another (e.g. commitment and identity is more likely to enhance process integration and vice versa). However, it is often the case that one is achieved at the expense of the other and this divergence will inevitably impact the potential for successful postmerger integration. To enable the integration process to be entirely successful, they maintain that operational synergies need to be realized but not at the expense of employee motivation. Equally, they stress that focusing on human integration may lead to satisfied employees at the

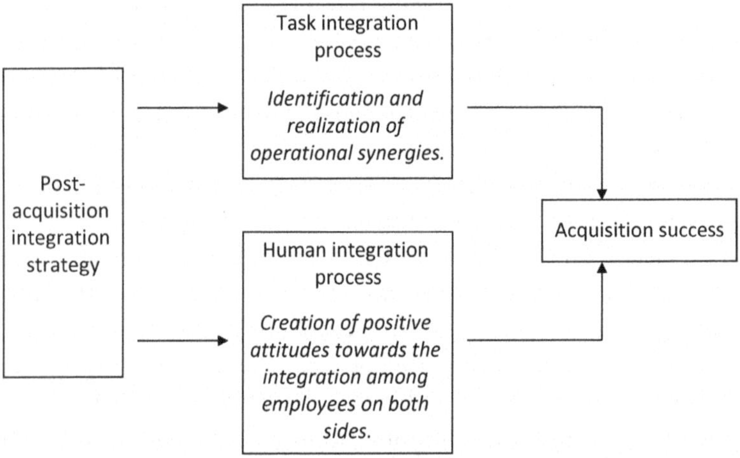

Fig. 2.1 Framework for integration management. (Note: Based on "Managing the post-acquisition integration process: How the human integration and task integration processes interact to foster value creation," by J. Birkinshaw, H. Bresman & L. Hakanson, 2000, *Journal of Management Studies, 37*, 395–425)

expense of operational synergies, which may be similarly detrimental (Birkinshaw et al., 2000).

These are important developments, although another essential finding from their empirical study was that in advance of any attempt to assimilate the first stage of operational functionalities, a bid to implement human integration will aid the success of task integration. An initial focus on positive attitude development such as trust within those key relationships is critical before asking members of each entity to cooperate on integrated systems and processes. The model draws emphasis on the need to avoid potential isolation of each process as management concentrate on complexities or potential risk factors associated with that process. For acquisition success to be realized, it should not be a case of operational synergies versus employee satisfaction, but eventually their management needs to encompass a reconciliation of each dimension. As Walker and Price (2000) identify, it is predominantly the case of those who fail to focus sufficiently on people-related issues in the integration plan that can be attributed to an overall failure in consolidation. Strategic scholars also highlight the urgency to focus on synergies such as enhancing learning (Leroy & Ramanantsoa, 1997) or transferring capabilities from one organization to another (Laamanen, 1997).

Summarizing, there are several human impact factors that are often neglected in practice during a merger or acquisition. The first relates to a more complete and integrated approach to both the planning process and any necessary remedial action. Second, a proactive preimplementation plan would appear essential for such a significant program of change. A positive correlation has been recognized between successful implementation and overall perceived success of the integration in 83% of cases (Hunt, Lees, Grumbar, & Vivian, 1987), making it, according to Hubbard and Purcell (2001), "the most decisive variable in success and failure" (p. 17). A framework for integration management, such as that proposed by Birkinshaw et al. (2000), is an example of this proposition. It is also evident that employee resistance has an influence on the success of the integration process. Whether there has been sufficient consideration of soft issues for the support of employees through the transition appears to play an influential role in the organization's concerted efforts to realize their strategic objectives from the integration. It would also appear that a failure to consider soft issues in the pre- and postimplementation plan may raise difficulties with task integration in addition to those raised with employee integration.

Therefore, an argument has been developed and supported for the proposition that success or failure of the integration plan is influenced by the consideration given to the needs and concerns of the employee throughout the process. There are four human factors that emerge as key performance indicators in the debates about effective merger implementation, consisting of culture, identity, fairness, and the PC. Of these, organizational justice has been identified as underresearched and an area at risk of lacking critical knowledge. Chapter 3 is dedicated to the concept of organizational justice, the dynamic relationships developed with other fundamental elements of the change process encountered through M&A, and any subsequent influence on employee attitudes and behaviors.

References

Adams, J. S. (1965). Inequity in social exchange. In L. Berkowitz (Ed.), *Advances in experimental social psychology* (pp. 267–229). New York: Academic Press.

Amiot, C. E., Terry, D. J., & Callan, V. J. (2007). Status, fairness, and social identification during an intergroup merger: A longitudinal study. *British Journal of Social Psychology, 46*, 557–577.

Amiot, C. E., Terry, D. J., Jimmieson, N. L., & Callan, V. J. (2006). A longitudinal investigation of coping processes during a merger: Implications for job satisfaction and organizational identification. *Journal of Management, 32*, 552–574.

Appelbaum, S. H., Gandell, J., Shapiro, B. T., Belisle, P., & Hoeven, E. (2000). Anatmoy of a merger: Behavior of organizational factors and processes throughout the pre-, during-, and post-stages. *Management Decision, 38*, 674–680.

Badrtalei, J., & Bates, D. L. (2007). Effect of organizational cultures on mergers and acquisitions: The case of DaimlerChrysler. *International Journal of Management, 24*(2), 303–317.

Barkema, H. G., Bell, J. H. J., & Pennings, J. M. (1996). Foreign entry, cultural barriers and learning. *Strategic Management Journal, 17*, 151–166.

Baruch, Y., & Hind, P. (1999). Perpetual motions in organizations: Effective management and the impact of the new psychological contracts on survivor syndrome. *European Journal of Work and Organizational Psychology, 8*(2), 295–306.

Baumeister, R. F., & Leary, M. R. (1995). The need to belong: Desire for interpersonal attachments as a fundamental human motivation. *Psychological Bulletin, 117*, 497–529.

Bellou, V. (2007). Psychological contract assessment after a major organizational change: The case of mergers and acquisitions. *Employee Relations, 29*(1), 68–88.

Birkinshaw, J., Bresman, H., & Hakanson, L. (2000). Managing the post-acquisition integration process: How the human integration and task integration processes interact to foster value creation. *Journal of Management Studies, 37*, 395–425.

Bligh, M. C., & Carsten, M. K. (2005). Post-merger psychological contracts: Exploring a multi-foci conceptualization. *Employee Relations, 27*(5), 495–510.

Brickson, S. L. (2005). Organizational identity orientation: Forging a link between organizational identity and organization's relations with stakeholders. *Administrative Science Quarterly, 50*, 576–609.

Buunk, B., & Janssen, P. (1992). Relative deprivation career issues, and mental health among men in midlife. *Journal of Vocational Behavior, 40*, 338–350.

Cartwright, S., & Cooper, C. L. (1992). *Mergers and acquisitions: The human factor*. Oxford, UK: Butterworth-Heinmann Ltd.

Cartwright, S., & Cooper, C. L. (1993). The psychological impact of merger and acquisition on the individual: A study of building society managers. *Human Relations, 46*, 327–347.

Cartwright, S., & Schoenberg, R. (2006). Thirty years of mergers and acquisitions research: Recent advances and future opportunities. *British Journal of Management, 17*, S1–S5.

Cartwright, S., Tytherleigh, M., & Robertson, S. (2007). Are mergers always stressful? Some evidence from the higher education sector. *European Journal of Work and Organizational Psychology, 16*(4), 456–478.

Chao, G. T., O'Leary-Kelly, A. M., Wolf, S., Klein, H. J., & Gardner, P. (1994). Organizational socialization: Its content and consequences. *Journal of Applied Psychology, 79*, 730–743.

Citera, M., & Rentsch, J. R. (1993). Is there justice in organizational acquisitions? The role of distributive and procedural fairness in corporate acquisitions. In R. Cropanzano (Ed.), *Justice in the workplace: Approaching fairness in human resource management* (pp. 211–230). Hilsdale, NJ: Erlbaum.

Clarke, N., & Salleh, N. M. (2011). Emotions and their management during a merger in Brunei. *Human Resource Development International, 14*(3), 291–304.
Conyon, M. J., Girma, S., Thompson, S., & Wright, P. W. (2001). Do hostile mergers destroy jobs? *Journal of Economic Behavior & Organization, 45*, 427–440.
Conyon, M. J., Girma, S., Thompson, S., & Wright, P. W. (2002). The impact of mergers and acquisitions on company employment in the United Kingdom. *European Economic Review, 46*, 31–49.
Cordery, J., Sevastos, P., Mueller, W., & Parker, S. (1993). Correlates of employee attitudes toward functional flexibility. *Human Relations, 46*, 705–723.
Deutsch, M. (1985). *Distributive justice: A social-psychological perspective*. New Haven, CT: Yale University Press.
Folger, R., & Cropanzano, R. (1998). *Organizational justice and human resource management*. Thousand Oaks, CA: Sage.
Folger, R., Rosenfield, D., Grove, J., & Cochran, L. (1979). Effects of 'voice' and peer opinions on responses to inequity. *Journal of Personality and Social Psychology, 37*, 2243–2261.
Galpin, T. J., & Herndon, M. (2007). *The complete guide to mergers and acquisitions: Process tools to support M&A integration at every level* (2nd ed.). San Francisco: Jossey-Bass.
Gouldner, A. W. (1960). The norm of reciprocity: A preliminary statement. *American Sociological Review, 25*, 161–178.
Haunschild, P. R., Moreland, R. L., & Murrell, A. J. (1994). Sources of resistance to mergers between groups. *Journal of Applied Social Psychology, 24*, 1150–1178.
Hitt, M. A., Hoskisson, R. E., Ireland, R. D., & Harrison, J. S. (1991). Effects of acquisitions on R&D inputs and outputs. *Academy of Management Journal, 34*, 693–706.
Hofstede, G. (2001). *Culture's consequences: Comparing values, behaviors, institutions and organizations across nations* (2nd ed.). Thousand Oaks, CA: Sage.
Horwitz, F. M., Anderssen, K., Bezuidenhout, A., Cohen, S., Kirsten, F., Mosoeunyane, K., et al. (2002). Due diligence neglected: Managing human resources and organizational culture in mergers and acquisitions. *South African Journal of Business Management, 33*(1), 1–10.
Hubbard, N. (2001). *Acquisition strategy and implementation*. Basingstoke, UK: Palgrave.
Hubbard, N., & Purcell, J. (2001). Managing employee expectations during acquisitions. *Human Resource Management Journal, 11*(2), 17–33.

Hunt, J. W., Lees, S., Grumbar, J., & Vivian, P. D. (1987). *Acquisitions: The human factor*. London: London Business School/Egon Zehnder International.
Huy, Q. N. (2002). Emotional balancing of organizational continuity and radical change: The contribution of middle managers. *Administrative Science Quarterly, 47*, 31–69.
Kaufman, J. D., Stamper, C. L., & Tesluk, P. E. (2001). Do supportive organizations make for good corporate citizens? *Journal of Managerial Issues, 13*, 436–449.
Kavanagh, M. H., & Ashkanasy, N. M. (2006). The impact of leadership and change management strategy on organizational culture and individual acceptance of change during a merger. *British Journal of Management, 17*(March Suppl), S81–S103.
Kickul, J. R., & Lester, S. W. (2001). Broken promises: Equity sensitivity as a moderator between psychological contract breach and employee attitudes and behavior. *Journal of Business and Psychology, 16*, 191–217.
Kirkman, B., Shapiro, D., Novelli, L., & Brett, J. (1996). Employee concerns regarding self managing work teams: A multidimensional justice perspective. *Social Justice Research, 9*(1), 47–67.
Klendauer, R., & Deller, J. (2009). Organizational justice and managerial commitment in corporate mergers. *Journal of Managerial Psychology, 24*(1), 29–45.
Konovsky, M., & Cropanzano, R. (1991). Perceived fairness of employee drug testing as a predictor of employee attitudes and job performance. *Journal of Applied Psychology, 76*, 698–707.
KPMG. (1999). *Unlocking shareholder value: The key to success, in mergers and acquisitions: A global research report*. London: Author.
Krug, J., & Hegarty, W. (1997). Postacquisition turnover among US top management teams: An analysis of the effects of foreign vs domestic acquisitions of US targets. *Strategic Management Journal, 18*, 667–675.
Laamanen, T. (1997). *The acquisition of technological competencies through the acquisition of new, technology-based companies*. Espoo, Finland: Helsinki University of Technology.
Larsson, R., Driver, M. J., Holmqvist, M., & Sweet, P. L. (2001). Career disintegration and reintegration in mergers and acquisitions: Managing confidence and motivational intangibles. *European Management Journal, 19*, 609–618.
Lee, D., Kim, K., Kim, T. G., Kwon, S., & Cho, B. (2013). How and when organizational integration efforts matter in South Korea: A psychological process perspective on the post-merger integration. *The International Journal of Human Resource Management, 24*(5), 944–965.

Leroy, F., & Ramanantsoa, B. (1997). Cognitive and behavioural dimensions of organizational learning in a merger: An empirical study. *Journal of Management Studies, 34*, 871–894.

Liao, H., & Rupp, D. E. (2005). The impact of justice climate and justice orientation on work outcomes: A cross-level multifoci framework. *Journal of Applied Psychology, 90*, 242–256.

Lind, E. A., & Tyler, T. R. (1988). *The social psychology of procedural justice*. New York: Plenum.

Lipponen, J., Olkkonen, M. E., & Moilanen, M. (2004). Perceived procedural justice and employee responses to an organizational merger. *European Journal of Work and Organizational Psychology, 13*, 391–413.

Louis, M. R. (1980). Surprise and sense-making: What newcomers experience in entering unfamiliar organizational settings. *Administrative Science Quarterly, 25*, 226–251.

Marks, M. L., & Mirvis, P. H. (1998). Rebuilding after a merger: Dealing with survivor sickness. *Organizational Dynamics, 21*(2), 18–32.

Mayer, D. M., Greenbaum, R. L., Kuenz, M., & Shteynberg, G. (2009). When do fair procedures not matter? A test of the identity violation effect. *Journal of Applied Psychology, 94*(1), 142–161.

Meyer, C. B. (2001). Allocation processes in mergers and acquisitions: An organizational justice perspective. *British Journal of Management, 12*(1), 47–66.

Mirvis, P. H. (1985). Negotiations after the sale: The roots and ramifications of conflict in an acquisition. *Journal of Occupational Behavior, 6*(1), 65–84.

Moorman, R. H. (1991). Relationship between organizational justice and organizational citizenship behaviors: Do fairness perceptions influence employee citizenship? *Journal of Applied Psychology, 76*, 845–855.

Moorman, R. H., Blakeley, G. L., & Niehoff, B. P. (1998). Does perceived organizational support mediate the relationship between procedural justice and organizational citizenship behavior? *Academy of Management Journal, 41*, 351–357.

Morrison, D. (1994). Psychological contracts and change. *Human Resource Management, 33*, 353–372.

Niehoff, B. P., Moorman, R. H., Blackley, G., & Fuller, J. (2001). The influence of empowerment and job enrichment on employee loyalty in a downsizing environment. *Group and Organization Management, 26*(1), 93–113.

Nikandrou, I., Papalexandris, N., & Dimitris, B. (2000). Gaining employee trust after acquisitions: Implications for managerial action. *Employee Relations, 22*(4), 334–348.

Nonaka, I. (1994). A dynamic theory of organizational knowledge creation. *Organization Science, 5*, 14–37.

Parvinen, P., & Tikkanen, H. (2007). Incentive asymmetries in the mergers and acquisitions process. *Journal of Management Studies, 44*(5), 759–787.

Pate, J., Martin, G., & Staines, H. (2000). Exploring the relationship between psychological contracts and organizational change: A process model and case study evidence. *Strategic Change, 9*(8), 481–493.

Piekkari, R., Vaara, E., Tienari, J., & Santii, R. (2005). Integration or disintegration? Human resource implications of a common corporate language decision in a cross-border merger. *International Journal of Human Resource Management, 16*(3), 330–344.

Restubog, S. L. D., & Bordia, P. (2006). Workplace familism and psychological contract breach in the Phillipines. *Applied Psychology: An International Review, 55*, 563–585.

Restubog, S. L. D., Bordia, P., & Bordia, S. (2009). The interactive effects of procedural justice and equity sensitivity in predicting responses to psychological contract breach: An interactionist perspective. *Journal of Business Psychology, 24*, 165–178.

Restubog, S. L. D., Bordia, P., & Tang, R. L. (2006). Effects of psychological contract breach on performance of IT employees: The mediating role of affective commitment. *Journal of Occupational and Organizational Psychology, 79*, 299–306.

Rhoades, L., & Eisenberger, R. (2002). Perceived organizational support: A review of the literature. *Journal of Applied Psychology, 87*, 698–714.

Richardson, P., & Denton, D. K. (1996). Communicating change. *Human Resource Management, 35*, 203–216.

Robinson, S. L. (1996). Trust and the breach of the psychological contract. *Administrative Science Quarterly, 41*, 574–599.

Robinson, S. L., & Morrison, E. W. (1995). Psychological contracts and OCB: The effect of unfulfilled obligations on civic virtue behavior. *Journal of Organizational Behavior, 16*, 289–298.

Rousseau, D. M. (1989). Psychological and implied contracts in organizations. *Employee Responsibilities and Rights Journal, 2*(2), 121–139.

Rousseau, D. M. (1995). *Psychological contracts in organizations: Understanding written and unwritten agreements*. Newbury Park, CA: Sage Publications.

Rousseau, D. M. (2001). Scheme promise and mutuality: The building blocks of the psychological contract. *Journal of Occupational and Organizational Psychology, 74*(4), 511–541.

Rousseau, D. M., & McLean Parks, J. (1993). The contracts of individuals and organizations. *Research in Organizational Behavior, 15*, 1–47.

Salancik, G. R., & Pfeffer, J. (1978). A social information processing approach to job attitudes and task design. *Administrative Science Quarterly, 23*, 224–253.

Schein, E. H. (1992). *Organizational culture and leadership: A dynamic view* (2nd ed.). San Francisco: Jossey-Bass.

Schweiger, D. M., & DeNisi, A. S. (1991). Communication with employees following a merger: A longitudinal field experiment. *Academy of Management Journal, 34*, 110–135.

Serpa, R. (1988). The often overlooked ethical aspects of mergers. *Journal of Business Ethics, 7*, 359–362.

Shapiro, D. L., & Kirkman, B. L. (1999). Employees' reaction to the change to work teams: The influence of "anticipatory" injustice. *Journal of Organizational Change Management, 12*(1), 51–66.

Shield, R., Thorpe, R., & Nelson, A. (2002). Hospital mergers and psychological contracts. *Strategic Change, 11*(7), 357–367.

Sitkin, S. B., & Bies, R. J. (1993). Social accounts in conflict situations: Using explanations to manage conflict. *Human Relations, 46*, 349–370.

Skitka, L. J. (2002). Do the means always justify the ends, or do the ends sometimes justify the means? A value protection model of justice reasoning. *Personality and Social Psychology Bulletin, 28*, 588–597.

Sorrentino, R. M., Nezlec, J. B., Yasunga, S., Houhara, S., Otsubo, Y., & Shuper, P. (2008). Uncertainty orientation and affective experiences: Individual differences within and across cultures. *Journal of Cross-Cultural Psychology, 39*(2), 129–146.

Sudarsanam, P. S. (2003). *Creating value from mergers and acquisitions: The challenges*. Harlow, UK: Pearson Education.

Tajfel, H., & Turner, J. C. (1979). An integrative theory of intergroup conflict. In W. G. Austin & S. Worchel (Eds.), *The social psychology of intergroup relations*. Monterey, CA: Brooks-Cole.

Teerikangas, S., & Very, P. (2006). The culture-performance relationship in M&A: From yes/no to how. *British Journal of Management, 17*, S31–S48.

Terry, D. J., Carey, C. J., & Callan, V. J. (2001). Employee adjustment to an organizational merger: An intergroup perspective. *Personality and Social Psychology Bulletin, 27*, 267–280.

Terry, D. J., & Hogg, M. A. (1996). Group norms and the attitude-behavior relationship: A role for group identification. *Personality and Social Psychology Bulletin, 22*, 776–793.

Tetenbaum, T. J. (1999). Beating the odds of merger and acquisition failure: Seven key practices that improve the chance for expected integration and synergies. *Organizational Dynamics, 28*(2), 22–36.
Thompson, J. A., & Bunderson, J. S. (2003). Violations of principle: Ideological currency in the psychological contract. *Academy of Management Review, 28*, 571–586.
Thornhill, A., & Saunders, M. N. K. (2003). Exploring employees' reactions to strategic change over time: The utilisation of an organisational justice perspective. *Irish Journal of Management, 24*(1), 66–86.
Tropp, L., & Wright, S. (1999). Ingroup identification and relative deprivation: An examination across multiple social comparisons. *European Journal of Social Psychology, 29*, 707–724.
Turner, J. C., Hogg, M. A., Oakes, P. J., Reicher, S. D., & Wetherell, M. S. (1987). *Rediscovering the social group: A self-categorization theory*. Oxford, UK: Blackwell.
Turnley, W. H., Bolino, M. C., Lester, S. W., & Bloodgood, J. (2003). The impact of psychological contract fulfilment on the performance of in-role and organizational citizenship behaviors. *Journal of Management, 29*(2), 187–206.
Turnley, W. H., & Feldman, D. C. (1999). The impact of psychological contract violations on exit, voice, loyalty, and neglect. *Human Relations, 52*, 895–922.
Tyler, T. R., & Blader, S. L. (2003). The group engagement model: Procedural justice, social identity, and cooperative behavior. *Personality and Social Psychology Review, 7*, 349–361.
Tyler, T. R., & De Cremer, D. (2005). Process-based leadership: Fair procedures and reactions to organizational change. *The Leadership Quarterly, 16*, 529–545.
Ullrich, J., Wieseke, J., & van Dick, R. (2005). Continuity and change in mergers and acquisitions: A social identity case study of a German industrial merger. *Journal of Management Studies, 42*(8), 1549–1569.
Unger, H. (1986). The people trauma of major mergers. *Journal of Industrial Management (Canada), 10*(17), 19–27.
Vaara, E. (2002). On the discursive construction of success/failure in narratives of post-merger integration. *Organization Studies, 23*(2), 211–248.
Valikangas, L., & Okumara, A. (1997). Why do people follow leaders? A study of a US and a Japanese change program. *Leadership Quarterly, 8*, 313–337.
van Dick, R., Ullrich, J., & Tissington, P. A. (2006). Working under a black cloud: How to sustain organizational identification after a merger. *British Journal of Management, 17*, S69–S79.

van Knippenberg, D., van Knippenberg, B., Monden, L., & de Lima, F. (2002). Organizational identification after a merger: A social identity perspective. *British Journal of Social Psychology, 41*, 233–252.

van Leeuwen, E., van Knippenberg, D., & Ellemers, N. (2003). Continuing and changing group identities: The effects of merging on social identification and ingroup bias. *Personality and Social Psychology Bulletin, 29*, 679–690.

Vince, R. (2006). Being taken over: Managers' emotions and rationalizations during a company takeover. *Journal of Management Studies, 43*(2), 343–365.

Walker, I., & Pettigrew, T. (1984). Relative deprivation theory: An overview and conceptual critique. *British Journal of Social Psychology, 23*, 301–310.

Walker, J. W., & Price, K. F. (2000). Why do mergers go right? *Human Resource Planning, 23*(2), 6–8.

Yoo, Y., Lyytinen, K., & Heo, D. (2007). Closing the gap: Towards a process model of post-merger knowledge sharing. *Information Systems Journal, 17*, 321–347.

3

Organizational Justice

3.1 Introduction

There is a belief among leaders that within a reciprocal relationship, perceptions of fairness will be rewarded by the employee through demonstrations of loyalty, commitment, and trust (Cobb, Vest, Hills, Frey, & Tamoff, 1991; Lind & Tyler, 1988). Although the extent of this behavior may depend on many moderating variables, these individuals are still more likely to display tendencies toward organizational citizenship behavior (OCB) within the workplace (Moorman, 1991) and, interestingly, will be better placed in adapting to change therein (Brookner, 1988; Konovsky & Folger, 1991; Martin & Bies, 1991). Other behaviors are also affected by perceptions of justice, such as group cohesion and cooperation, but there is also a greater aptitude for resolution of inter- and intra-group disputes when justice is in evidence (Deutsch, 1985; Lind & Tyler, 1988; Thibaut & Walker, 1975). Folger and Cropanzano (1998) maintain, "Fair treatment … breeds commitment … and helpful citizenship behaviors that go beyond the call of formal job duties" (p.xii). Essentially, employees should be entitled to the same levels of justice they had come to expect before the implementation of change. Their perception of continuous justice through and beyond a change program is vital as this will appreciably influence

N. Jackson, *Organizational Justice in Mergers and Acquisitions*,
https://doi.org/10.1007/978-3-319-92636-0_3

resistance to change, organizational commitment, and turnover intentions (Shapiro & Kirkman, 1999).

The chapter begins with an illustration of how organizational justice has developed as a concept through the latter stages of the twentieth century, from its origins in relative deprivation (RD) and equity theory and its introduction to the workplace. This is followed by an outline of its development from a single-factor to a three-factor model, considering the implications of each factor and its multiple dimensions. The analysis then moves on to investigate the dynamics of the relationship between perceived fairness and the three important influential concepts of organizational culture, identity, and the psychological contract. An account of antecedents recognized as having a major influence on an individual's perception of fairness precedes a discussion about employee outcomes that will have an impact within the organization.

3.2 Origins of Organizational Justice

One of the earliest forms of organizational justice was the concept *Relative Deprivation Theory* (Stouffer, Suchman, DeVinney, Star, & Williams, 1949). Briefly, RD theory is based on the following belief: (i) the individual receives, or anticipates receiving, some outcome; (ii) the individual ascertains the worth of this outcome by comparing it to some form of standard, usually an outcome obtained by a similar other; and (iii) if the obtained outcome is less than the standard, the individual feels a sense of moral outrage or dissatisfaction (Pettigrew, 1967). The perceived importance of the outcome will influence the level of moral outrage or dissatisfaction (i.e. high level of importance, high level of dissatisfaction). The concept of RD theory can be compared to *distributive justice* (fair allocation of outcomes) and *Equity Theory* (Adams, 1965), one of the earliest frameworks of justice to be applied within an organizational setting.

Prior to 1975 much of the investigative work carried out in relation to justice was within the realms of the fairness of distributions or outcomes. At this time, Thibaut and Walker's (1975) seminal work on procedural justice, emphasizing the process of how distributions are determined, was an addition to the overall framework of justice. In an organizational setting, justice theory was not studied with any significance until the 1980s and has since been recognized as a framework with three distinct constructs: *distributive*, *procedural*, and *interactional*.

3.2.1 The Development of Organizational Justice

During the same year as Thibaut and Walker's seminal work on procedural justice, an extended framework for distributive justice was developed by Deutsch (1975), followed by Leventhal's (1976) *justice judgment model*, as limitations of Adams' (1965) work were exposed. Equity theory had been proposed as a unitary dimension that was dependent on justice determined by merit. However, in his development of distributive justice, Leventhal also identified two further allocation rules of *equality* and *need*. Allocations based on merit, and therefore distributed using the equity rule, are associated with a primary goal of economic productivity. However, this unidimensional approach disengages other potential situations where fairness of distributions may also be called into question. For example, the impact of distributions among group members where the perspective of cohesion and the development of social relations is of primary purpose may be better served by the rule of equality in allocations. Even if we return to the concept of distribution for economic purpose we can see there are similar limitations to applying the single approach of merit when we consider other situations where the principle of need is applied (e.g. the distribution of welfare and personal development in the workplace).

Along with Thibaut and Walker's contribution outlining the value of procedures in the decision-making process, the development of a tripartite framework for distributive justice provided a major advance toward understanding the key determinants of fairness arising from allocations made within the organizational context. Similarly, early understanding of procedural justice was expanded beyond a two-dimensional level of process and decision control to be considered from a more multidimensional perspective. In doing so, Leventhal (1980) applied the concept of procedural justice to an organizational setting and proposed a justice judgment framework highlighting its significance within the act of workplace fairness.

The communication of decision outcomes, an aspect of the allocation process largely undeveloped until the mid-1980s, was brought to prominence as a dimension of justice by Bies and Moag (1986) and became the third element of the organizational justice framework. There developed a much-contested discussion whether fairness in communication (*interactional justice*) was a single independent factor of organizational justice or a second dimension of procedural justice. Interactional justice and procedural justice were perceived as the social and formal aspect of a single construct (Greenberg, 1990). However, defining it as an independent concept, the premise of interactional justice was further refined by Bies and Moag, who proposed a two-dimensional construct consisting of *interpersonal justice*, representing dignity and propriety, and *informational justice*, representing truthfulness and justification. Following the logicality that if two variables predict different criteria, then they should be viewed as separate constructs (Cronbach & Meehl, 1955), it would appear justifiable to identify interactional justice as an independent dimension of organizational justice. This is a conclusion that has been supported consistently with the opinion of others in organizational justice research (Bies, 2001; Cropanzano, Prehar, & Chen, 2002).

A summary of organizational justice as a three-dimensional framework is presented in Table 3.1.

The term "systemic justice" has been applied to the overarching concept that incorporates all the three key components and applies to the

Table 3.1 The constructs of organizational justice

Construct and subdimensions	Definition	Organizational impact
Distributive justice Equity Equality Need	Perceived fairness of the distribution or allocation of outcomes	Response to policies of the organization as a whole, particularly those with a personal outcome—person referenced (e.g. pay and job satisfaction)
Procedural justice	Perceived fairness of formal procedures used in allocation decision-making	Response to policies of the organization as a whole—system referenced (e.g. commitment and valuation of authorities)
Interactional justice Interpersonal justice Informational justice	Perceived fairness of the interpersonal treatment received from the decision-makers	Response to interpersonal treatment by authorities of the organization

social systems found within an organization and forming part of the organizational culture.

These three dimensions of organizational justice, their subdimensions, and their implications in the workplace are considered in more detail.

3.3 The Dimensions of Organizational Justice

Distributive, procedural, and interactional justice are now discussed in more depth with emphasis on their interactive relationship with organizational outcomes.

3.3.1 Distributive Justice

The concept of distributive justice relates to policies of the organization (Weiss, Suckow, & Cropanzano, 1999), and because the organization's systems determine outcomes, it has been classed as a structural component of justice (Ambrose, Seabright, & Schminke, 2002). Most of the important work outcomes influenced by it can be categorized under the two broad headings of attitudes (e.g. commitment, satisfaction, and trust) and behaviors (e.g. performance, citizenship (OCB), and withdrawal). It has been argued that distributive justice is more influential than the other two justice dimensions in determining overall fairness judgments and that it will predominate by explaining more variance over the other constructs (Conlon, 1993; Leventhal, 1980; Lind & Tyler, 1988). In applying their two-factor model, Sweeney and McFarlin (1993) provided evidence that distributive justice was more suited to predicting person-referenced outcomes such as satisfaction with a pay rise or performance appraisal, rather than system-referenced outcomes.

Equity, Equality, and Need

Of the three rules identified within the framework of distributive justice, equity, which relies on a system of selection by contribution rather than equal distribution, has been identified as the dominant rule that guides perceptions of distributive fairness (Meyer, 2001; Sampson, 1975). The equity rule sets out to achieve several outcomes. For instance, it will strongly reinforce those recipients whose behavior is most useful and beneficial, and they will have greatest access to essential resources. Conversely, the equity rule provides low reinforcement to those whose behavior is least useful, although it does encourage them to change their behavior by offering an opportunity for them to increase their rewards by working harder and improving their performance.

Equality governs a fair distribution regardless of contribution, and the third justice norm, need, refers to distribution by satisfying legitimate desires and therefore preventing an individual suffering in the event of nonallocation. A greater emphasis on the needs rule should be applied in situations of high interdependence where a primary concern is the sense of responsibility for the welfare of the recipient, and the principal goal is development of the individual (Kabanoff, 1991). Referred to as a norm of Marxian justice, because of its objective to reward recipients according to their needs, this dimension of distribution is influenced by the norm of social responsibility (Leventhal, 1976).

Rawls (1971) takes the philosophical viewpoint of justice and delineates equity and equality by comparing to the two principles of *difference* and *liberty*. The liberty principle he proposes "requires that all citizens have an equal right to take part in, and to determine the outcome of, the constitutional process that establishes the laws with which they are to comply" (p. 221). In this sense liberty has been associated with the rule of equality. However, there is also an early association here with the principle of *voice*, which is discussed in more detail in Sect. 3.4.1. Rawls' second principle is the difference principle, which takes the position that within social systems inequalities are acceptable so long as they benefit the whole of that society, and the lowest members of that society. In this system, there would not be a voice for all, whereas the libertarian/equality principle provides voice for all.

Further discussion surrounding the dynamics of distribution by the principle of equality or equity has focused on the influence each has on the organizational relationship. Equality has been found to foster lasting social relationships, and the equity principle is applied in situations where economic productivity is the main priority (Kabanoff, 1991;

Lind & Tyler, 1988; Mannix, Neale, & Northcraft, 1995), a concept that can also be applied with similar effect to procedural justice (Lind & Tyler, 1988). Further support of this situational context is also reported by Meindl (1989), who found that a social cohesion policy was more responsive to the equality rule, and when individual productivity was the priority, a weighting toward the equity rule was more beneficial. A question of compromise is therefore raised between the need to be productive and efficient and a need to build harmonious relationships, fostering group loyalties and commitment. This is perhaps illuminated by Birkinshaw, Bresman, and Hakanson's (2000) framework of integration management, discussed in Chap. 2, and the principles surrounding both the task integration process and the human integration process.

An argument proposed by Cobb, Wooten, and Folger (1995) indicates that when the equity criterion is applied in its traditional format, it lends itself more to the *transactional* nature of stable organizations rather than the *transformational* needs of changing ones. They state:

> To be applied both effectively and fairly, the equity norm assumes knowledge of, and some general agreement about, which contributions are of more value to the enterprise. In the context of profound change however, there often exists ambiguity, confusion and disagreements about the priority of objectives to pursue and about the means to best achieve them. (p. 252)

This seems to suggest that equality rather than equity as a criterion is the more appropriate distributive rule to be applied during specific change, such as that encountered in mergers or acquisitions. In addition, the use of equity as an allocation principle also tends to refer to past contributions and achievements (Mannix et al., 1995). Meyer (2001) adds, "In mergers this principle relies upon detailed knowledge of both parties' employees. Furthermore, it presumes that yesterday's success criteria are the same as tomorrow's. These presumptions are likely to be violated in times of profound change" (p. 52).

Evidence points toward a need for managers to consider the balance between merit and equality. In circumstances of a merger or acquisition, equal distribution demonstrates to employees that they will be treated fairly and with respect regardless of whether they belong to the acquiring or target organization. Furthermore, the perceived state of equality indicates that different members of a relationship have equal value as individuals and, consequently, emphasizes a common fate for these members, which promotes solidarity and social cohesiveness (Kabanoff, 1991). Because of their disadvantaged position, lower-status partners in a merger are less likely to consider equity as fair and are more likely to prefer equality as the mode of distribution (Meyer, 2001). But, consequently, equal distribution also discriminates against merit as well as prolonging the integration process (Schweiger, Ridley, & Martini, 1992). This raises the prospect of an imbalance in fairness perceptions for those who are from the perceived higher-status partner and feel aggrieved at having to share the outcomes from integration.

An Exchange Relationship

The equity distribution rule (Adams, 1965) depends on a social exchange theory framework to evaluate fairness (Colquitt, Conlon, Wesson, Porter, & Ng, 2001). An individual will look to receive rewards consistent with inputs they have contributed to a distribution situation in comparison to those made by a referent other. A referent comparison can be in relation to several criteria such as (i) another person (ii), a generalized other (e.g. an occupational group), (iii) comparison to own previous input/output ratios, and (iv) input/output ratio specified for the situation (Adams). It is proposed that an individual's relationship with the organization is based on the social exchange framework, which will continue until unfairness is evidenced, at which point the individual will reinterpret the relationship as fundamentally economic rather than social (Organ, 1990). Similarly, when allocators expect future interactions with recipients, then the equality rule is more likely to be given greater consideration than the equity rule (Shapiro, 1975), and are likely to be more generous when their success depended on them (Bryant & Hansen, 1979).

The review of justice moves on to take a closer look at how procedural justice has evolved within the organizational context, and its effect within the changing environment of a merger or acquisition.

3.3.2 The Role of Procedural Justice

The discussion so far has focused on distributive justice and its potential outcomes. However, individuals are not just concerned about the outcome of decisions (i.e. distributive justice); they are also affected by the perceived fairness of procedures used in making those distribution decisions. This argument is presented by Greenberg (1990), who highlights that distributive justice does not consider or address the pursuit of fair procedure by an individual. Indeed, it has been proposed that an individual's perception of procedural justice may be independent of any observations they have for related distributive justice (McFarlin & Sweeney, 1992). Resultant behavior determined from perceived inequities of procedural justice reveals an individual's inclination to less commitment, lower performance, resignation, fewer OCBs, and, with reference to deviance, increased likelihood of theft (Folger & Cropanzano, 1998). Evidence suggests that leaders are perceived as more legitimate and competent when they make decisions based on fair procedures, leading to circumstances where employees will be more accepting of organizational change. This relationship will become increasingly evident for those who experience a greater identity with the organization (Tyler & De Cremer, 2005).

In a similar vein to distributive justice, the concept of procedural justice relates to policies of the organization. However, while distributive justice is focused on allocation outcomes (e.g. pay satisfaction), procedural justice relates to attitudes toward the overall organization (Sweeney & McFarlin, 1993), such as organizational identification (Meyer, 2001). Therefore, an individual's identity with the organization is influenced by the perceived fairness of its procedures. From this it is postulated that the long-term maintenance of positive social relationships within groups is fostered crucially by evidence of procedural justice (Lind & Tyler, 1988).

Three Streams of Procedural Justice

There are three distinct streams of research that have been identified in the procedural justice literature: Thibaut and Walker (1975), role of process control; Leventhal (1980), list of procedural rules; and Bies and Moag (1986), the role of interactional justice.

In a situation of dynamic change, procedural aspects of the justice process may become more critical toward the outcome evaluation. Crucially, communication of procedural standards, including employee voice within the process, can affect the favorability of employee attitudes. It is argued that allowing affected individuals an input or influence in the decision-making process is one of the most successful techniques used to encourage fairness perceptions (Folger, 1977), in part because it provides opportunity to demonstrate the individual's knowledge, skills, and abilities (Gilliland, 1993). However, these fairness perceptions will not be enabled unless the decision-maker acknowledges and shows consideration of the individual's input. A criticism of Thibaut and Walker's process control model is that it doesn't account for the interactional, noninstrumental effects of procedural justice (e.g. see Kickul, Lester, & Finkl, 2002). For instance, the *value-expressive* element of voice has been offered where value was still evident in cases when the contributors were aware that their input had little or no influence on the decisions made (Tyler, Rasinski, & Spodick, 1985). This was evident even if the opportunity for input came after the decision was made (Lind, Kanfer, & Earley, 1990), which demonstrates an interpersonal value to process input. Considering the potentially complex process of change during the implementation of a merger or acquisition, interpersonal relationships between authorities and employees may have a substantive influence on how fairness in this process is perceived. This suggests that mechanisms designed to manage the procedure of employee voice may have an important role within this experience.

Leventhal's (1980) expansion of Thibaut and Walker's framework contemplated the significance of fair procedures in decision-making and how this could be applied to the context of an organizational setting. Within this situation he proposed six rules that could be recognized as imperative toward governing the concept of fair procedure: *consistency*, *bias*, *accuracy*, *correctability*, *ethicality*, and *representativeness*. *Consistency* of allocative procedures over people and time is closely related to the notion of equality, at least over the short term. Applying doctrinaire views or personal self-interest (e.g. serving as a judge in one's own case) during decision-making is considered as *bias* and should be suppressed from the process. *Accuracy* includes accountability and relates to the appropriateness of the actual information collected, and from whom the information is collected. Review and modification of procedures built into the process at various stages allowing formal and informal appeals as a *correctability* rule. If allocative procedures violate personal standards of ethics and morality then perceived fairness will be reduced, and this is expressed in the *ethicality* rule. *Representativeness* of the individual's basic concerns and values through participatory decision-making and consultation with management may also affect their judgments of procedural fairness. This final point mirrors the process control or "voice" proposed by Thibaut and Walker within the decision-making process.

Influential Factors

It has been acknowledged that procedural justice will become more important when a decision does not meet with the recipient's approval, in which case the procedures are more likely to be carefully scrutinized. Conversely, when outcome favorability is high, then procedures are less likely to be of significance (Brockner & Wiesenfeld, 1996). There is also evidence that procedural justice is more important when there is a divergence from the equality norm toward the equity norm. This is particularly the case when there is an aim to foster long-term relationships, which may well be challenged when the equity rule is applied since this is more conducive toward promoting productivity than social relationships (Meyer, 2001). Similarly, procedures become more significant to the recipient of a decision outcome when they experience uncertainty. Such procedures matter more to those experiencing the uncertainty of radical change as opposed to only minor change (van den Bos, 2001), which makes them more likely to be central during the transformational change of a merger or acquisition.

3.3.3 Interactional Justice

The construct of organizational justice concerned with the social exchange of the superior-subordinate relationship is known as interactional justice and relates specifically to the treatment of employees during the enactment of procedural justice (Bies & Moag, 1986). Therefore, in difference to distributive justice and procedural justice, which form an exchange relationship between the employee and the organization, perceptions of interactional injustice lead to resentment toward the offender rather than the organization (Schweiger, Ivancevich, & Power, 1987). If perceived unfairness is related specifically to an individual's supervisor or manager rather than at the organization level, then the justice record of that individual will be taken into consideration rather than that of the organization's (Choi, 2008). However, there is also evidence to support the proposition that interactional justice will influence relationships held between the employee and the organization. For instance, it is argued that the interpretation of psychological contract breach will be influenced by perceived interactional fairness (Morrison & Robinson, 1997).

Greenberg (1993) defines and categorizes interactional justice as consisting of two important dimensions: *informational justice* (recognized as the social determinant of procedural justice) and *interpersonal justice* (recognized as the social aspect of distributive justice, that is, showing concern for individuals following distributive outcomes they have received). These two rules have been developed further into four subrules. Informational justice has been defined as *justification* of the decisions made, and *truthfulness* (honesty and deception avoidance) in communication of those decisions, which is recognized as not only genuine in intent but also based on sound reasoning (Bies & Moag, 1986). Interpersonal justice has been defined as displaying a *respect* for individual rights and *propriety* of behavior (e.g. an authority demonstrating genuine concern when an individual receives an unfavorable outcome). Each of these factors is an important consideration for authorities due to their ability to influence perceptions of fairness, acceptance of decisions, and organizational attitudes (Konovsky & Cropanzano, 1991; Korsgaard, Schweiger, & Sapienza, 1995).

However, discussion has also been indecisive with respect to whether interactional justice is an independent dimension of organizational justice (Bies & Moag, 1986) or if it simply represents an interpersonal construct of procedural justice (Greenberg, 1993). Early research took the view that it was merely a social form of procedural justice (Cropanzano & Greenberg, 1997). As a further consideration, not all studies have recognized an independent definition of either procedural or distributive justice. There are several studies that have revealed a high correlation between the two. For example, correlations of 0.72 (Sweeney & McFarlin, 1993) and 0.74 (Welbourne, Balkin, & Gomez-Mejia, 1995) were calculated, leading to Ambrose and Cropanzano (2003) proposing that the distinction between procedural and distributive justice can be overemphasized and others (e.g. Martocchio & Judge, 1995) making no attempt to separate the two, carrying out their study from a purely one-dimensional organizational justice perspective.

An important contribution to the debate was made by Colquitt et al. (2001), who found during their separate meta-analyses of 183 empirical studies that procedural, interpersonal, and informational justice are distinct constructs and distinguishable empirically. This adds considerable weight to the argument in favor of a structure of independence for each of the three constructs: distributive, procedural, and interactional justice.

The discussion now moves on to take a more analytical view of why individuals form certain perceptions of justice from the organizational decision-making process.

3.4 Antecedents of Justice

In the world of social science, justice is a subjective phenomenological activity that is dependent upon individual perception (Folger & Cropanzano, 1998). Judgments made from an individual's perceptions of justice are then memorized and applied when forming attitudes. Greenberg and Wiethoff (2001) refer to a person's perception of a situation as a *frame*, uniquely shaped by the cognitive vantage point through which they view it. An individual's frame has been described by Tannen (1979) as the way a person "organizes knowledge about the world and uses this knowledge to predict interpretations and relationships regarding new information, events and experiences" (pp. 138–139). Such perceptions are influenced by (i) outcome distributions, (ii) organizational practices (procedures and quality of interactions), and (iii) characteristics of the perceiver (Cohen-Charash & Spector, 2001). In addition, if *a priori* expectations are violated, then it is considered that this will influence an individual's perceptions (Adams, 1965) and how that individual reacts to situations of perceived injustice.

In this context, frames are a method of developing an overall concept from which an individual can evaluate and base judgments on the fairness of an outcome, a process to form the antecedents of perceived organizational justice. Greenberg and Wiethoff (2001) propose a formal process that individuals will engage in to form a justice frame. This process consists of three general categories:

- Context cues

The influence of human interaction and setting of social contexts, which include social comparison and the use of referent others to form justice perceptions. Any violation of established rules and norms can trigger perceptions of injustice (i.e. established expectations of how interactions in the environment will occur). Failure to receive expected or promised outcomes can trigger perceptions of injustice.

- Information cues

Type and timing of information can influence the initiation of justice-based framing initial information, which has implications for individual assessments of justice.

- Individual differences

Differences between individuals such as reactions, perceptions of inequity, gender, personality, individual predisposition, self-efficacy, and personal ethical frameworks can all play a key role in determining how individuals assess fairness in a situation. These are acknowledged as perceiver characteristics and can be categorized as demographic characteristics, or personality traits.

The frameworks of Cohen-Charash and Spector, and Greenberg and Wiethoff provide an informative context from which to comprehend the cognitive process of evaluation and judgment. In relation to these frameworks, the main antecedents of perceived organizational justice can be developed and discussed.

3.4.1 Voice

Personal control has been defined as "a psychological construct reflecting an individual's beliefs, at a given point in time, in his or her ability to effect a change, in a desired direction, on the environment" (Greenberger & Strasser, 1986, p. 165). The significance of voice (or process control) in the realm of procedural justice is exemplified by van den Bos and van Prooijen (2001), who point us toward a convincing body of research emphasizing its role as a central determinant in the evaluation of whether a procedure is fair or unfair. Houlden, LaTour, Walker, and Thibaut (1978) affirm that individuals will prefer scenarios where authorities retain a level of control over making the final decision (*decision control)* but prefer to retain process control for themselves (i.e. control over the process of providing evidence toward the final decision). This would suggest a level of exchange from outcome to meaningful interaction in the process is acceptable for the individual. The level of expected meaningful interaction will be dependent upon various factors, of which one will be the environment and its extremities (e.g. dictatorship vs. democracy). Examples of such institutions are autocratic regimes, or hierarchically structured organizations, and evidence has been provided that an individual's reaction to voice procedures will be moderated by the strength of outcome dependence (van Prooijen, van den Bos, & Wilke, 2007). Even if the individual does not ultimately influence the final decision being allowed, voice has value because it demonstrates a willingness of authorities to consider the recipient's views and show politeness and respect (Tyler & Blader, 2003; Tyler & Lind, 1992). An authority's willingness to demonstrate respect and consideration relates to interpersonal fairness within interactional justice. As previously discussed, this represents the noninstrumental value of voice and is highlighted in Tyler and Lind's *relational model* of authority, which connects the effect upon an individual's self-worth to the value they place on an authority's willingness to allow them to engage in voice procedures.

Power-distance values (an individual's tolerance of large differences in status, or concentration of power where high power-distance is representative of high tolerance) are another example that will affect the emphasis placed on an individual's perception of their treatment by authorities (Tyler, Lind, & Huo, 2000). Those from high power-distance cultures will place less emphasis on their level of procedural voice (Brockner et al., 2001). Consequently, those from low power-distance cultures (i.e. individuals who fear concentrations of power and have low tolerance to differences in status) will be influenced more by their access to voice in procedure setting because they expect authorities to share their power (van Prooijen et al., 2007). As proposed by Brockner et al. (2001): "It is not the lack of voice per se to which people object … It is when the lack of voice violates cultural norms that people respond unfavorably" (p. 301). In laboratory experiments, they tested commitment levels against low and high voice conditions within both high power-distance and low power-distance cultures. Low voice had the effect on individuals from low power-distance cultures of lowering their organizational commitment levels.

3.4.2 Group Influence

We can see evidence that the context of culture will influence an individual's expectations and desire to engage with the process of decision-making through their level of voice. Similarly, there is evidence that an individual's perceptions of procedural justice and the expectancy of being allowed voice is affected by their group membership characteristics (van Prooijen, van den Bos, & Wilke, 2004). The relational model of authority (Lind & Tyler, 1988; Tyler & Lind, 1992) attempts to highlight the importance of group membership for the individual and influence a sense of belonging, security, self-esteem, social identity, and confirmation of worldviews. The framework professes that the way an individual is treated by group authorities (Tyler, Degoey, & Smith, 1996) will have an impact on their group membership (i.e. if treated with dignity and respect), but this may also be affected by social inclusion or exclusion by peers within the group (Gardner, Pickett, & Brewer, 2000; Williams, Cheung, & Choi, 2000). There is evidence that an individual's level of inclusion within a group (social inclusion) moderates their perceived levels of procedural fairness and effects of voice procedures become stronger at higher levels of inclusion (van Prooijen et al., 2004).

An individual's justice perceptions are also influenced by group members when coworkers are denied voice in the procedure-setting process (Lind, Kray, & Thompson, 1998). It has been reported that fairness perceptions of the supervisor were negatively impacted when team members learned that other individuals in the group had been denied voice, although the impact wasn't as great as when they themselves were denied (Lind, Kray, and Thompson). Further support for fairness judgments relating to an individual's team has been provided and related to outcomes such as job satisfaction, OCB, commitment, and turnover (Liao & Rupp, 2005; Mossholder, Bennet, & Martin, 1998; Naumann & Bennett, 2000; Simons & Robertson, 2003). In addition, Lind et al. (1998) found group polarization detrimentally affected fairness ratings of an event when individuals were placed in a group and shared their injustices.

Social influence and its effect on an individual's perceptions is discussed by Salancik and Pfeffer (1978) in their proposed framework, social information processing. They contend that individuals will form evaluations and perceptions of organizational characteristics by using information from other people in the same environment. The cornerstone of their theory is that individuals will rely more on "relevant others" for information upon which to base their evaluations and perceptions when there is ambiguity in the task or event, where ambiguity means employees are unclear which information to use, and there is also difficulty obtaining and using that information in assessing an event. Social influence in both evaluation and perception formation will increase along with the ambiguity.

3.4.3 Trust and Uncertainty

Uncertainty, in this context, has been defined as "an individual's perceived inability to predict something accurately" (Bordia, Hunt, Paulsen, Tourish, & DiFonzo, 2004, p. 348).

A framework of uncertainty management is offered by van den Bos and Lind (2002), who remonstrate that a loss of trust leading toward uncertainty of authorities leads to a negative impact of perceived procedural fairness. Because change has the potential to significantly erode trust in both management and organization, an individual's trust in authorities is a significant factor in the determination of whether a change program is deemed to be successful (Dirks & Ferrin, 2002; Kirkman, Jones, & Shapiro, 2000). One of the consequences of eroded trust is that individuals are more likely to withdraw from participating in the organization's efforts to implement the change program (Mishra & Spreitzer, 1998). If, due to a lack of information, an individual is uncertain whether to trust an authority, it is proposed that they will base their decision of fairness on the procedures used to determine the outcome. In which case this will increase their need for procedural fairness information (van den Bos, 2001). The proposition is therefore supported that procedural fairness matters less when an individual is certain whether they can or cannot trust the authority making the decision. However, it is of importance when this information is not available. If the individual is faced with a situation guided by an authority they are not familiar with, then there will be an increase in their need to experience just and fair procedures used to form any outcome allocations. This determines that the salience of uncertainty is a key antecedent of this process and why fairness matters so much to people within the realms of social justice.

Schweiger and DeNisi (1991) maintain that the uncertainties of change are more stressful for employees than the change itself and that there are three main causes of perceived uncertainty. These three causes are: the inability to estimate the likelihood of an event, the lack of information about a cause-effect relationship, and the inability to predict what the outcomes of a decision will be. If at this point the underlying assumptions of process control are considered, it is noticeable that there is a distinct similarity between these and the causes of uncertainty discussed by Schweiger and De Nisi. Employee participation in the decision-making process may provide insights to the likelihood of events and offer some control over the outcome of decisions, therefore reducing uncertainty.

Extending the concept of participation to the broader remit of employee-employer communication, it has been asserted that knowledge, a method of mitigating uncertainty, is essential if control is to be achieved and subsequent aims fulfilled from interpersonal interactions (Bordia et al., 2004). There is evidence that uncertainty in a change scenario has the potential to be reduced through communication with authorities (interactional justice) and as the level of control increases for the individual in that relationship (process control).

3.4.4 Affective State of the Individual

In a study of the psychology of justice judgments, van den Bos (2003) maintains that situations of information-uncertainty raise the event that in absence of information they can trust individuals will form justice perceptions influenced by their affective state prior to, and even unrelated to, the justice event itself. He recognizes that the phenomenon of affect in justice judgments has been a much-neglected area of research, particularly the conditions where individuals are most likely to use affective feelings as input, and takes the argument to the debate between rationalist and intuitionalist models of moral judgment (Haidt, 2001). In situations where directly relevant information is available, and individuals are in a position of information-certainty, then their affective state (positive or negative) will have less bearing on their justice judgments. Yet, if this is not available there is evidence that individuals may, while passing justice judgments, use affect as the criteria of assessment and fill the void left by a lack of information, or a situation of information-uncertainty. In such cases, rather than an individual's justice judgments being informed by the level of logicality and objectivity originating from information related directly to the case, it is replaced by a level of subjectivity that is dictated by the incident, when affect becomes the controlling variable. The assumptions of this contrast between rational-cognitive (Kohlberg, 1969; Turiel, 1983) and subjective-affective processes (Haidt; Kagan, 1984; Wilson, 1993) in the formation of justice judgments are that affective processes are steeped in subjectivism, and therefore a more stable rational model of cognitive justice should be aimed for. However, this may only be achieved if management secure an environment of trust and information-certainty.

Support for the notion that an individual will use other information to base their judgments (a *heuristic substitute*) in an environment of insufficient or untrustworthy information is purported in a model proposed by van den Bos and Lind (2002). The *uncertainty management model* depicts a situation where the level of information-certainty becomes a moderator in the relationship between affect and perceived justice. Similarly, Barsky and Kaplan (2007) found that perceptions of justice are formed from influence of phenomenological states of feeling on fundamental cognitive and social-information processes, such as memory and schemata. Both levels of uncertainty and the affective state experienced by an individual will increase the likelihood of such subjective influence. These are important contributions to the debate because during situations of information-uncertainty, individuals with positive mood rate allocation procedures as being fairer than those in a negative mood (van den Bos, 2003).

This point is highlighted by Wanberg, Bunce, and Gavin (1999), who report individuals who experience high negative trait affectivity are more likely to perceive unfair treatment than those experiencing low negative trait affectivity, because of their tendency to focus on the negative aspects of the situation. Similarly, individuals who suffer from low self-esteem will form different perceptions toward justice outcomes than those who experience high self-esteem (Cohen-Charash & Spector, 2001). There are two perspectives on this. *Attribution theory* predicts that in some instances negative outcomes determined by unjust procedures will either reduce low self-esteem or increase it because such outcomes will not be attributed to low personal ability (Schroth & Pradhan Shah, 2000; van den Bos, Bruins, Wilke, & Dronkert, 1999). In addition, the Group Value Model (Lind & Tyler, 1988; Tyler, 1994) emphasises that the level of respect individuals receive from other group members will influence feelings of self esteem via the mechanisms of perceived fairness. The GVM also predicts that individuals who feel more uncertain about their status in a group will place greater emphasis on procedural fairness in decisions made within the group (Roberts & Markel, 2001).

3.4.5 Anticipatory Justice

Even though the large body of research on organizational justice has been acknowledged (e.g. Lind & Tyler, 1988), most of this research tends to investigate the specific processes of justice from a psychological perspective once the individual has experienced an event and its outcomes. Anticipatory justice has been identified and defined by Shapiro and Kirkman (1999) as a phenomenon that is prevalent as either an expression or fear from those who have experienced a form of change in recent times but have not yet received the outcomes or distributions aligned to the event. After this earlier work, there has been further support in more recent times distinguishing it from the literatures recognizing justice that has already been experienced (Bell, Wiechmann, & Ryan, 2006; Ritter, Fischbein, & Lord, 2005).

The arguments proposed are founded on the basis that as organizations struggle to adapt to change, their members will anticipate that organizational injustices are likely to occur within everyday work processes. Greenberg (1990) points out that we tend to know much more about the consequences of experienced justice than how perceived justice will develop certain reactions. It is often discussed in terms of anticipatory *injustice*, or those who have an expectation that they may not be treated fairly in a given situation. This will take the form of an expectation of unfair outcomes pertaining to one of the three recognized forms of justice concerning distributions, procedures, communication, and/or interpersonal treatment regarding the outcomes of the situation. Examples of anticipated undesired outcomes may include the loss of a currently satisfying job or working relationship. Furthermore, these anticipated interactional, procedural, and distributive injustices will lead to counterproductive and self-defeating behavior on the part of organizational members (Harrison, Hopeck, Desrayaud, & Imboden, 2013). For example, it has been proffered that there is a significant positive correlation between anticipatory injustice and withdrawal behavior relating to change resistance and turnover intentions and a negative correlation with employee commitment (Shapiro & Kirkman, 1999).

The principles of anticipatory (in)justice can be related to those of the psychological contract that is formed between the employee and the employing organization. The psychological contract has been discussed briefly in Chap. 2 and will be investigated in greater depth within Chap. 11. Here, we can see the relationship with expectations of the employee, which will, in part, be founded on past experiences that can be referred to and used as a comparison other. Of course, there is no surety that those expectations are formed through a just process, and could be subject to cognitive process predispositions, such as confirmatory bias, or the tendency to view events as we expect to see them (Snyder & Swann, 1978a, 1978b). Therefore, a situation arises where an individual's perceptions of justice may well be more contingent upon their expectations rather than their actual experiences, leaving the concept of anticipatory justice as a critical factor in the overall process of acceptance or rejection of the object of focus.

The predictors of anticipatory injustice relating to procedural and interactional justice have been considered and Rodell and Colquitt's (2009) investigation determined that, to some extent, these were dependent on the quality of the relationship between an employee and their supervisor. This will be dependent on the justice reputation of the person responsible for administering the distributions (i.e. if they are deemed to have a fair reputation, then this increases the presence of perceived anticipatory justice). In this sense we can see that previous contexts have a significant influence and decisions about predicted fairness are dependent on situational factors that can also be relational. Perceptions such as these are developed through our socially constructed environments, which will be of significant influence in the process of shaping and determining our justice judgments. Whether this process is fair or not is largely subjective and perhaps sets a basis for our early preconceived ideas that are then subject to change and iterations as the impact of the outcomes are revealed over time. The criticality of impact from the supervisory relationship is clear from Rodell and Colquitt's research and demonstrates the importance of this role and the supervisor's reputation for fairness in previous interactions. Considering the outcome that anticipated justice impacts the level of experienced justice, these are important factors. In other words, how influential constructs such as voice, consistency, bias suppression, sincerity, respect, truthfulness, and justification are shaped by the event occurring will be affected not only by what is experienced, but also by what was anticipated in advance of the event occurring. Within these relationships there is also a need to consider the influence of trust and how this will impact the expectations of employees in situations of anticipated distributions. It should also be noted that consistent with previous findings (see Bies & Tyler, 1993; Greenberg, 1990) Shapiro and Kirkman (1999) found that perceived procedural justice moderated the relationship between anticipated distributive injustice, the prospect of employee resistance to change, and their organizational commitment. This is an important facet of the justice principle that offers mitigation of perceived unfair distributions whether these are exacted or anticipated and demonstrates the value in visibility of fair process.

3.5 Outcomes of Perceived Justice

While considering the antecedents of perceived justice it is an opportune point to reflect on potential outcomes, particularly in a context that recognizes the impact it has on relationships formed between an employee and their organization: the attitudinal and behavioral outcomes.

3.5.1 The Relationship Between Power and Resistance

Since the power in a superior-subordinate relationship usually resides with the superior, where there has been an injustice enacted upon the subordinate, the opportunity for them to respond directly and restore justice is usually limited (Homans, 1961). An approach that is often adopted, particularly if it is the only option available to the subordinate in this relationship, is to try and exercise their power and restore justice by resisting the change being imposed (Jermier, Knights, & Nord, 1994). In fact, the actual change itself may warrant resistance because apart from being unjust it may also be incorrect. Folger and Skarlicki (1999) argue that the organization may be "doing the wrong thing or doing it wrong" (p. 37). Where this is the case, as Fiorelli and Margolis (1993) propose, an organization can benefit from some level of resistance to change.

Because of their disadvantage within the employer-employee exchange relationship, employees are aware they run a high risk that their efforts will fail to be adequately compensated in that relationship. According to Shore and Shore (1995), this is because (i) the employee is the less powerful partner in the exchange, (ii) there is often a delay inherent in employer fulfillment of obligations, and (iii) there are multiple agents both intrinsic and extraneous to this relationship that may influence whether obligations are fulfilled. As mentioned, this imbalance can be partly mitigated by the potential threat of employee actions such as reducing effort, absenteeism, and quitting. However, the impact of these withdrawal behaviors on the organization is unlikely to be of parity in comparison to the outcomes of any action that may be bestowed upon the employee. This disparity in reciprocal actions by each party also has the converse effect when employees who feel slighted by the smallest act of perceived unjust behavior toward them by the organization respond with more extreme examples of negativity or withdrawal behavior toward the organization.

Continuing the theme of employees engaging with resistance as an exercise of power, Folger and Skarlicki (1999) propose that justice is a psychological mechanism that acts as a mediator of an individual's resistance to change. Referring to their framework as *resentment-based workplace resistance* they define resistance as "employee behavior that seeks to challenge, disrupt, or invert prevailing assumptions, discourses, and power relations" (Folger and Skarlicki, p. 36). Considering resistance as a response to perceived consequential injustices from managerial control, it becomes evident why this should be particularly severe during a period of organizational change. For instance, drawing from earlier discussion, it has been asserted that individuals will compensate for negative emotional experiences during organizational change (e.g. job values, job security, and fair treatment) by withdrawing from the organization and its representative agents (Turnley & Feldman, 2000).

3.5.2 Influence of Perceived Justice upon Emotion

Previous studies acknowledge cognitive events can influence affective reactions and that work attitudes and behaviors are influenced by both affect and cognition (see Cropanzano & Folger, 1989 and Weiss et al., 1999). There is support for the notion that justice perceptions influence positive and negative emotions, although negative emotions are normally experienced from an unfair outcome if both the outcome and procedure are perceived to be unjust. As part of a study into the emotional response to change, Paterson and Cary (2002) focused on anxiety. They found evidence that a positive evaluation directly reduced anxiety about the change, and indirectly, by increasing the perceived fairness of the outcome. They found that during a change program the importance of specific events is likely to adapt with newly-communicated information, effects of the change procedures, and perceptions of justice influencing the individual's evaluation of the event, resulting in fluctuating emotions and eventual outcomes.

However, the concept of perceived justice having a causal relationship with emotion has been evidenced as far back as Adams (1965), who proposed through the tenets of equity theory that when an individual is underrewarded they will feel anger, and when they are overrewarded will experience feelings of guilt.

3.5.3 Organizational Commitment

There is considerable support that a relationship is formed between an individual's perceptions of organizational justice and their commitment toward the organization, although existing research is indecisive toward which of the three justice dimensions makes the greatest contribution. Judgments that employees make about procedural fairness of decisions and interactional treatment of those members by the organization have been found to influence the level of organizational commitment they experience (Rupp & Cropanzano, 2002). Similar studies also recognize that distributive justice has been found most influential on more specific person-referenced outcomes such as satisfaction with a pay rise or performance evaluation (McFarlin & Sweeney, 1992; Sweeney & McFarlin, 1993) than system-referenced outcomes such as organizational commitment. Tyler (1990) argues that procedural justice is more influential toward employee support for institutions than distributive justice and within the two-factor model of justice this is reinforced in other studies (Folger & Konovsky, 1989); Sweeney & McFarlin, 1993). Conversely, distributive justice has been identified as having the stronger relationship with organizational commitment when compared with the dimensions of procedural and interactional justice, leaving the academic arguments open (Greenberg, 1994; Lowe & Vodanovich, 1995).

3.5.4 Organizational Citizenship Behavior

OCB has been defined as behavior that is discretionary but not explicitly rewarded, with the purpose of improving organizational functioning (Organ, 1990) and motivated largely by fairness perceptions. Being a fundamental element of the employee-employer social exchange relationship, OCBs have been found to have a stronger connection with procedural justice than with distributive justice (Ball, Trevino, & Sims, 1994; Moorman, 1991). There is also evidence that OCBs are related to exchanges with organizational agents (i.e. supervisors, line managers), and therefore they may also be influenced by interactional justice perceptions (Skarlicki & Latham, 1996).

3.5.5 Intention to Leave

Surprisingly, there have been few studies into the effects of organizational justice on an employee's intentions to leave (for an exception, see Dailey & Kirk, 1992), a situation emphasized by Loi, Hang-yue, and Foley (2006), who advise "the underlying processes through which organizational justice leads to employee turnover remain largely unknown" (p. 102). Their investigation into the effects of perceived organizational support as a mediator in the relationship between a two-factor model of distributive and procedural justice and intention to leave offered evidence of a significant relationship. These results provide further supporting evidence of the importance of organizational justice in the employee-employer social exchange relationship and further insight into the mechanisms through which this is essentially maintained.

3.6 Summary

The perception of fairness is bound within a reciprocal relationship between an employee and their organization. It is within this relationship of social exchange that important employee attitudes and behaviors are influenced by the perceived fairness of the organization's actions. Three dimensions of organizational justice have been identified as, distributive justice, procedural justice, and interactional justice. Each has been developed and recognized within the workplace as independent constructs, although interactional justice is considered the enactment of procedural justice. Important workplace outcomes have been identified with organizational justice such as the attitudes of commitment, satisfaction, and trust, along with the behaviors of citizenship, withdrawal, job performance, and intention to leave. Influential antecedent relationships of organizational justice include the trust and uncertainty, voice, affective state of the individual, group influence, and anticipatory justice.

It is evident from this research review that there are many gaps in the body of knowledge associated with the realms of organizational justice and within the specific context of a merger or acquisition. It is also apparent that, following a period of change in the workplace, an individual's perception of how fairly they and others are treated by the organization (organizational justice) because of decision outcomes will have a subsequent affect upon their attitudes and behaviors. Within this context there is a need to extend our understanding about the mechanisms of perceived fairness, its development, its importance to the individual when evaluating decision outcomes, and its subsequent influence on their attitudes and behaviors. Evidence points toward the impact on organizational outcomes, such as the company's ability to meet its strategic objectives, which, in turn, supports a need to understand these concepts in more detail and develop our knowledge of the human barriers to integration and how they are caused.

In Parts II and III of this text, I move on to develop the frameworks discussed in Chaps. 2 and 3 and, in doing so, consider their implications within the specific change environment of a merger or acquisition and the successful implementation of an integration plan.

References

Adams, J. S. (1965). Inequity in social exchange. In L. Berkowitz (Ed.), *Advances in experimental social psychology* (pp. 267–229). New York: Academic Press.

Ambrose, M. L., & Cropanzano, R. (2003). A longitudinal analysis of organizational fairness: An examination of reactions to tenure and promotion decisions. *Journal of Applied Psychology, 88*(2), 266–275.

Ambrose, M. L., Seabright, M. A., & Schminke, M. (2002). Sabotage in the workplace: The role of organizational justice. *Organizational Behavior and Human Decision Processes, 89*, 947–965.

Ball, G. A., Trevino, L. K., & Sims, H. P., Jr. (1994). Just and unjust punishment: Influences on subordinate performance and citizenship. *Academy of Management Journal, 37*, 299–322.

Barsky, A., & Kaplan, S. A. (2007). If you feel bad, it's unfair: A quantitative synthesis of affect and organizational justice perceptions. *Journal of Applied Psychology, 92*(1), 286–295.

Bell, B. S., Wiechmann, D., & Ryan, A. M. (2006). Consequences of organizational justice expectations in a selection system. *Journal of Applied Psychology, 91*, 455–466.

Bies, R. J. (2001). In: Byrne, Z. S., & Cropanzano, R. (2001). The history of organizational justice: The founders speak. In Cropanzano, R. (Ed.), *Justice in the workplace: From theory to practice* (Vol. 2, pp. 3–26). Mahwah, NJ: Lawrence Erlbaum Associates, Inc.

Bies, R. J., & Moag, J. F. (1986). Interactional justice: Communication criteria of fairness. In R. J. Lewicki, B. H. Sheppard, & M. H. Bazerman (Eds.), *Research on negotiations in organizations* (Vol. 1, pp. 43–55). Greenwich, CT: JAI Press.

Bies, R. J., & Tyler, T. T. (1993). The litigation mentality in organizations: A test of alternative psychological explanations. *Organization Science, 4*(3), 352–366.

Birkinshaw, J., Bresman, H., & Hakanson, L. (2000). Managing the post-acquisition integration process: How the human integration and task integration processes interact to foster value creation. *Journal of Management Studies, 37*, 395–425.

Bordia, P., Hunt, E., Paulsen, N., Tourish, D., & DiFonzo, N. (2004). Uncertainty during organizational change: Is it all about control? *European Journal of Work and Organizational Psychology, 134*, 345–365.

Brockner, J., Ackerman, G., Greenberg, J., Gelfand, M. J., Francesco, A. M., Chen, Z. X., et al. (2001). Culture and procedural justice: The influence of power distance on reactions to voice. *Journal of Experimental Social Psychology, 37*, 300–315.

Brockner, J., & Wiesenfeld, B. M. (1996). An integrative framework for explaining reactions to decisions: Integrative effects of outcomes and procedures. *Psychological Bulletin, 120*(2), 189–208.

Brookner, J. (1988). The effects of work layoffs on survivors: Research theory and practice. In B. M. Staw & L. L. Cummings (Eds.), *Research in organizational behavior*. Greenwich, CT: JAI Press.

Bryant, B. K., & Hansen, B. K. (1979). The interpersonal context of success: Differing consequences of independent and dependent success of sharing behavior among boys and girls. *Representative Research in Social Psychology, 9*, 103–113.

Choi, J. (2008). Event justice perceptions and employees' reactions: Perceptions of social entity justice as a moderator. *Journal of Applied Psychology, 93*(3), 513–528.

Cobb, A. T., Vest, M., Hills, F., Frey, F. F., & Tamoff, K. (1991). *Procedural justice: Source attributions and group effects in performance evaluations.* Proceedings, Southern Management Association.

Cobb, A. T., Wooten, K. C., & Folger, R. (1995). Justice in the making: Toward understanding the theory and practice of justice in organizational change and development. *Research in Organizational Change and Development, 8*, 243–295.

Cohen-Charash, Y., & Spector, P. E. (2001). The role of justice in organizations: A meta-analysis. *Organizational Behavior and Human Decision Processes, 86*, 278–321.

Colquitt, J. A., Conlon, D. E., Wesson, M. J., Porter, C. O. L. H., & Ng, K. Y. (2001). Justice at the millennium: A meta-analytic review of 25 years of organizational research. *Journal of Applied Psychology, 86*, 425–445.

Conlon, D. E. (1993). Some tests of the self-interest and group value models of procedural justice: Evidence from an organizational appeal procedure. *Academy of Management Journal, 36*, 1109–1124.

Cronbach, L. J., & Meehl, P. H. (1955). Construct validity in psychological tests. *Psychological Bulletin, 52*, 281–302.

Cropanzano, R., & Folger, R. (1989). Referent cognitions and task decision autonomy: Beyond equity theory. *Journal of Applied Psychology, 74*, 293–299.

Cropanzano, R., & Greenberg, J. (1997). Progress in organizational justice: Tunneling through the maze. In C. Cooper & I. Robertson (Eds.), *International review of industrial and organizational psychology* (pp. 317–372). New York: Wiley.

Cropanzano, R., Prehar, C. A., & Chen, P. Y. (2002). Using social exchange theory to distinguish procedural justice from interactional justice. *Group and Organizational Management, 27*, 324–351.

Dailey, R. C., & Kirk, D. J. (1992). Distributive and procedural justice as antecedents of job dissatisfaction and intent to turnover. *Human Relations, 45*, 305–317.

Deutsch, M. (1975). Equity, equality and need: What determines which value will be used as the basis of distributive justice? *Journal of Social Issues, 31*, 137–149.

Deutsch, M. (1985). *Distributive justice: A social-psychological perspective.* New Haven, CT: Yale University Press.

Dirks, K. T., & Ferrin, D. L. (2002). Trust in leadership: Meta-analytic findings and implications for research and practice. *Journal of Applied Psychology, 87*, 611–628.

Fiorelli, J. S., & Margolis, H. (1993). Managing and understanding large systems change: Guidelines for executives and change agents. *Organization Development Journal, 11*(3), 1–13.

Folger, R. (1977). Distributive and procedural justice: Combined impact of "voice" and improvement on experienced inequity. *Journal of Personality and Social Psychology, 35*, 108–119.

Folger, R., & Cropanzano, R. (1998). *Organizational justice and human resource management.* Thousand Oaks, CA: Sage.

Folger, R., & Konovsky, M. A. (1989). Effects of procedural and distributive justice on reactions to pay raise decisions. *Academy of Management Journal, 32*(1), 115–130.

Folger, R., & Skarlicki, D. P. (1999). Unfairness and resistance to change: Hardship as mistreatment. *Journal of Organizational Change Management, 12*(1), 35–50.

Gardner, W. L., Pickett, C. L., & Brewer, M. B. (2000). Social exclusion and selective memory: How the need to belong influences memory for social events. *Personality and Social Psychology Bulletin, 26*, 486–496.

Gilliland, S. W. (1993). The perceived fairness of selection systems: An organizational justice perspective. *Academy of Management Review, 18*, 694–734.

Greenberg, J. (1990). Organizational justice: Yesterday, today and tomorrow. *Journal of Management, 16*, 399–432.

Greenberg, J. (1993). The social side of fairness: Interpersonal and informational classes of organizational justice. In R. Cropanzano (Ed.), *Justice in the workplace: Approaching fairness in human resource management* (pp. 79–103). Englewood Cliffs, NJ: Erlbaum.

Greenberg, J. (1994). Using socially fair treatment to promote acceptance of a work site smoking ban. *Journal of Applied Psychology, 79*, 288–297.

Greenberg, J., & Wiethoff, C. (2001). Organizational justice as proaction and reaction: Implications for research and application. In R. Cropanzano (Ed.), *Justice in the workplace: From theory to practice* (pp. 271–302). Mahwah, NJ: Erlbaum.

Greenberger, D. B., & Strasser, S. (1986). Development and application of a model of personal control in organizations. *Academy of Management Review, 11*(1), 164–177.

Haidt, J. (2001). The emotional dog and its rational tail: A social intuitionist approach to moral judgment. *Psychological Review, 108*, 814–834.

Harrison, T. R., Hopeck, P., Desrayaud, N., & Imboden, K. (2013). The relationship between conflict, anticipatory procedural justice, and design with intentions to use ombudsman processes. *International Journal of Conflict Management, 24*(1), 56–72.

Homans, G. C. (1961). *Social behavior: Its elementary forms.* New York: Harcourt, Brace and World.

Houlden, P., LaTour, S., Walker, S., & Thibaut, J. (1978). Preference for modes of dispute resolution as a function of process and decision control. *Journal of Experimental Social Psychology, 14*, 13–30.

Jermier, J. M., Knights, D., & Nord, W. (1994). *Resistance and power in organizations.* London: Routledge.

Kabanoff, B. (1991). Equity, equality, power and conflict. *Academy of Management Review, 16*, 416–441.

Kagan, J. (1984). *The nature of the child.* New York: Basic Books.

Kickul, J., Lester, S. W., & Finkl, J. (2002). Promise breaking during radical organizational change: Do justice interventions make a difference? *Journal of Organizational Behavior, 23*(Special Issue S1), 469–488.

Kirkman, B. L., Jones, R. G., & Shapiro, D. L. (2000). Why do employees resist teams? Examining the 'resistance barrier' to work team effectiveness. *International Journal of Conflict Management, 11*(1), 74–92.

Kohlberg, L. (1969). Stage and sequence: The cognitive-developmental approach to socialization. In D. A. Goslin (Ed.), *Handbook of socialization theory and research* (pp. 347–480). Chicago: Rand McNally.

Konovsky, M., & Cropanzano, R. (1991). Perceived fairness of employee drug testing as a predictor of employee attitudes and job performance. *Journal of Applied Psychology, 76*, 698–707.

Konovsky, M. A., & Folger, R. (1991). The effects of procedures, social accounts, and benefits level on victims' layoff reactions. *Journal of Applied Social Psychology, 21*, 630–650.

Korsgaard, M. A., Schweiger, D., & Sapienza, H. (1995). Building commitment, attachment and trust in strategic decision-making teams: The role of procedural justice. *Academy of Management Journal, 38*(1), 60–84.

Leventhal, G. S. (1976). The distribution of rewards and resources in groups and organizations. In L. Berkowitz & E. Walster (Eds.), *Advances in experimental social psychology* (Vol. 9). New York: Academic Press.

Leventhal, G. S. (1980). What should be done with equity theory? New approaches to the study of fairness in social relationships. In K. J. Gergen, M. S. Greenberg, & R. H. Willis (Eds.), *Social exchange, advances in theory and research* (pp. 27–55). New York: Plenum.

Liao, H., & Rupp, D. E. (2005). The impact of justice climate and justice orientation on work outcomes: A cross-level multifoci framework. *Journal of Applied Psychology, 90*, 242–256.

Lind, E. A., Kanfer, R., & Earley, C. (1990). Voice, control, and procedural justice. *Journal of Personality and Social Psychology, 59*, 952–959.

Lind, E. A., Kray, L., & Thompson, L. (1998). The social construction of injustice: Fairness judgements in response to own and others' unfair treatment by authorities. *Organizational Behavior and Human Decision Processes, 75*, 1–22.

Lind, E. A., & Tyler, T. R. (1988). *The social psychology of procedural justice.* New York: Plenum.

Loi, R., Hang-yue, N., & Foley, S. (2006). Linking employees' justice perceptions to organizational commitment and intention to leave: The mediating role of perceived organizational support. *Journal of Occupational and Organizational Psychology, 79*, 101–120.

Lowe, R. H., & Vodanovich, S. J. (1995). A field study of distributive and procedural justice as predictors of satisfaction and organizational commitment. *Journal of Business and Psychology, 10*, 99–114.

Mannix, E. A., Neale, M. A., & Northcraft, G. B. (1995). Equity, equality or need? The effects of organisational culture on the allocation of benefits and burdens. *Organizational Behavior and Human Decision Processes, 63*, 276–286.

Martin, C. L., & Bies, R. J. (1991, August). Just laid off, but still a 'good citizen'? Only if the process is fair. In D. Eskaw (Ed.), *The role of organizational justice in organizational citizenship behaviors*. Miami Beach, FL: Symposium conducted at the annual meeting of the Academy of Management.

Martocchio, J. J., & Judge, T. A. (1995). When we don't see eye to eye: Discrepancies between supervisors and subordinates in absence disciplinary decisions. *Journal of Management, 21*(2), 251–278.

McFarlin, D. B., & Sweeney, P. D. (1992). Distributive and procedural justice as predictors of satisfaction with personal and organizational outcomes. *Academy of Management Journal, 35*, 626–637.

Meindl, J. R. (1989). Managing to be fair: An exploration of values, motives, and leadership. *Journal of Applied Psychology, 34*, 252–276.

Meyer, C. B. (2001). Allocation processes in mergers and acquisitions: An organizational justice perspective. *British Journal of Management, 12*(1), 47–66.

Mishra, A. K., & Spreitzer, G. M. (1998). Explaining how survivors respond to downsizing: The role of trust, empowering, justice, and work redesign. *Academy of Management Review, 23*, 567–588.

Moorman, R. H. (1991). Relationship between organizational justice and organizational citizenship behaviors: Do fairness perceptions influence employee citizenship? *Journal of Applied Psychology, 76*, 845–855.

Morrison, E. W., & Robinson, S. L. (1997). When employees feel betrayed: A model of how psychological contract violation develops. *The Academy of Management Review, 22*(1), 226–256.

Mossholder, K. W., Bennet, N., & Martin, C. L. (1998). A multilevel analysis of procedural justice context. *Journal of Organizational Behavior, 19*, 131–141.

Naumann, S. E., & Bennett, N. (2000). A case for procedural justice climate: Development and test of a multilevel model. *Academy of Management Journal, 43*, 881–889.

Organ, D. W. (1990). The motivational basis of organizational citizenship behavior. *Research in Organizational Behavior, 12*(1), 43–72.

Paterson, J. M., & Cary, J. (2002). Organizational justice, change anxiety, and acceptance of downsizing: Preliminary tests of an AET-based model. *Motivation and Emotion, 26*(1), 83–103.

Pettigrew, T. F. (1967). Social evaluation theory: Convergence and applications. In D. Levine (Ed.), *Nebraska symposium on motivation* (Vol. 15, pp. 241–315). Lincoln, NE: University of Nebraska Press.

Rawls, J. (1971). *A theory of justice*. Cambridge, MA: Belknap Press.

Ritter, B. A., Fischbein, R. L., & Lord, R. G. (2005). Implicit and explicit expectations of justice as a function of manager and subordinate race. *Human Relations, 58*, 1501–1521.

Roberts, K., & Markel, K. S. (2001). Claiming in the name of fairness: Organizational justice and the decision to file for workplace injury compensation. *Journal of Occupational Health Psychology, 6*(4), 332–347.

Rodell, J. B., & Colquitt, J. A. (2009). Looking ahead in times of uncertainty: The role of anticipatory justice in an organizational change context. *Journal of Applied Psychology, 94*(4), 989–1002.

Rupp, D. E., & Cropanzano, R. (2002). The mediating effects of social exchange relationships in predicting workplace outcomes from multifoci organizational justice. *Organizational Behavior & Human Decision Processes, 89*(1), 925–946.

Salancik, G. R., & Pfeffer, J. (1978). A social information processing approach to job attitudes and task design. *Administrative Science Quarterly, 23*, 224–253.

Sampson, E. E. (1975). On justice as equality. *Journal of Social Issues, 31*, 45–64.

Schroth, H. A., & Pradhan Shah, P. (2000). Procedures: Do we really want to know them? An examination of the effects of procedural justice on self-esteem. *Journal of Applied Psychology, 85*, 462–471.

Schweiger, D. M., & DeNisi, A. S. (1991). Communication with employees following a merger: A longitudinal field experiment. *Academy of Management Journal, 34*, 110–135.

Schweiger, D. M., Ivancevich, J. M., & Power, F. R. (1987). Executive actions for managing human resources before and after acquisitions. *Academy of Management Executive, 1*, 127–137.

Schweiger, D. M., Ridley, J. R., & Martini, D. M. (1992). Creating one from two: The merger between Harris Semiconductor and General Electric Solid State. In S. E. Jackson et al. (Eds.), *Diversity in the workplace: Human resource initiatives*. New York: The Guildford Press.

Shapiro, E. G. (1975). Effect of expectations of future interaction on reward allocations in dyads: Equity or equality. *Journal of Personality and Social Psychology, 31*, 873–880.

Shapiro, D. L., & Kirkman, B. L. (1999). Employees' reaction to the change to work teams: The influence of "anticipatory" injustice. *Journal of Organizational Change Management, 12*, 51–66.

Shore, L. M., & Shore, T. H. (1995). Perceived organizational support and organizational justice. In R. Cropanzano & K. M. Kacmar (Eds.), *Organizational politics, justice, and support: Managing social climate at work* (pp. 149–164). Westport, CT: Quorum Press.

Simons, T., & Robertson, Q. (2003). Why mangers should care about fairness: The effects of aggregate justice perceptions on organizational outcomes. *Journal of Applied Psychology, 88*, 432–443.

Skarlicki, D. P., & Latham, G. P. (1996). Increasing citizenship behavior within a labour union: A test of organizational justice theory. *Journal of Applied Psychology, 81*, 161–169.
Snyder, M., & Swann, W. B., Jr. (1978a). Behavioral confirmation in social interaction: From social perception to social reality. *Journal of Experimental Social Psychology, 14*, 148–162.
Snyder, M., & Swann, W. B., Jr. (1978b). Hypotheses-testing processes in social interaction. *Journal of Personality & Social Psychology, 36*, 1202–1212.
Stouffer, S. A., Suchman, E. A., DeVinney, L. C., Star, S. A., & Williams, R. M. (1949). *The American soldier: Adjustment during army life* (Vol. 1). Princeton, NJ: Princeton University Press.
Sweeney, P. D., & McFarlin, D. B. (1993). Workers evaluation' of the "ends" and the "means": An examination of four models of distributive and procedural justice. *Organizational Behavior and Human Decision Processes, 55*, 23–40.
Tannen, D. (1979). What's in a frame? Surface evidence of underlying expectations. In R. Freedle (Ed.), *New dimensions in discourse processes* (pp. 137–181). Norwood, NJ: Ablex.
Thibaut, J., & Walker, L. (1975). *Procedural justice: A psychological analysis.* Hillsdale, NJ: Erlbaum.
Turiel, E. (1983). *The development of social knowledge: Morality and convention.* Cambridge, UK: Cambridge University Press.
Turnley, W. H., & Feldman, D. C. (2000). Re-examining the effects of psychological contract violations: Unmet expectations and job dissatisfaction as mediators. *Journal of Organizational Behavior, 21*(1), 25–42.
Tyler, T. R. (1990). *Why people obey the law: Procedural justice, legitimacy, and compliance.* New Haven, CT: Yale University Press.
Tyler, T. R. (1994). Psychological models of the justice motive: Antecedents of distributive and procedural justice. *Journal of Personality and Social Psychology, 67*, 850–863.
Tyler, T. R., & Blader, S. L. (2003). The group engagement model: Procedural justice, social identity, and cooperative behavior. *Personality and Social Psychology Review, 7*, 349–361.
Tyler, T. R., & De Cremer, D. (2005). Process-based leadership: Fair procedures and reactions to organizational change. *The Leadership Quarterly, 16*, 529–545.

Tyler, T. R., Degoey, P., & Smith, H. (1996). Understanding why the justice of group procedures matters: A test of the psychological dynamics of the group-value model. *Journal of Personality and Social Psychology, 70*, 913–930.

Tyler, T. R., & Lind, E. A. (1992). A relational model of authority in groups. In M. Zanna (Ed.), *Advances in experimental social psychology* (Vol. 25, pp. 115–292). San Diego, CA: Academic Press.

Tyler, T. R., Lind, E. A., & Huo, Y. J. (2000). Cultural values and authority relations: The psychology of conflict resolution across cultures. *Psychology, Public Policy, and Law, 6*, 1138–1163.

Tyler, T. R., Rasinski, K., & Spodick, N. (1985). The influence of voice on satisfaction with leaders: Exploring the meaning of process control. *Journal of Personality and Social Psychology, 48*, 72–81.

van den Bos, K. (2001). Uncertainty management: The influence of uncertainty salience on reactions to perceived procedural fairness. *Journal of Personality and Social Psychology, 80*, 931–941.

van den Bos, K. (2003). On the subjective quality of social justice: The role of affect as information in the psychology of justice judgments. *Journal of Personality and Social Psychology, 85*, 482–498.

van den Bos, K., Bruins, J., Wilke, H. A. M., & Dronkert, E. (1999). Sometimes unfair procedures have nice aspects: On the psychology of the fair process effect. *Journal of Personality and Social Psychology, 77*, 324–336.

van den Bos, K., & Lind, E. A. (2002). Uncertainty management by means of fairness judgements. In M. P. Zanna (Ed.), *Advances in experimental social psychology* (Vol. 34, pp. 1–60). San Diego, CA: Academic Press.

van den Bos, K., & van Prooijen, J.-W. (2001). Referent cognitions theory: The role of closeness of reference points in the psychology of voice. *Journal of Personality and Social Psychology, 81*, 616–626.

van Prooijen, J.-W., van den Bos, K., & Wilke, H. A. M. (2004). Group belongingness and procedural justice: Social inclusion and exclusion by peers affects the psychology of voice. *Journal of Personality and Social Psychology, 87*, 66–79.

van Prooijen, J.-W., van den Bos, K., & Wilke, H. A. M. (2007). Procedural justice in authority relations: The strength of outcome dependence influences people's reactions to voice. *European Journal of Social Psychology, 37*, 1286–1297.

Wanberg, C. R., Bunce, L. W., & Gavin, M. B. (1999). Perceived fairness of layoffs among individuals who have been laid off: A longitudinal study. *Personnel Psychology, 52*, 59–84.

Weiss, H. M., Suckow, K., & Cropanzano, R. (1999). Effects of justice conditions on discrete emotions. *Journal of Applied Psychology, 84*, 786–794.

Welbourne, T. M., Balkin, D. B., & Gomez-Mejia, L. R. (1995). Gainsharing and mutual monitoring: A combined agency-organizational justice interpretation. *Academy of Management Journal, 38*(3), 881–899.

Williams, K. D., Cheung, C. K. T., & Choi, W. (2000). Cyberostracism: Effects of being ignored over the internet. *Journal of Personality and Social Psychology, 79*, 748–762.

Wilson, J. Q. (1993). *The moral sense.* New York: Free Press.

Part II

The Organization System

4

Change

4.1 Introduction

The necessity for organizations to manage a continual need to renew and change themselves, remain innovative, and maintain a competitive edge is one of the challenges of the corporate world (Leonard-Barton, 1995; D'Aveni, 1994). As discussed in Chap. 1, mergers and acquisitions (M&A) provide a tempting opportunity for organizations to seek opportunities for renewal by avoiding the restrictions imposed by forms of organic growth. However, this method of expansion brings with it a challenge to effectively manage the process of change encountered at both human and systems level. In many cases, M&A are disruptive events that cause immense uncertainty, which can lead to increasing variants of human anxiety. Organizational culture (discussed in more depth in Chap. 5) has a way of encouraging its organizational members to develop ritualistic behaviors that enshroud them with predictability and certainties, providing safety and comfort at a psychological level. However, the change experienced in M&A can be ruthless in its tendency to influence processes that discourage and even disband ritualistic behaviors, crushing those continuities much sought after by those who partake in them.

N. Jackson, *Organizational Justice in Mergers and Acquisitions*,
https://doi.org/10.1007/978-3-319-92636-0_4

The level of disruption is dependent on several contextual factors that will be specific to each case (many of these have been identified and discussed in Chap. 1). The impact of change will help determine the response of organizational members from senior management down to those working at operational level. Those tasked with designing the change strategies will often depend on those in middle management to act as messengers and implement the structures and formations of the new world order, while also joining the rank and file with their own uncertainties of what the changes being implemented will mean to them.

4.2 Models of Change

Even though there is agreement about a steady incline in the rate of organizational change over recent decades (see, for example, Burnes, 2004), there has been a protracted debate about whether change brings the expected benefits to organizations or their members. If we consult the literature, there are two mainstream approaches to change: the planned and the emergent models. One of the key criticisms of the planned model is that it offers change as a concept that can be organized into an ordered and linear sequence, whereas, in reality, change is something that is unpredictable, messy, and untidy. In relation to the emergent model, Weick (2000) argues that it consists of ongoing accommodation, adaptation, and alteration that will produce fundamental change without *a priori* intentions to do so. Both the planned and emergent approaches indicate that change in any form is unpredictable and unstable and in many cases fails to achieve its objectives.

The uncertainties generated by moving from the known to the unknown may well depend on the nature of the change and level of impact this will have on the organizations. For instance, Miller and Friesen (1982) distinguish between evolutionary, revolutionary, and quantum changes, while Weick and Quinn (1999) discuss the differences to emerge from episodic and continuous change. As an example, integration may form part of a much wider program of change or, equally, it may follow a period of inertia in the integrating organizations and be recognized as revolutionary or even quantum change. The extent of change experienced in a merger or

Unfreezing → Movement → Refreezing

Fig. 4.1 Three-step procedure for episodic change. (Note: Based on "Group decision and social change," by K. Lewin, 1958. In W. B. Burke (1992). *Organization development: A process of learning and changing,* (2nd ed.). Reading, MA: Addison-Wesley Publishing Company)

acquisition will be dependent on many of the factors discussed relating to strategic objectives, methods of integration, and typologies (e.g. deeper integration from horizontal acquisition).

Pertinent to episodic change is Kurt Lewin's (1958) three-step procedure model, which is depicted in Fig. 4.1. This model demonstrates a linear process of *Unfreezing* the original situation, *Movement* during the period when the change is introduced, and, finally, *Refreezing* to capture the changes that have been made. Lewin's model represents episodic change.

Burke (1992) explains the stages of Lewin's model and describes unfreezing the present level of behavior, followed by movement "to take action that will change the social system from its original level of behaviour" (p. 55) and finally refreezing by "establishing process that will make the new level of behavior relatively secure against change." One of the key facets of the model that helps to explain this form of change is that it illustrates the emphasis placed on the need to "unfreeze" a current situation before any form of change can be successfully applied. As Bratton (2015) explains, to enable this stage the agents of change will need to either focus on increasing the drivers of change, reducing the inhibitors, or apply a mixture of the two. By increasing or emphasizing the drivers of change, adherents may alter the will of those who are currently identified as inhibitors or resistors of change by raising awareness of the benefits or potential consequences of not accepting the need to move forward and change. This is a useful contribution when considering the debates between organizations and their members encompassing the multitude of factors identified as drivers and inhibitors of change.

Others have argued that change in organizations tends to be more of a continuous pattern of events that are complex and unpredictable, and form a more dynamic process (e.g. see Weick, 2000; Dawson, 1994). The dominant framework up to the 1970s for this more emergent rather than planned approach to change was the perspective that change in organizations is incremental and related to different subsets of an organization and their specific goals (Burnes, 2004). More akin to local internal and external environments, managers could deal with these episodes of change within their own operating environments while recognizing that change is not unidimensional but is dynamic and situation specific. Consequently, different change initiatives will require a more open mind, and when considering the most appropriate conceptual approach, there is also a need to acknowledge the nuances from an intra-organizational perspective. Change may impact specific areas of a business in different ways and may also be more acceptable to some organizational members operating at different levels of the business (e.g. geographical territory, business unit, and department/local teams). Inevitably, perception of change at an employee level will therefore be extremely subjective and dependent on individual circumstance. Nonetheless, it is likely that how change is perceived and interpreted by organizational members at this level will be appreciably influenced by how it is received within the immediate social environment and, indeed, the wider social system.

When considering the model of continuous change, one of the facets is that there is no discernible beginning or end point to the process (Orlikowski, 1996). It is better understood as a series of fast mini-episodes of change and therefore represents change on a micro-level as opposed to the macro-level characteristics of episodic change (Weick & Quinn, 1999). In contrast to the Lewin episodic change process model, the continuous change framework looks to freeze the ongoing change so that any sequence is visible and readily analyzable to investigate what is happening. This follows a period of rebalance to reinterpret, inform, and make any necessary changes to the situation, and then followed by a period of unfreezing to continue with a better-informed process. Weick and Quinn's model of continuous change is illustrated in Fig. 4.2.

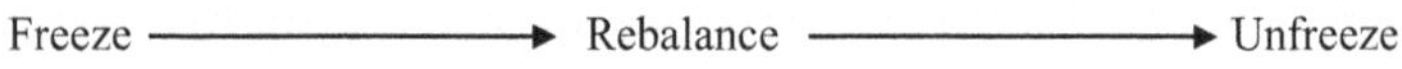

Fig. 4.2 Three-step procedure for continuous change. (Note: Based on "Organizational change and development," by K. E. Weick and R. E. Quinn, 1999. *Annual Review of Psychology*, *50*, 361–386)

Lewin's episodic change model is driven by inertia in a situation where it is necessary to create change, an ideal example being an underperforming target in a proposed merger or acquisition transaction. Alternatively, a target may be the outperformer being purchased because of its unique capabilities, offering an acquirer the opportunity to escape from a period of inertia. In this example, the acquisition is perhaps motivated by a reactive change to the acquirer's environment. It becomes possible that the nature of the change is very different for either target or acquirer and the appropriate framework will be contingent upon the individual circumstances of the integration.

Two concepts that emerged from the 1980s were the punctuated equilibrium model, and the more radical approach to change that set the early seeds for what we now readily refer to as transformational change. Although each concept has its own distinctions, there are similarities in that they both depict change following periods of stability and inertia within the organization. The similarity continues in that each concept proffers a model of change that is revolutionary in nature. The main differentiator is that the punctuated equilibrium model is presented as a pattern of revolutionary change that will occur in short bursts and follow periods of continuity or inertia. In this model the periods of revolutionary change are presented as bearing characteristics that will "disrupt established activity patterns and install the basis for new equilibrium periods" (Romanelli & Tushman, 1994, p. 1141). However, advocates of the transformational change model present a version of organizations that are in continuous need for radical change to adapt and survive on a daily basis (Burnes, 2004). It may be helpful to consider these two models in an applied situation and how they may represent the practical aspect of change in organizations if we consider context-specific criteria, such as different types of industry or technology used in the process of production (Brown & Eisenhardt, 1997).

It is useful to understand the process of change through the lens of the two abstract depictions of episodic and continuous change and then apply some of the various models and frameworks that have been developed as the focal points of discussion and debate in the realms of change management over recent years. For example, Kotter's (2012) eight-stage model helps to recognize some of the more generic factors that encourage both inhibitors and drivers of change, including the importance of communicating an overall vision of the new world postchange and the need to create short-term wins. Engaging employees in change is also recognized for its contribution and the links here with employee voice (see Chap. 3) are notable.

As already alluded to, recognizing change as multidimensional rather than a "one-size fits all" is critical if effective solutions are to be proposed. Defining the scale of change is a primary consideration and viewing this from a perspective of surface change at one end of the spectrum to transformational change at the other enables strategists and implementers to categorize first and then gain insight to the level of changes that will be needed. Table 4.1 shows the increasing depths of change that may occur based on the likely impact to the business.

Drawing from the spectrum of change categories presented in Table 4.1, we can see that, in extremis, the scale of change may be classified as transformational, and it would be fair to say that many mergers involve this form of reshaping corporate identity. However, this is not always the case. Numerous mergers and acquisitions are formed around the auspices of little more than a corporate name change and do not always include the upheaval associated with radical change to ways of

Table 4.1 Depth of organizational change

Depth of change	Impact on organization
Surface	Fine-tuning: focus on efficiency Restructure: centralize, decentralize
Shallow	Reallocate resources: grow some departments, cut others Improve business planning: symbolize a shift in thinking
Penetrating	Change the leadership: new CEO with major change remit Change the organization's definition of success: create new goals, objectives, targets to change behavior
Deep	Change the mission, vision, values, and philosophy: symbolize a radical shift in thinking and behavior
Transformational	Paradigm shift: change how we think, how we solve problems, how boundaries are defined, the way we do business—frame-breaking, mold-breaking, fundamental, strategic change

Note: Adapted from "Organizational Behaviour (8th edn.)," by A. A. Huczyhnski & D. A. Buchanan, 2013. Harlow (UK): Pearson Education Limited working and an overhaul of operating systems. Even so, the strategic implications for most cases of integration are designed to capitalize on the benefits of synergy gained from combining both human knowledge and system practices, retained from methods of working in existing operations, which will necessitate a much deeper form of change strategy.

4.3 Emotional and Behavioral Reaction to Change

If we are to understand the influence of emotion in exacting a reaction to the type of change experienced through a merger or acquisition, then we should turn to some of the change literature that focuses on emotional outcomes. Kiefer (2002), who has conducted studies in this field, identifies organizational change in general terms as "Alterations to an organization's structure, its processes and/or its social system" (p. 877). Change may alter structure such as hierarchy and the functioning of departments (Porras & Silvers, 1991), work processes and work structure, and the perceptions of fair treatment the individual receives as an event of the change (Kiefer). From the results of her research, Kiefer asserts that negative emotions are not experienced because of the change per se, but the individual's evaluations and constructed perception of the specific events leading to a potentially harmful or threatening outcome for that individual. For example, senior managers going through a takeover were recognized for demonstrating several emotional responses including powerlessness, fear, pain, anger, shame, and purposelessness (Vince, 2006).

Such emotional outcomes are activated by the feelings of intense anxiety, loss, and stress that mergers provoke in those who go through them (Cartwright, Tytherleigh, & Robertson, 2007), in part because of the changes experienced to the distinctiveness of the premerger group identity (van Dick, Ullrich, & Tissington, 2006). Loss of psychological attachment resulting in problems with identity and culture orientation is recognized as a common source of merger problems. In turn, these problems are associated with increased levels of stress among employees and impact on critical attitudes, such as affective organizational commitment (van Dick, Ullrich, & Lemmer, 2008; Appelbaum, Bailey, Berg, & Kalleberg, 2000). In addition to these outcomes, the uncertainty aroused by change to both personal and organizational circumstances associated with the fallout from mergers and acquisitions elicits negative responses to other important workplace attitudes such as job satisfaction and trust (Schweiger & DeNisi, 1991). This is occurring at a time when maintaining positivity among the workforce will be critical if individual effort is not only sustained but increased in an attempt to successfully implement system and human integration strategies.

Kiefer (2002) maintains that emotions are an expression of the underlying difficulties an individual is experiencing during the implementation of change rather than the cause of the problems. There is a difference between the individual's emotion and mood, where an emotion involves an appraisal of an object or event (Frijda, 1993) and a mood generally lacks focus and a contextual stimulus (Weiss & Cropanzano, 1996). The effect of change on the individual is described as a trigger event (Isabella, 1993) that is perceived as potential harm/loss, threat, or challenge (Lazarus, 1999). These are the antecedents of emotions experienced by the individual as a reaction to changes in the working environment and relate to how that individual evaluates the triggering event caused by the change (Kiefer, 2005). For example, due to a perceived harmful or threatening outcome a manager who is experiencing the effect of restructuring in their organization is likely to display withdrawal behaviors as an outcome of that change, or triggering event, by searching for another job or portraying other acts of disloyalty (Turnley & Feldman, 1998). The outcome, or behavior, is guided by the central mechanism of emotion experienced from the antecedent (Weiss, Suckow, & Cropanzano, 1999); in other words, emotion is the conduit.

It is important to understand the impact of emotion, because negative emotion (e.g. pain, fear, shame, and anger) is one of the drivers of resistance to change. Different types of merger may impact both organizational and employee outcomes very differently, and, as a consequence, these will lead to different reactions. For example, if we return to the discussion in Chap. 1, here it was discussed whether the integration was a merger or acquisition of one organization by another and whether it was horizontal or vertical. These are a few of the critical factors that will influence the structure and format of the senior board, the level of redundancies, and, ultimately, who are the key decision-makers in the deal.

4.3.1 Resistance to Change

Negative emotion may lead to withdrawal behaviors that form a resistance to the changes that evolve. Resistance is a phenomenon that slows the change process by hindering its implementation and, as an outcome of such behavior, increases costs. The consequences of resistance can be detrimental at best and catastrophic at worst, meaning that there is a need for change agents to recognize not only the most obvious factors that will encourage such behavior, but also the nuances that can be harder to detect and will not be generic activators to all undergoing the change. Some of the more common drivers of resistance will include economic fears, uncertainty, inconvenience, threats to interpersonal relationships, the impact on social functions, and change to the routinization of daily operations, including the disruption to internal processes and systems. The impact from perceived threats to rituals and routinized behavior is discussed in the next section and, in greater depth, in Chap. 5.

Cultural change and the process of transforming identities often leads to various forms of employee resistance as power struggles begin to errupt with the organization machine. This form of activity is often a key antagonist of change, developing barriers to integration and impeding the social functioning of an organization (e.g., see Larsson, 1990; Lipponen, Olkkonen, & Moilanen, 2004). For many years there has been a widespread claim that over half of all M&As failing to meet their strategic objectives do so because of difficulties originating from the attempted combination of employees from the integrating organizations (Davy, Kinicki, Kilroy, & Scheck, 1988; Marks & Cutcliffe, 1988). Full integration should result in the emergence of a new organization that assimilates the working practices and policies of the old organizations and a transformation for employees from those organizational identities to a new organizational identity that encompasses a shared cultural meaning. However, barriers are often created by an employee resistance to these changes, resulting in an endeavor by authorities to drive through the necessary combining of operational functions without the full support of employees. Identifying and understanding the reasons why individuals resist the change to a new organization is therefore important if they are to be encouraged to transfer their identities and embrace the developing shared meaning of the new organizational culture.

Hambrick and Cannella Jr. (1989) propose three distinctions of the kind of resistance individuals enter into. They talk about the following: blind resistance, where people are afraid and intolerant of any change; political resistance, a belief that they stand to lose something of value; and ideological resistance, a belief that the planned change is ill-fated or in violation of deeply held values. It is therefore important for integrating organizations to understand the type of change they are entering into, and how this change may affect their employees' behavior. However, we also need to balance this notion that resistance is mostly considered negative because this perspective does not portray a complete story. Change is not necessarily beneficial to the organization, and resistance can reveal to managers important aspects of the situation that have not been properly considered. Change can generate deep resistance in employees and organizations, which makes it difficult and sometimes impossible to implement change processes and this can also be beneficial to the organization.

The effects upon an individual from a merger change program are discussed by Cartwright and Cooper (1992), and in a more extreme form they relate this to the Kubler-Ross (1969) change, or personal bereavement, model. The model recognizes five stages of loss that people go through when faced with terminal illness and while severity of outcomes are not comparable, there are distinct similarities in the effects of the change process for the individual. The five stages are as follows: (i) shock and denial, (ii) anger, (iii) bargaining, or attempts to postpone the inevitable, (iv) depression, and (v) acceptance. According to the model, some people do not move through all the stages with some failing to go beyond denial. Adopting this framework, often in a merger situation it is characteristic of individuals to develop a fixation within the earlier stages of the process, which inevitably leads to an attempt on their part to deny or resist the situation (Cartwright & Cooper, 1992). Preoccupation with the early orders of the model may lead to unproductive behavior or, in extreme cases, for the employee to leave the organization. Kavanagh and Ashkanasy (2006) add, "Unless these different stages are recognized [by the change agent(s)] and dealt with astutely, employees will resent change, will have difficulty reaching the acceptance stage, and the risk of merger failure is increased significantly" (S86). Following on this theme, Burke (2002) discusses the effect of loss from change and associates this with the subject of resistance. He states:

> The phenomenon of resistance to change is not necessarily that of resisting the change per se but is more accurately a resistance to losing something of value to the person .... loss of the known and tried in the face of being asked, if not forced, to move into the unknown and untried (p. 92).

In conformity with this approach, Levinson (1976) alludes to the fact that all change is portrayed as a loss experience whether resisted or embraced, especially when the loss involves familiar routines.

Cartwright and Cooper (1992) discuss Freud's considerations that "collective grief" powerfully maintains a sense of community and increases cohesiveness. They state that there are implications within an organizational setting, "which arguably makes new culture and managerial practices even more difficult to introduce...The challenge for acquiring management is to attach that cohesion to a new organizational leader or goal" (pp. 38–39). This perhaps implies that those who do resist the movement phase of Lewin's model, or the rebalance phase proposed by Weick, will create a two-tier (or two-speed) readiness for change among the workforce that may be compounded by a cohesive state among those who are not ready to move on.

This potential for collective resistance is highlighted by several mechanisms within the workplace. Schein (1992) discusses situational appraisals and subsequent emotions often shared by groups of individuals who identify with a common culture. Group influence can provide an individual with a sense of increased power while, at the same time, the perception of anonymity also emboldens them due to their place in the group (Huy, 2002). Furthermore, when employees are faced with similar outcomes, their cohesion and affiliative needs are increased by the perceived threats from radical change (Gump & Kulick, 1997) and displays of empathy can then become commonplace (Huy).

4.3.2 Ritualistic Behavior and Resistance to Change

Rituals are usually seen as conservative in function (no matter how colorful the example) and, therefore, a challenge to change. Given this, the simple enjoyment derived from ritual practices, and their fundamental roles in building identity and community, Bell's (2009, p. 211) conclusions that "ritual activities tend to resist change and to do so more effectively than other forms of social custom" is then unsurprising. Contrary to this, if we look to specific examples of contemporary ritual, for example, graduation ceremonies or the investiture of a political officer, or those associated with age-group change, rituals also signify change, instilling new "norms" and values acting as a positive vehicle for and facilitator *of* change. Certainly, rituals are viewed as fundamental in individual transition from one social role to the next, and Van Gennep (1909/1960) argued that the ritual framing of transitions is fundamental to restoring social equilibrium in the context of constant change. This may, for example, relate to marriage or, indeed, death but, given the cross-cultural and cross-context applicability of ritual, could equally apply in the circumstance of organizational change.

Whatever the magnitude of difference of intra-organizational norms and values, these are likely to be magnified at the interorganizational level. Hence, the shared meaning and ritualization of values attached to social identity, social interaction, and cultural ties are likely to form a common bond between employee and organization and form a potential barrier to any threat from external change initiatives (albeit instigated internally). A good example here is the hostile takeover where acquired employees are more likely to form a defense of their organization and become invested in its preservation. As this occurs, their identification with the cultural symbols of the old organization will remain strong at a time when management will be attempting to transfer identities to the newly-formed organization (Citera & Rentsch, 1993). In this type of change initiative, there is a sense of loss that threatens the in-group or community and subsequent resistance to change is likely to be high. Indeed, this resistance is not only relevant in the context of hostile takeover but cited as one of the key aspects of why mergers and acquisitions are prone to fail (see, for example, Cartwright & Cooper, 1992; Schoenberg, 2006).

Rituals offer a focal point for collective action, which is often demonstrated through the form of traditional symbolic routines (e.g. annual awards ceremony). In this scenario, rituals generate a strong sense of organizational community that leads to a form of social control through the transmission of messages about appropriate attitudes and behaviors (Anand & Watson, 2004), and the potential abolishment of an important ritual practice—however seemingly benign in nature—could become a force to block change in almost any situation. Overall, there is an abundance of evidence that ritualistic type behavior is an impediment to change because of its inherent nature to promote resistance.

Conversely, if we turn to consider the findings of Kertzer (1988) and Wollschleger (2012), who also proposed the solidarity perspective of ritualistic behavior and emphasize the ability of rituals to unify diverse groups of individuals, then the advantages they can offer in support of change in organizational life are also identifiable. A good example would be the formation and unification of a new work team. Where change leaders are conscious of its utility, it is therefore possible to engage ritual to advantage as an enabler of change. Taking this perspective, rituals can also be recognized for their aptitude to emphasize stability, as well as being identified for their ability to manage anxiety and therefore help in the transition of periods of change. In cultural terms, they have been considered a valuable mechanism for transmitting values and beliefs to either out-groups or new group members. Scholars have explored how rituals are able to maintain social order within communities (e.g. see Radcliffe-Brown, 1952), supporting the Durkheimian contention that ritual behavior emphasized the unity of the group and minimized individual distinctions. Promoting unified action reduces the opportunity for instances of rebellion if the in-group can be brought onside and encouraged to see the positive outcomes of change. According to Rappaport (1999), because rituals help to accurately communicate the intentions of performers, the communicative function of ritual assists solidarity and helps promote trust and cooperation within communities. Capturing this provides the basis of a critical framework for change leaders to develop a working relationship within their community that will support and enable change. It is important that agents tasked with the responsibility of implementing and enabling change are aware that there is considerable evidence that "ritual" practice can function as a major obstacle to successful change. However, it should also be acknowledged that ritual practice can also be facilitative of change.

One of the recognized levers of employee resistance is whether they feel the changes being undertaken in the workplace have been fairly applied (Folger & Cropazano, 1998; Thornhill & Saunders, 2003). As referred to at greater length in Chap. 3, organizational justice, the psychological concept of fairness in the workplace, is defined by the three dimensions of outcome distribution, the procedures by which those distributions are determined, and the communication of distributions. Support for the notion that perceived organizational justice has been identified as an influence of workplace attitudes and behaviors has led to researcher intrigue within the realms of change. The interaction of perceived justice, changing culture, and identity with a tendency for lower commitment and resistance through withdrawal behaviors has been pursued in a few studies (e.g. see Saunders & Thornhill, 2003). The procedures used in the merger implementation will also have a direct consequence upon how the employee makes judgment on those changes, and their importance is now considered. Bearing in mind the potential impact of perceived fairness in the M&A process, it is perhaps not surprising that it has developed into a topic of increasing concern in the debate surrounding the substandard performance of organizations within this context.

4.3.3 Reducing Resistance Through Employee Involvement

While resistance is a reaction from employees feeling threatened by the changes to their environment, positive attitudes and behaviors associated with successful change have been reported for individuals who perceive they have experienced fair treatment during the integration program (Cobb, Wooten, & Folger, 1995). If an employee is engaged in the process of decision-making, this often has the desired effect of raising an individual's commitment to change because of their participation with it. Individuals will particularly value participation, which leads to increasing their control, partly because it ensures the reliability that effort will lead to a positive outcome (Bandura, 1986). Participation raises the possibility for an individual to gain authority over their behavior and move toward a position of equality from subordinacy in a relationship (Pasmore & Fagans, 1992). Lines (2004) advises, "It is assumed that involvement of those affected by a change strategy will reduce organizational resistance and create a higher level of psychological commitment among employees towards the proposed changes" (p. 193). These are the employee attitudes agents of change need to inspire to encourage positive behaviors in the organization's mission to achieve their objectives of integration.

Case in Question

Because of the merger, many employees indicated a level of anxiety due to changes to organizational policies and practices and insecurity about future uncertainties. This affected their *locus of control*, leading to further uncertainty and insecurity, which may have been partly mitigated had there been an effective mechanism of *process control* (voice) embedded in the merger implementation plan. According to the conversations in Phase 2 of the study, one of the main instigators of perceived unfairness was the lack of employee involvement in the decision-making process, which supported their *a priori* expectations that there would be little clarity and openness in the development of policy and procedure. An ineffective mechanism of process control was deemed as disingenuous and again confirmed *a priori* expectations of little trust in the leadership.

4.4 Uncertainty Avoidance

Uncertainty has been defined as "an individual's perceived inability to predict something accurately" (Milliken, 1987, p. 136). Research has identified that this inability to predict events can be attributed to ambiguous (Putnam & Sorenson, 1982) or contradictory information, or a simple lack of information (Berger & Calabrese, 1975). Regardless of the preceding event, uncertainty has traditionally been a dis-preferred state which motivates people to engage in coping strategies aimed at reducing such perceptions (Berger & Bradac, 1982). However, the theory of uncertainty management offers a conceptualization of the construct in which uncertainty is not defined singly as a negative state (Brashers, 2001). Instead, it is argued some individuals may perceive uncertainty positively in particular contexts. Evidence supporting the theory of uncertainty management has been found in health contexts, demonstrating information-seeking behaviors can be used to reduce the experience of uncertainty that is distressing or to increase uncertainty and consequently optimism and hope (Brashers, Goldsmith, & Hsieh, 2002). It is argued that uncertainty may provide a sense of hope or optimism regarding the impending outcome, rather than the certainty of a negative outcome. An example that can be applied within the context of organizational change may be where corporate restructuring affects employees. In such a scenario the uncertainty of not knowing the outcome of the restructure may provide a preferred state to the certainty of an announcement about job losses. A value of uncertainty management theory is that it acknowledges the range of possible responses individuals may have when experiencing uncertainty, providing a more comprehensive understanding of the construct and how it operates across different contexts. Not everyone will be disadvantaged by uncertainty in comparison to the alternative and, to some extent, this will be context dependent.

4.4.1 Communication and Uncertainty Avoidance

A critical factor in the management of uncertainty is the value of communication. How much an organization recognizes and invests in effective communication during a period of change could be the most important contribution toward achieving change objectives. Kitchen and Daly professed that communication was the link between "what gets said and what gets done" (p. 46). The role of both senior management and frontline managers (FLMs) will have a critical impact in various guises upon communicating the change. Both groups will have capacity to influence employee outcomes and their journey of sense-making about the changes being imposed once they have been transmitted. Huy (2002) found that FLMs who received greater levels of support from senior management were more likely to show higher levels of commitment to the program of change. This will help the group develop motivational aspirations to the change, which will have more influence in supporting those at lower levels in the organization who encounter FLMs to develop similar attitudes. We mustn't forget the significance of FLMs and the role they will play and that actions of senior management should not only focus support on those from the lower levels in the organization, but that attitudes of change agents and their levels of support for the change will be pivotal for effective implementation.

Therefore, we can see that a positive relationship between the two forms of management that is intensely interactive during key stages of the change process is crucial and helps to communicate important aspects such as the vision and need for change. FLMs become pivotal, and if they are to perform this role effectively they will be tasked with not only transmitting the messages of vision and functions of the change, but also being able to form these often indecipherable messages from senior management into something that can be interpreted by those at operational level. FLMs are seen as being closer to the needs and requirements of this group and should be better positioned to communicate to those at ground level while also being better placed to interpret their messages and filter these back to senior bodies in the organization.

It is likely that managers at all levels may have exclusive access to pockets of information that will assist their interaction and engagement with a range of activity (e.g. decision-making) that will play a critical role in the effective management of uncertainty (e.g. Brashers, 2001). Employees will feel fully justified about their expectations that these individuals will manage interactions effectively. For example, there is an expectation that FLMs who can partake in decision-making will have access to valuable information and will be willing to dissemainte this in a timely and accurate manner to organizational members. In turn, they will also be expected to work with others and develop mechanisms in the workplace to help those who are struggling to cope with the changes they are experiencing. Three levels of support are identified by Malecki and Demaray (2003) as instrumental (providing the necessary resources), appraisal (evaluative feedback), and informational support (information and advice). While the need for both instrumental and informational support is more obvious, there is often a tendency to overlook the value of providing feedback to those who are perhaps having to cope with new systems of operating. This may be particularly relevant to those in the position of having to communicate the change (FLMs) among employees, since feedback is identified as an important element of motivation. Support mechanisms form part of the overall process model of the change, which should aim to provide a step-by-step guide to help those involved to understand what is required and the expected impact on organizational members at different stages of implementation (Armenakis & Bedeian, 1999).

4.5 Case in Question

For employees of the premerger business school, control had become manifest in their expectation to manage their own publishing strategy and relating this to their own career preferences. Procedures become more important to the recipient of a decision outcome when they experience uncertainty, and increasingly so when this uncertainty is a consequence of radical change (van den Bos, 2001). Fair procedures are important to the fostering of positive social procedures within groups, and increase an individual's perception of leader legitimacy, paving the way to an increasing prospect of them accepting organizational change (Lind & Tyler, 1988; Tyler & de Cremer, 2005). It is clear from the conversations held that the perceived injustice experienced at the premerger business school can be partly attributed to two related but distinct forms of control. The change to publishing strategy had been imposed on the academic staff, and it appeared from conversations that there had been no consultation and therefore little, if any, employee involvement (process control) in the process. The uncertainty and insecurity expressed by certain members of academic staff at the premerger business school was a direct consequence of this loss of control and was being articulated as sequestering of their basic rights as academics. It appeared to the individual that without consultation the senior management was being authoritarian in its approach to a change in terms and conditions, and this denial of process control had impacted the individual's locus of control. Consequently, this had led to uncertainty and insecurity leading to a frustration with management that was being expressed, in extreme, with an intention to leave the organization. Support for these propositions was provided in the Phase 3 and 4 surveys where evidence of a significant relationship between employees' experiences of process control and identification of a breach in their psychological contract was provided. Thibaut and Walker (1975) discussed the relationship between participation in the decision-making process and its ability to alleviate uncertainty for those individuals, and it is professed that one of the three main causes of employee uncertainty is the lack of information about a cause and effect relationship (Schweiger & DeNisis, 1991). It is therefore clear from the research conversations that for control to be achieved knowledge is an essential element in the elimination of uncertainty, and as a further implication of the study this should be considered in future research.

In addition to the dispersion of knowledge and alleviation of uncertainty, involvement also transmits a message of respect from the management to the employee that they are valued enough to be kept informed and that their knowledge, skills, and abilities are recognized as adding value to the process. The Phase 2 interviews provided positive examples of this proposition where individuals had been asked to participate, as well as negative examples ranging to the extreme of anger and emotion at being treated disrespectfully with no contact or involvement for the employee. Even if the individual does not ultimately influence the final decision being allowed, participation has value because it demonstrates a willingness of authorities to consider the recipient's views and show politeness and respect (Tyler & Blader, 2003). This is demonstrated within the case study in question. An emphasis on treating employees with dignity and respect should be taken for granted. However, in the time of radical change where judgments of fair treatment by authorities are important this becomes of increasing relevance. When individuals feel they are treated with respect their sense of self-worth is strengthened and their attachment to the group is reaffirmed (Huo, Smith, Tyler, & Lind, 1996). This relational model of justice is particularly important when an individual identifies strongly with a group and that group is represented by the authority because the authority's actions toward them carry information about their value and position within that group (Tyler & Lind, 1992). Therefore, the notion that the leadership had demonstrated a complete disregard toward their respect and dignity was of anguish to staff from the premerger management college who had demonstrated in Phase 1 a deep-seated attachment to organizational identity. This behavior led to a great deal of resentment toward the management. In the survey conducted during Phases 3 and 4, there was a strong correlation between the variable respect and dignity, a dimension of interactional justice, and psychological contract breach. This assertion demonstrated that in both cases of field research the act of disrespectful behavior portrayed by management was experienced by staff, and where this was the case it was deemed to affect their perceptions of a psychological contract breach by the organization.

Evidence suggests that process control offers the employee a form of empowerment, increasing their feelings of control at a time of uncertainty. Such influence has also been found to increase their levels of participation in a change process (Jha & Nair, 2008), and strengthen the individual's self-efficacy belief (Conger & Kanungo, 1988). These behavioral and attitudinal effects appeared particularly pertinent at the premerger management school, where cases of extremely low morale appeared to be connected to a feeling of low levels of mutual respect with the leadership. In line with the dynamics of interactional justice, this indicates the level of respect they command within the group and promotes pride in group membership. This helps to develop the relationship between identity and perceived fairness and influencing organizational identification with the newly-merged group (Amiot, Terry, Jimmieson, & Callan, 2006).

References

Amiot, C. E., Terry, D. J., Jimmieson, N. L., & Callan, V. J. (2006). A longitudinal investigation of coping processes during a merger: Implications for job satisfaction and organizational identification. *Journal of Management, 32*, 552–574.

Anand, N., & Watson, M. R. (2004). Tournament rituals in the evolution of fields: The case of the grammy awards. *Academy of Management Journal, 47*(1), 59–80.

Appelbaum, E., Bailey, T., Berg, P., & Kalleberg, A. (2000). *Manufacturing advantage: Why high-performance work systems pay off.* Ithaca, NY: ILR Press.

Armenakis, A. A., & Bedeian, A. G. (1999). Organizational change: A review of theory and research in the 1990s. *Journal of Management, 25*(3), 293–315.

Bandura, A. (1986). *Social foundations of thought and action*. Englewood Cliffs, NJ: Prentice Hall.

Bell, C. (2009). *Ritual: Perspectives and dimensions*. Oxford, UK: Oxford University Press.

Berger, C., & Bradac, J. (1982). *Language and social knowledge: Uncertainty in interpersonal relations*. London: Edward Arnold.

Berger, C., & Calabrese, R. J. (1975). Some explorations in initial interaction and beyond: Toward a developmental theory of interpersonal communication. *Human Communication Research, 1*(2), 99–112.

Brashers, D. E. (2001). Communication and uncertainty management. *Journal of Communication, 51*(3), 477–497.

Brashers, D. E., Goldsmith, D. J., & Hsieh, E. (2002). Information seeking and avoiding in health contexts. *Human Communication Research, 28*(2), 258–271.

Bratton, J. (2015). *Introduction to work and organizational behaviour* (3rd ed.). New York: Palgrave Macmillan.

Brown, S. L., & Eisenhardt, K. M. (1997). The art of continuous change: Linking complexity theory and time-paced evolution in relentlessly shifting organizations. *Administrative Science Quarterly, 42*, 1–34.

Burke, W. B. (1992). *Organization development: A process of learning and changing* (2nd ed.). Reading, MA: Addison-Wesley Publishing Company.

Burke, W. B. (2002). *Organization change: Theory and practice*. Los Angeles: Sage Publications, Inc.

Burnes, B. (2004). Emergent change and planned change – Competitors or allies? The case of XYZ construction. *International Journal of Operations & Production Management, 24*(9/10), 886–902.

Cartwright, S., & Cooper, C. L. (1992). *Mergers and acquisitions: The human factor*. Oxford, UK: Butterworth-Heinmann Ltd.

Cartwright, S., Tytherleigh, M., & Robertson, S. (2007). Are mergers always stressful? Some evidence from the higher education sector. *European Journal of Work and Organizational Psychology, 16*(4), 456–478.

Citera, M., & Rentsch, J. R. (1993). Is there justice in organizational acquisitions? The role of distributive and procedural fairness in corporate acquisitions. In R. Cropanzano (Ed.), *Justice in the workplace: Approaching fairness in human resource management* (pp. 211–230). Hilsdale, NJ: Erlbaum.

Cobb, A. T., Wooten, K. C., & Folger, R. (1995). Justice in the making: Toward understanding the theory and practice of justice in organizational change and development. *Research in Organizational Change and Development, 8*, 243–295.

Conger, J. A., & Kanungo, R. N. (1988). The empowerment process: Integrating theory and practices. *Academy of Management Review, 13*, 471–482.

D'Aveni, R. A. (1994). *Hypercompetition*. New York: Free Press.

Davy, J. A., Kinicki, A., Kilroy, J., & Scheck, C. (1988). After the merger: Dealing with peoples' uncertainty. *Training and Development Journal, 42*(11), 57–61.

Dawson, P. (1994). *Organizational change: A processual approach*. London: Paul Chapman Publishing.

Folger, R., & Cropanzano, R. (1998). *Organizational justice and human resource management*. Thousand Oaks, CA: Sage.

Frijda, N. H. (1993). Moods, emotion episodes, and emotions. In M. Lewis & J. M. Haviland (Eds.), *Handbook of emotions* (pp. 381–403). New York: Guildford Press.

Gump, B. B., & Kulick, J. A. (1997). Stress, affiliation, and emotional contagion. *Journal of Personality and Social Psychology, 72*(2), 305–319.

Hambrick, D. C., & Cannella, A. A., Jr. (1989). Strategy implementation as substance and selling. *Academy of Management Executive, 3*(4), 278–285.

Huczynski, A. A., & Buchanan, D. A. (2013). *Organizational behaviour* (8th ed.). Harlow, UK: Pearson Education Limited.

Huo, Y. J., Smith, H. J., Tyler, T. R., & Lind, E. A. (1996). Superordinate identification, subgroup identification, and justice concerns: Is separatism the problem; is assimilation the answer? *Psychological Science, 7*(1), 40–45.

Huy, Q. N. (2002). Emotional balancing of organizational continuity and radical change: The contribution of middle managers. *Administrative Science Quarterly, 47*, 31–69.

Isabella, L. A. (1993). Managing the challenges of trigger events: The mindsets governing the adaptation to change. In T. D. Jick (Ed.), *Managing change: Cases and concepts*. Homewood, AL: Irwin.

Jha, S. S., & Nair, S. K. (2008). Influence of locus of control, job characteristics and superior-subordinate relationship on psychological empowerment. *Journal of Management Research, 8*(3), 147–161.

Kavanagh, M. H., & Ashkanasy, N. M. (2006). The impact of leadership and change management strategy on organizational culture and individual acceptance of change during a merger. *British Journal of Management, 17*(March Suppl), S81–S103.

Kertzer, D. (1988). *Ritual, politics and power*. New Haven, CT: Yale University Press.
Kiefer, T. (2002). Understanding the emotional experience of organizational change: Evidence from a merger. *Advances in Developing Human Resources, 4*(1), 39–61.
Kiefer, T. (2005). Feeling bad: Antecedents and consequences of negative emotions in ongoing change. *Journal of Organizational Behavior, 26*, 875–897.
Kotter, J. P. (2012). *Leading change*. Boston: Harvard Business Review Press.
Kubler-Ross, E. (1969). *On death and dying*. New York: Macmillan.
Larsson, R. (1990). *Coordination of action in mergers and acquisitions: Interpretive and systems approaches towards synergy*. Lund, Sweden: Lund University Press.
Lazarus, R. (1999). *Stress and emotion: A new synthesis* (1st ed.). London: Free Association Books.
Leonard-Barton, D. (1995). *Wellspring of knowledge: Building and sustaining the sources of innovation*. Boston: Harvard Business School Press.
Levinson, H. (1976). *Psychological man*. Cambridge, MA: The Levinson Institute.
Lewin, K. (1958). Group decision and social change. In W. B. Burke (Ed.) (1992), *Organization development: A process of learning and changing* (2nd ed.). Reading, MA: Addison-Wesley Publishing Company.
Lind, E. A., & Tyler, T. R. (1988). *The social psychology of procedural justice*. New York: Plenum.
Lines, R. (2004). Influence of participation in strategic change: Resistance, organizational commitment and change goal achievement. *Journal of Change Management, 4*, 193–215.
Lipponen, J., Olkkonen, M. E., & Moilanen, M. (2004). Perceived procedural justice and employee responses to an organizational merger. *European Journal of Work and Organizational Psychology, 13*, 391–413.
Malecki, C. K., & Demaray, M. K. (2003). What type of support do they need? Investigating student adjustment as related to emotional, informational, appraisal and instrumental. *School Psychology Quarterly, 18*(3), 231–252.
Marks, M. L., & Cutcliffe, J. G. (1988). Making mergers work. *Training and Development Journal, 42*(4), 30–36.
Miller, D., & Friesen, P. H. (1982). Structural change and performance: Quantum versus piecemeal-incremental approaches. *Academy of Management Journal, 25*, 867–892.
Milliken, F. J. (1987). Three types of perceived uncertainty about the environment: State, effect, and response uncertainty. *Academy of Management Review, 12*(1), 133–143.

Orlikowski, W. J. (1996). Improvising organizational transformation overtime: A situated change perspective. *Information Systems Research, 7*(1), 63–92.

Pasmore, W. A., & Fagans, M. R. (1992). Participation, individual development, and organizational change: A review and synthesis. *Journal of Management, 18*, 375–397.

Porras, J. I., & Silvers, R. C. (1991). Organizational development and transformation. *Annual Review of Psychology, 42*, 51–78.

Putnam, L. L., & Sorenson, R. L. (1982). Equivocal messages in organizations. *Human Communication Research, 8*(2), 114–132.

Radcliffe-Brown, A. (1952). *Structure and function in primitive society*. London: Cohen and West.

Rappaport, R. A. (1999). *Ritual and religion and the making of humanity*. Cambridge, UK: Cambridge University Press.

Romanelli, E., & Tushman, M. L. (1994). Organizational transformation as punctuated equilibrium: An empirical test. *Academy of Management Journal, 37*(5), 1141–1166.

Saunders, M. N. K., & Thornhill, A. (2003). Organisational justice, trust and the management of change: An exploration. *Personnel Review, 32*(3), 360–375.

Schein, E. H. (1992). *Organizational culture and leadership: A dynamic view* (2nd ed.). San Francisco: Jossey-Bass.

Schoenberg, R. (2006). Measuring the performance of corporate acquisitions: An empirical comparison of alternative metrics. *British Journal of Management, 17*, 361–370.

Schweiger, D. M., & DeNisi, A. S. (1991). Communication with employees following a merger: A longitudinal field experiment. *Academy of Management Journal, 34*, 110–135.

Thibaut, J., & Walker, L. (1975). *Procedural justice: A psychological analysis*. Hillsdale, NJ: Erlbaum.

Thornhill, A., & Saunders, M. N. K. (2003). Exploring employees' reactions to strategic change over time: The utilisation of an organisational justice perspective. *Irish Journal of Management, 24*(1), 66–86.

Turnley, W. H., & Feldman, D. C. (1998). Psychological contract violations during corporate restructuring. *Human Resource Management, 37*(1), 71–83.

Tyler, T. R., & Blader, S. L. (2003). The group engagement model: Procedural justice, social identity, and cooperative behavior. *Personality and Social Psychology Review, 7*, 349–361.

Tyler, T. R., & De Cremer, D. (2005). Process-based leadership: Fair procedures and reactions to organizational change. *The Leadership Quarterly, 16*, 529–545.

Tyler, T. R., & Lind, E. A. (1992). A relational model of authority in groups. In M. Zanna (Ed.), *Advances in experimental social psychology* (Vol. 25, pp. 115–292). San Diego, CA: Academic Press.

van den Bos, K. (2001). Uncertainty management: The influence of uncertainty salience on reactions to perceived procedural fairness. *Journal of Personality and Social Psychology, 80*, 931–941.

van Dick, R., Ullrich, J., & Lemmer, G. (2008). Research note: The winds of change – Multiple identifications in the case of organizational mergers. *European Journal of Work & Organizational Psychology, 13*(2), 121–138.

van Dick, R., Ullrich, J., & Tissington, P. A. (2006). Working under a black cloud: How to sustain organizational identification after a merger. *British Journal of Management, 17*, S69–S79.

Van Gennep, A. (1960). *Rites of passage* (M. B. Vizedom & G. L. Caffee, Trans.). Chicago: University of Chicago Press (Original work published 1909).

Vince, R. (2006). Being taken over: Manager's emotions and rationalizations during a company takeover. *Journal of Management Studies, 43*(2), 343–365.

Weick, K. E. (2000). Emergent change as a universal in organizations. In M. Beer & N. Nohria (Eds.), *Breaking the code of change*. Boston: Harvard Business School Press.

Weick, K. E., & Quinn, R. E. (1999). Organizational change and development. *Annual Review of Psychology, 50*, 361–386.

Weiss, H. M., & Cropanzano, R. (1996). Affective events theory: A theoretical discussion of the structure, causes and consequences of affective experiences at work. *Research in Organizational Behavior, 18*, 1–74.

Weiss, H. M., Suckow, K., & Cropanzano, R. (1999). Effects of justice conditions on discrete emotions. *Journal of Applied Psychology, 84*, 786–794.

Wollschleger, J. (2012). Interaction ritual chains and religious participation. *Sociological Forum, 27*(4), 896–912.

5

Organization Culture

5.1 Introduction

Cultural compatibility is recognized as one of the key contributing factors for those organizations that fail to meet their preintegration objectives (Kavanagh & Ashkanasy, 2006). Moreover, it is still recognized for its influential bearing whether culture change involves the simple action of an adjustment to the corporate name or the myriad of complexities involved in fully integrating organizational resources and processes, often referred to as *organizational fit* (Hubbard, 2001). As previously alluded to, employee practices, social norms, and expectations, such as organizational routines and social identities, are widely affected by the integration of systems and processes (both operational and human in origin), and any interference will therefore be of central importance. Disruptions to routines and the transfer of an individual's identity from the old organization to the newly-integrated organization may increase the tendency for resistance as a consequence (Johnson & Scholes, 2002; van Knippenberg, van Knippenberg, Monden, & de Lima, 2002). These are some of the typical concerns employees will experience arising from culture change, which will have implications for the success of organizational merger objectives.

N. Jackson, *Organizational Justice in Mergers and Acquisitions*,
https://doi.org/10.1007/978-3-319-92636-0_5

A strong culture will exist when similar dominant values are held by most organizational members, and it is clear from this that the strength of the organizational culture will have an impact upon the level of resistance to proposed change. Indeed, it is acknowledged that the strength of an organization's culture can be determined by the alignment of its espoused values, which provide a common direction and guidance for employee behavior, and the enacted values of its members (Schein, 2004). A method of effectively transmitting values is using organizational rites and rituals, defined by Dennett (2006) as culturally constructed systems of symbolic communication. Rituals are the routines of daily organizational life and a form of symbolic expression through which beliefs, emotions, and identities can be formed and changed, and a vehicle by which to examine culturally rich phenomena compressed into relatively short periods (Islam & Zyphur, 2009). Therefore, rituals offer an important opportunity for scholars attempting to develop an awareness of an organization's culture and its dynamic relationship with member attitudes and behaviors in the context of an organizational merger or acquisition.

Organizational culture can be observed and investigated from many perspectives, but this chapter is dedicated to the two key aspects that emerged as dominant in the mergers considered in the two cases in question. Value systems, particularly in relation to the impact on developed routinized and ritualistic behavior, were paramount to the attitudes of members in the business school merger and were therefore fundamental in the behaviors that emerged in the early days of their postmerger world. The impact this had on the social foundations of the premerger management college was considerable and went to the very heart of the fabric of their social structure. First, the relationship between different approaches to the process of integrating organizations and the culture experienced therein is considered for its potential impact on employee behavior.

5.2 The Relationship Between Integration Strategy and Culture

The cultural compatibility of integrating organizations is recognized as being an important element of their successful incorporation. It has been examined as a multifaceted phenomenon that bears influence from the complexities of combining multinational organizations through to a simple corporate name change. The combining of resource and processes is often described as *organizational fit* which is acknowledged by Hubbard (2001) for its implications toward the realization of premerger objectives. An prime example of failing to achieve a premerger objective due to a *misfit* in the combination would be an unsuccessful attempt to gain meaningful synergies due to an incompatibility between industry and geographic knowledge. A problem often associated with a diversification strategy. In raising the problem of cultural fit, Hubbard discusses how successful implementation of the integration is difficult without addressing such an issue. Further inference to cultural fit is acknowledged by Johnson, Scholes, and Whittington (2011), who advise that the following options are available to integrating organizations:

(i) *Parent* culture remains predominant and efforts are made to assimilate the partner company into that culture.
(ii) Combine the features of both organizations into a *hybrid* culture.
(iii) Keep the previous cultures intact and separate.

The third option is only realistic if the integration of business activities is not of prime importance.

Similarly, a tripartite framework of contrasting cultural fit strategies with striking connotations is also recognized by Larsson (1990). Larsson and Finkelstein (1999) refer to these as: (i) *hard/controlling*, which can be approximated to Johnson, Scholes, and Whittington's parent culture; (ii) *co-competence*, akin to a combination, or hybrid culture; and (iii) *soft/avoiding* or keeping the cultures intact.

These strategies are presented in Table 5.1.

Co-competence is the superior approach for accomplishing the required level of integration, partly because it is perceived as being more equitable. The main stipulation is the recognition of both organizations' core competencies and attempts to exploit these within the newly-formed entity (Larsson, 1990; Larsson & Finkelstein, 1999). Focus is on combining the best complementary competences from both and therefore tends to somewhat overcome the label of prejudice and bias. Such dimensions may have important implications toward fairness in the process and how this is perceived by employees from both target and acquiring organizations.

Table 5.1 Approaches to integration

Strategic approach to integration	Characteristics
Hard/controlling	Attempts to eliminate possible culture clashes and employee resistance as quickly as possible Concentrates on implementing acquirer's methods of operating Achievement of functional integration is rapid but at the expense of promoting an atmosphere of employee resistance
Co-competence	Focuses on exploiting the competences of both firms Requires constructive and learning interaction between the integrating organizations
Soft/avoiding	Aims to preserve existing values of integrating firms Integration develops slowly as the joining firms learn about each other and establish trust Approach minimizes employee resistance but at the expense of full integration

Note: Based on "Coordination of action in mergers and acquisitions: Interpretive and systems approach towards synergy," by R. Larsson, 1990. Lund, Sweden: Lund University Press

In consideration of the other two approaches, the soft/avoiding approach, while evading early conflict, is only a realistic possibility in situations of low or zero integration. As an example of the hard/controlling method of integration, it has been recognized that to impose their will, dominant organizations sometimes dismiss senior management from the target company to establish their own culture (*monoculturism*) on the newly-integrated organization (Cartwright & Cooper, 1992). It is also asserted that such a move will encourage resistance of the integration by target employees and lower the chances of them being willing to identify with the new organization (van Knippenberg et al., 2002).

Employee reaction to the management of acquisition change is deemed to be the cause of many acquisition failures that can lead to stress and ambiguity within the workforce. In relation to this, studies have found effective communication during acquisition reduces ambiguity and employee stress, thereby increasing chances of success (Napier, Simmons, & Stratton, 1989).

5.3 Case in Question

The alignment of personal and organizational values meant an experience of culture congruence and shared identity for the employees of both premerger organizations. A perceived attack on this relationship of shared values was a substantive issue for employees from both preexisting organizations with a diminution of social and organizational interaction (predominantly from the premerger management college), and a change to the publishing strategy from the premerger business school. Both these issues had been divisive to the extreme and had brought several employees to claim that they were considering leaving the new organization.

5.3.1 The Role of Values in Fairness

At the business school the shared meaning attached to brand identity, publishing strategy, and the ritualization of social interaction, formed a common bond between employee and organization that was of primary importance to the individual and was to form a barrier to transferring their identification to the new organization. The change in practices from old to new was a cause of resentment and subsequent resistance that materialized into negative workplace attitudes and behaviors, such as a lowering of affective commitment, and indications of an intention to leave.

It is helpful to recall Larsson's (1990) framework of strategic approach to integration and cultural fit of integrating organizations, consisting of the three approaches: (i) hard/controlling (one best method, usually controlled by acquirer), (ii) co-competence (interactive, exploiting the competences of both firms), (iii) soft/avoiding (preserve existing values at expense of full integration). It is useful to recall these strategies when considering the three main cultural and identification changes at the business school, and the problems with cultural integration at the NHS Trust. Of the three strategies, the closest fit to the business school model was that of hard/controlling where changes were enforced by an autocratic leadership with the intention of achieving a rapid functional integration. However, as acknowledged within Larsson's framework, this strategy risks provoking an atmosphere of employee resistance because the human element of integration tends to be of secondary concern.

Considering the business school merger, it became evident that an attempt to implement a hard/controlling strategy of integration was inappropriate, and this is perhaps all too common in other examples of M&A that are forged around similar auspices. Where employees experience a strong emotional attachment to their existing organization and this is compounded by a binding of their personal and organizational identities, a hard/controlling strategy of integration is likely to meet with employee resistance, as evidenced in this study. In this instance, there were two elements of integration policy that were incompatible, not only with each other but with the deeply held convictions and values of employees across the business school. Policy changes were introduced without an effective mechanism of consultation procedure and were therefore perceived as enforced through authoritarian rule. On the other hand, the integration of staff and working practice for academics was largely avoided, resembling the soft/avoiding strategy of integration in Larsson's model. In this case it appears that the form of integration strategy has been confused between the extremes of a partial attempt to impose a rapid integration of policy even though little attempt has been made to bring together the workforce and break down the cultural barriers of human integration. One is again reminded of Birkinshaw, Bresman, and Hakanson's (2000) warning that where task integration precedes human integration suspicions are raised of acquisition motives and there will be a threat to acquisition success. In this, there are stark similarities to employee concerns at both the business school and the NHS Trust.

Which of Larsson's three strategies is best fit will be contingent upon the specific circumstances of the merger or acquisition, but what would seem of equal importance is that consistency of the strategy engaged throughout the merger implementation process is applied throughout. If strategies of rapid and deep integration are used for any significant element of policy or task integration, it is important early in the process to bring together those individuals who will be either directly, or indirectly, involved in their implementation.

5.3.2 Rituals, Routines, and Organizational Values

It is perhaps first worth noting the observations of Reger, Mullane, Gustafson, and DeMarie (1994), who offered a vision of organizations as social systems comprising work, people, and formal and informal systems. They proposed that the key to choosing the right approach to culture change is to understand that organizations are inherently resistant to change and designed to neutralize its impact. The issue of moving people through the transition from an organization's past to its future will often fail because, in addition to assumptions that are taken for granted, it is restricted by long-held beliefs that constrain their understanding and support of the new initiatives. Indeed, it is suggested that groups of individuals within the organization social system will automatically use resistance to neutralize any efforts to implement change strategies (Kavanagh & Ashkanasy, 2006). However, we also know that even where there are early positive responses toward an integration partner, these often quickly dissolve into a *them-and-us* attitude (Cartwright & Cooper, 1996), and the characteristics of the integrating organizations have been found to seriously impact the dynamics of this situation. For example, as well as the depth of integration the balance of power may influence continuity of important brand and social identity. Encouraging employees to accept the merger or acquisition partner and identify with the new organization to emerge is likely to have a substantive influence on attitudes and behaviors and reducing resistance to change.

It is recognized in either a merger or acquisition that a dominant partner will demonstrate a stronger sense of continuity than the subordinate partner whose members are deemed to experience the integration as more threatening (Gleibs, Mummendey, & Noack, 2008). Therefore, the threat of change to identity is not only common in the subordinate merger or acquisition partner. This may also be exacerbated where there is a situation of common fate and access to rewards for the high status, or dominating organization is perceived to be diminished through integration with a less prestigious, or subordinate, organization (Hornsey, van Leeuwen, & van Santen, 2003). This may be particularly prevalent where members of that common group have been subject to the same decision rules, or the rule of equality has been applied during decision-making

(Brewer, 2000). In addition, of course, this may also apply where the organizational culture is particularly strong—the strength of which may be quite different for the two merging organizations. The point being, where employees perceive changes affect the cultural ambience of the workplace, particularly where individuals feel a sense of shared identity with the organization, then resistance to the changes being imposed may be considerable.

Organizational rituals, "symbolic practices and communal rites together with their ceremonial enactment," offer a method of expressing such symbolic meaning to the organization's internal and external environments (Smith & Stewart, 2011, p. 114). They have been described quite succinctly as providing a medium that illuminates organizational behavior as well as offering the ability to entrench existing cultural values. Ritual behavior, that is, "*a form of social action in which a group's values and identity are publicly demonstrated or enacted in a stylized manner, within the context of a specific occasion or event*" (Islam & Zyphur, 2009, p. 116), has been identified with the promotion of both organizational change and stability, allowing individuals to transit between roles, to maintain organizational status, or to build solidarity with the organization.

In earlier work, Trice and Beyer (1984) conceptualized organizational culture as having two basic components, namely its substance, or the networks of meanings contained in its ideologies, norms and values and its forms, and the practices whereby these meanings are expressed, affirmed, and communicated to members. In an attempt to cover the broad spectrum of outcomes, Trice and Beyer identified six rites in their original taxonomy consisting of the following: *Rites of passage*—a ritual event marking a person's progress from one status to another (e.g. socialization of a new employee); *Rites of degradation*—removing an individual from their social role and to one of a lower status (e.g. for wrongdoing or failure); *Rites of enhancement*—elaborate ceremonials given to those employees of an organization that perform exceptionally well (e.g. model employee rewarded through recognition and reinforcement); *Rites of renewal*—symbolic actions geared toward reaffirming existing structures and organizational values (e.g. annual meetings and functions, development activities, and team-building workshops); *Rites of conflict reduction*—public attempts to resolve conflict (e.g. collective bargaining and problem-solving groups); *Rites of integration*—committing organizational members to a social system by encouraging and reviving common feelings that bind them together (e.g. social gatherings). Subsequently, Trice and Beyer (1985, 1993) expanded their working taxonomy, including three additional categories consisting of the following: *Rites of creation*—establishing new roles within the organization; *Rites of transition* (Trice & Beyer, 1993)—to accompany changes in structure or technology in the organization; *Rites of parting* (Trice & Beyer, 1993)—to accompany permanent loss of organizational culture through death or merger.

The taxonomy offers a guiding framework for the investigation of organizational rituals and their dynamic interaction with workplace cultural assumptions and values, together with an examination of specific behaviors associated with the cultural change experienced from a merger or acquisition of organizations. Considering existing research, there is ample support for the proposition that cultural integration is one of the most emotive subjects for members of an organization embroiled in the process of a merger or acquisition. Along with other forms of cultural expression, rites and rituals have an implicit meaning to organizational members that will be dependent on context, and therefore specific to situational factors within the workplace.

Rituals that have been examined within the business school case study can be identified as having a level of implicit meaning that was particularly significant as they demonstrated the whole ethos of a strong corporate culture endorsed by a closely aligned identity between an organization and its members. As graphically detailed within the interviews, the ending of those rituals instigated an emotional outcry that exhibited a great deal of frustration and anger by some members of staff that their shared meaning and sense of purpose with the organization had been impaired. It is proposed from this research that the bonding of people through alliances and relationships at the management college was assisted and reinforced by the rituals of social gatherings, particularly those conducted daily within the restaurant and lounges. These routines played an integral part in encouraging social interaction and the subsequent development of relationships that crossed hierarchical and departmental boundaries as well as those between supplier and client. It is proposed that these routines were fundamental in removing interpersonal barriers and maintaining a culture of low-power distance.

It is accepted that to some extent the economic loss experienced by individuals from the withdrawal of free lunch and drinks was the cause of some dissatisfaction, and this was also implied during the staff interviews. However, there can be little doubt that the main impact on the employee-organization relationship was not an outcome of a realignment in the economic exchange, but a consequence of a perceived breakdown in the social exchange. There is considerable evidence that the free flow of information that had been a product of communication across organizational boundaries was crucial to the knowledge sharing and networking ethos that was a fundamental element of the management college culture. In the restaurant and lounges, the daily rituals of meeting and exchanging information had been removed, and in doing so there was a feeling that opportunities to reaffirm a sharing of values and identities had been lost. These ritualistic events created an environment of integration and homogeneity, removing vertical and horizontal barriers to the extent where in-groups and out-groups were not allowed to form a substantive part of the management college culture. Indeed, with consideration to their perceived elevated status there was a distinct impression that staff recognized the organization to which they closely identified as the in-group.

The two most distinct themes to emerge from the discussions with employees in the business school merger were shared values and social structure. Overwhelmingly, these two dimensions depicted the purpose of the daily ritualistic events at the management college, and they are defined in further depth by other interrelated themes identified in the final analysis. Returning to Trice and Beyer's (1984, 1985, 1993) taxonomy of rites and rituals, there are four specific categories that can be closely identified to the case of the management college and are therefore emphasized as being particularly influential. Informed by the four categories of Trice and Byer's taxonomy, focus now turns to the two key themes of shared values and social structure and their subthemes.

Shared Values

The shared meaning and ritualization of values attached to brand identity, social interaction, and the networking ethos formed a common bond between employee and organization that was of primary importance to the individual and was to form a barrier toward the transference of their identification to the new organization. The change in practices from old to new was a cause of resentment and subsequent resistance that materialized into negative workplace attitudes and behaviors, such as a lowering of affective commitment, and indications of an intention to leave.

Trice and Beyer (1984) discuss rites of integration and identify a major manifest consequence of this phenomenon where

> potentially divergent subsystems increase their interaction with each other during common participation in the rite, and thus revive shared feelings that bind them together and commit them to the larger system. (p. 662)

In the current research, the larger system was the management college and, as discussed, this created a situation where barriers were eroded and potential in-group/out-group situations were alleviated as individuals found a common ground to share their identity with the organization (the larger social system). This cohesive force was developed around the common identification with the brand itself, which then became the entity that employees increasingly aligned their personal identities to and formed an affective bond. There was an indication during the interviews of a perceived "special status" attached to the management college. Being a part of this enabled staff to enjoy a perceived elevated status that they then aligned to their own personal identity. This perceived elevated status was reaffirmed through the daily rituals of silver service three-course lunches, unlimited use of the coffee lounges with relaxing comfy chairs, and the annual reaffirming of shared values at the annual Christmas party.

The almost "family-like" atmosphere generated throughout the college, where potentially disparate groups of individuals interacted and networked with few impediments, can be related to Trice and Beyer's (1984) depiction of rites of integration. Their assertions that this promotes equality and community through the narrowing of social distance was identified at the college as a low-power distance culture where, even though there was a genuine respect for authority and a delineation between management and worker existed, there was also a perception of equality in vertical as well as horizontal relationships. Again, it was expressed that the daily rituals not only encouraged this atmosphere but were responsible for its occurrence and recalled images of the Japanese social model (i.e. where inclusivity is encouraged by such examples as morning exercise routines).

Social Structure

Before discussing the importance of the events surrounding social interaction at the management college, first it is appropriate to consider Durkheim's (1902) view that social structure consists of people in a society considered as a system organized by a characteristic pattern of relationships and that the shared system of beliefs regulates social relations. Durkheim further outlines social structure as being characterized by "a system of homogenous segments that are similar to one another" (p. 157).

Although forming an important part of employee opinions at the management college, communication between management and employees during the merger was considered a subtheme of the broader spectrum definition of *social exchange*. The main overriding issue to emerge during the staff interviews at the premerger management college was the loss of benefits they had previously received before the merger. This situation gives rise to a potential conflict of economic exchange (Blau, 1964) between the organization and its staff. However, the consequence of the withdrawal of benefits, including free drinks and lunches, went far deeper than questions surrounding the relationship of economic exchange. It went to the very heart of the historic values and culture developed within the original management college, in which the staff played an integral part. This is depicted by a long-tenured employee, who stated:

> There was a culture where all the faculty had lunch together and you even had your names on serviette rings. The faculty would have lunch together with students and clients all in the same room…it was almost like one of those rituals where for a certain period everybody would get together and would be sharing and reaffirming the [management college] culture. (MC-PT 24)

Increasingly, drink breaks and lunches in the postmerger world of the management college were now taken by members of staff within their own offices because social arrangements at these times had been curtailed with the new arrangements. The design of the college building did not allow for contemporary open plan office environments and most employees worked in the small teams they were affiliated to. Unless purposefully arranged, contact with other employees was minimal. The importance of this networking and social ethos was again presented by a staff member who remarked:

> Decisions about payment for car parking and coffee etc. are big issues because they were very much a part of the [management college] culture, and you would meet people over coffee and lunch. You would have opportunity to share information, catch up, problem solve, quickly maintain networks. (MC-PT 6)

Unless an effort was made to purposefully bring people together, under the new arrangements this was unlikely to happen. From the interviews conducted, there appeared to be a sense of anger toward this challenge upon their perceived rights to network and socialize with different levels of management, and with the students of the college. Discussing how they wanted to articulate their frustrations to senior management about the loss of benefits, one employee commented:

> Don't you understand how important they were? It's not about benefits or salaries, or it may be for some people, but it was more about this is how [the management college] worked…people don't meet as much as they did. The networking isn't as good, so a lot of the actual benefits of the approach have been lost. (MC-PT 1)

There was a distinct feeling that a collective camaraderie that went to the heart of the organization's culture had been severely damaged and perhaps even destroyed. It also appeared to have the effect of distancing and separating individuals at a time of great uncertainty and unease. They believed they had a right to these benefits and that this was built into their informal contract with the organization. This was highlighted by an individual, who observed: “With a lot of people there was a psychological contract that said I am working here not because the pay is great but because there are these other benefits” (MC-PT 5).

Because the social structure of the management college was dependent on the continuation of the daily rituals of renewal and integration of the values and beliefs that the members shared with each other and with the organization, it then becomes evident how the removal of those daily rituals would have such a detrimental impact on their sense of purpose and identity. This challenges Trice and Beyer’s (1984) original purpose for the rites of renewal, which referred to a cyclical or periodical recurring form of renewal. Evidence from the current research study indicates that activities intended to refurbish or strengthen existing social structures were conducted daily over a long time period. If we consider activities at the management college, such as the offering of free silver service lunches, which closely represent the definition of rites of renewal, then the original framework of renewal rites appears limited. This should be extended to recognize either the timing beyond the limitations of a cyclical or periodical basis, or a new category recognizing that there are no limitations on the timing of renewal rituals.

However, within their taxonomy Trice and Beyer (1984) recognized that individuals operating within a social system also progress through states or passages that lead to different end points. Based on a seminal analysis by Van Gennep (1960), they recognized that these rituals resembled “rites of passage,” forming three distinct and consecutive subsets of behaviors defined as rites of separation, rites of transition, and rites of incorporation. The intended consequence of completing the three-rite process is to enable members within a social system that have experienced a transition from one social role to another, to reestablish equilibrium in their social relations. The transition can be favorably compared to a period of socialization, and, indeed, Trice and Beyer exemplify with a case from the US army where myths and folktales are exchanged as part of the process. To draw from this analogy and exemplify the management college, then there is a case to propose that a continuation of the daily rituals of meals and drinks could have served the purpose of a rite of passage. Much of the anxiety among employees originated from the uncertainty caused by the merger which was then amplified by the withdrawal of the daily gatherings to share their experiences and knowledge. Information flows were curtailed but this gathering of organizational members could have, at very least, acted as an event to share concerns, overcome some of the misapprehensions, and alleviate some of the more misguided anxieties. At best, this may have orchestrated Trice and Byer's rites of passage by encouraging the transition of identity and values from the past to the future. This could have been encouraged by inviting members from their merger partner to join them and form the basis from which to develop a new social structure.

Commitment, Citizenship, and Intention to Leave

Organizational culture and identity are recognized as two important concepts that are influential in shaping employee attitudes and behaviors during the change process of a merger or acquisition (Hubbard, 2001; van Dick, Ullrich, & Tissington, 2006). Perhaps there is no surprise that where actions impede relationships so closely aligned as the values and identities of organizations and their members, this can instigate radical forms of behavior change. There was evidence from conversations with employees from the management college that for some individuals there had been a change of commitment from a form of affective commitment to a much weaker form of either normative or continuous commitment. At least for the time being, emotional attachment to the organization had been curtailed. It is thought that there are a few reasons why this may be the case and why the change in commitment can be associated with the ending of the daily ritual of free lunch and drinks. First, these rituals reaffirmed the commitment to organizational values through a process of renewal and integration, a process that involved a sharing of values and identities with other organizational members. This had been developed around the spirit of community and society and was therefore contingent on the presence of the social system itself.

Second, the act of removing those rituals was responsible for impacting the social structure of the organization, damaging the equilibrium. Turning once again to the definition of social structure, we can see from the example of the management college that it is developed around those relationships that are regulated by a shared system of beliefs. This example provided further supporting evidence that maintenance of such relationships is a critical function of social structure. At the management college, the daily rites of renewal and integration were fundamental to maintaining the shared system of beliefs and the consequential relationships that resulted, but also the shared identities that have already been discussed. Organizational identity has been recognized as a key determinant of commitment (Bartels, Douwes, de Jong, & Pruyn, 2006) and is therefore a highly significant factor during the merger or acquisition process when there may be an escalation of employee resistance due to increased anxieties.

Third, ownership of the college brand, as depicted through the logo, now acknowledged the University, and this act was perceived by many of those interviewed as a diminution of its status. Because the brand was perceived as having superordinate status and was such an integral element of the strong culture experienced at the management college, there was a deep feeling of loss resonating from the members, which even extended to the college alumni. It has been acknowledged that members of the high-status group will be motivated to maintain their identity (Amiot, Terry, & Callan, 2007) and avoid a situation of reduced status from their merger or acquisition partner (Hornsey et al., 2003). Consequently, the closely aligned identity between the organization and its members resulted in the feeling of personal loss and emotions that may be ascribed to this event. Again, there is evidence that the close relationship recognized between an individual's identity and commitment influenced the members' affective commitment because of the detrimental impact on the relationship between personal, social, and organizational identities.

As may be expected, where there is a move from an affective form of commitment to a more normative or continuous form of commitment among organizational members, a subsequent change in behavior, or intended behavior, was also experienced. A persistent message received from the interviews was that an attitude of less inclination to work beyond contractual obligations had developed. A change in behavior of this nature is particularly pertinent in this example when considering the emphasis on citizenship. This form of behavior had been part of the College culture and, indeed, the presence of citizenship had developed into an expectation of organizational members. The message within the newly-developing culture was less affective commitment and less citizenship behavior. Even more alarming was that among those organizational members who experienced a weaker form of emotional attachment, there was a clear indication of an intention to leave the organization in the near future.

5.4 Conclusions

When considering previous examples of cultural issues in mergers and acquisitions, it is perhaps inevitable that the experience at the management college would result in such a negative response from its members. A strong culture such as that experienced in this example where the espoused and enacted values are so inextricably linked will undoubtedly present a sensitive case in situations where management attempt to enforce behavior change using such a radical and extreme approach without the support of employees. However, this example is not just about the effect of culture change in a merger or acquisition. It presents an opportunity to examine the dynamics of ritualistic behavior that became the conduit of the cultural ethos in an organization and was subsequently fundamental to the shared values, purpose, and identity of its members. Subsequently, it is also the case that because this example is the consequence of an organizational merger, the opportunity presented is relatively unique to the study of cultural rituals. Therefore, what can be concluded from the experience for each party of the merger?

First, although rites of renewal and rites of integration have been identified by Trice and Beyer (1984), as important concepts in the maintenance of organizational culture they appear to hold significance during an organizational merger or acquisition and perhaps in the broader context of organizational change. The relevance here is because the uncertainty often associated with mergers and acquisitions raises anxiety in organizational members, especially where their previous identities are threatened with the formation of a new organizational identity along with the formation of a new company. However, while it is important to consider these rites, it is also important to recognize that a simple continuation of the routines may provide a barrier to change, particularly to changing the loyalties and identities of organizational members. If we consider the tenets of the rites of passage, which demonstrate the importance of transition from one social state to another, it becomes evident that where a new social structure is necessary, previous rituals should be adapted to include elements of it (i.e. in consideration of the rites of passage, rituals that demonstrate rites of renewal and rites of integration are still important, but must be adapted to include elements of the new order).

Second, it is evident that both rites of renewal and rites of integration are an important aspect of reinforcing shared values between an organization and its members. While employees from the university also experienced shared values, these were not demonstrated through an engagement with organizational rituals. Shared values between the management college and its members provided a strength that became the backbone of the organization and may even have been critical to its survival over recent years. In addition, these shared values were embedded in a perception that the organization had an elevated status within its industry which, along with a closely related personal, social, and organizational identity, resulted in a sense of loss for the employees at the thought of having to share their brand with the university. Where a strong culture exists and, as in the example case at the management college, identities are closely aligned, rituals of renewal and integration can form an impervious barrier to change because of the resistance encountered from employees. This simply wasn't the case for members of the university, where a much weaker form of culture existed, based on a commitment to career occupation rather than organization. In situations such as the example at the management college, it would appear critical that the continuation of these rituals should receive careful consideration, not least because of the influence they have over the behavior of the individuals involved. However, as the current case has exemplified, the total withdrawal of these rituals may also have an equally devastating effect, resulting in negative attitudes and behavior from organizational members. Once again, an alternative solution is to enable a continuation of the ritual with a redefined format to include elements of the new social structure, incorporating a visible presentation of values from both organizations that can be effectively integrated within the new social order.

References

Amiot, C. E., Terry, D. J., & Callan, V. J. (2007). Status, fairness, and social identification during an intergroup merger: A longitudinal study. *British Journal of Social Psychology, 46*, 557–577.

Bartels, J., Douwes, R., de Jong, M., & Pruyn, A. (2006). Organizational identification during a merger: Determinants of employees' expected identification with the new organization. *British Journal of Management, 17*, S49–S67.

Birkinshaw, J., Bresman, H., & Hakanson, L. (2000). Managing the post-acquisition integration process: How the human integration and task integration processes interact to foster value creation. *Journal of Management Studies, 37*, 395–425.

Blau, P. (1964). *Exchange and power in social life*. New York: Wiley.

Brewer, M. B. (2000). Superordinate goals versus superordinate identity as the bases of intergroup cooperation. In D. Capozzo & R. Brown (Eds.), *Social identity processes: Trends in theory and research* (pp. 117–132). London: Sage.

Cartwright, S., & Cooper, C. L. (1992). *Mergers and acquisitions: The human factor*. Oxford, UK: Butterworth-Heinmann.

Cartwright, S., & Cooper, C. L. (1996). *Managing mergers, acquisitions and strategic alliances: Integrating people and cultures*. Oxford, UK: Butterworth-Heinmann.

Dennett, D. (2006). *Breaking the spell: Religion as a natural phenomenon*. New York: Viking.

Durkheim, E. (1902). The division of labour in society. In S. Lukes (Ed.), *Emile Durkheim, his life and work: A historical and critical study*. New York: Penguin Books.

Gleibs, I. H., Mummendey, A., & Noack, P. (2008). Predictors of change in postmerger identification during a merger process: A longitudinal study. *Journal of Personality and Social Psychology, 95*(5), 1095–1112.

Hornsey, M. J., van Leeuwen, E., & van Santen, W. (2003). Dragging down and dragging up: How relative group status affects responses to common fate. *Group Dynamics: Theory, Research and Practices, 7*, 275–288.

Hubbard, N. (2001). *Acquisition strategy and implementation*. Basingstoke, UK: Palgrave.

Islam, G., & Zyphur, M. J. (2009). Rituals in organizations: A review and expansion of current theory. *Group and Organization Management, 34*(1), 114–139.

Johnson, G., & Scholes, K. (2002). *Exploring corporate strategy* (6th ed.). Harlow, UK: Prentice Hall.

Johnson, G., Scholes, K., & Whittington, R. (2011). *Exploring strategy: Text & cases* (9th ed.). Harlow, UK: Prentice Hall.

Kavanagh, M. H., & Ashkanasy, N. M. (2006, March). The impact of leadership and change management strategy on organizational culture and individual acceptance of change during a merger. *British Journal of Management, 17*(Suppl), S81–S103.

Larsson, R. (1990). *Coordination of action in mergers and acquisitions: Interpretive and systems approaches towards synergy*. Lund, Sweden: Lund University Press.

Larsson, R., & Finkelstein, S. (1999). Integrating strategic, organizational, and human resource perspectives on mergers and acquisitions: A case survey of synergy realization. *Organization Science, 10*, 1–26.

Napier, N. K., Simmons, G., & Stratton, K. (1989). Communication during a merger: The experience of two banks. *Human Resource Planning, 12*(2), 105–122.

Reger, R. K., Mullane, J. V., Gustafson, L. T., & DeMarie, S. M. (1994). Creating earthquakes to change organizational mindsets. *Academy of Management Executive, 8*(4), 31–43.

Schein, E. H. (2004). *Organizational culture and leadership* (3rd ed.). San Francisco: Jossey-Bass.

Smith, A. C. T., & Stewart, B. (2011). Organizational rituals: Features, functions and mechanisms. *International Journal of Management Reviews, 13*, 113–133.

Trice, H. M., & Beyer, J. M. (1984). Studying organizational cultures through rites and ceremonials. *Academy of Management Review, 9*(4), 653–669.

Trice, H. M., & Beyer, J. M. (1985). Using six organizational rites to change cultures. In R. H. Kilmann, M. J. Saxton, & R. Serpa (Eds.), *Gaining control of the corporate culture* (pp. 370–399). San Francisco: Jossey-Bass.

Trice, H. M., & Beyer, J. M. (1993). *The cultures of work organizations*. Englewood Cliffs, NJ: Prentice Hall.

van Dick, R., Ullrich, J., & Tissington, P. A. (2006). Working under a black cloud: How to sustain organizational identification after a merger. *British Journal of Management, 17*, S69–S79.

Van Gennep, A. (1960). *Rites of passage* (M. B. Vizedom & G. L. Caffee, Trans.). Chicago: University of Chicago Press (Original work published 1909).

van Knippenberg, D., van Knippenberg, B., Monden, L., & de Lima, F. (2002). Organizational identification after a merger: A social identity perspective. *British Journal of Social Psychology, 41*, 233–252.

6

Social and Organization Identity

6.1 Introduction

There seems to be overwhelming evidence that the consistently high rate of failure for merging organizations to achieve their integration objectives is inextricably bound to the misunderstandings of managing people through the transition of change. Early positive employee responses toward an integration partner are often quickly dissolved into a *them-and-us* attitude (Cartwright & Cooper, 1996). This may lead to reactions such as an intention to leave (Mottola, Gaertner, Bachman, & Dovidio, 1997; van Knippenberg & van Leeuwen, 2001), stress (Lipponen, Olkkonen, & Moilanen, 2004; Terry, Callan, & Sartori, 1996), lower productivity and illness (Cartwright & Cooper, 1993), and lower job satisfaction (Lipponen et al., 2004). The propensity for individuals to switch their allegiance to the new organization and the social systems that operate within and around the entity is essential, and the process of developing a sense of identity will play a key role. Mael and Ashforth (1992) define organizational identity as "the perception of oneness with or belongingness to an organization, where the individual defines him- or herself in terms of the organization(s) in which he or she is a member"

N. Jackson, *Organizational Justice in Mergers and Acquisitions*,
https://doi.org/10.1007/978-3-319-92636-0_6

(p. 104). Encouraging employees to accept the merger partner and identify with the newly-formed organization will be pivotal in this process and, subsequently, the attitudes and behaviors organization members develop.

Depending on the level of integration, members of an organization will need to *disidentify* with the premerger organization when it is dissolved (Chreim, 2002). As well as the depth of integration, the balance of power may influence continuity of identity. Because the integration creates a perceived threat to the organization's identity and, in turn, the employees' social identification with their organization, it may also pose negative connotations toward their collective identity and self-esteem (van Dick, Ullrich, & Tissington, 2006). The whole phenomenon of organizational identification draws on the desire to fulfill social needs, and the social group individuals belong to form a significant part of their self-concept (Tajfel & Turner, 1986). An increase in an individual's identification with a group will extend the influence the group has over that individual's attitudes and behaviors (Hogg & Abrams, 1988; Tajfel & Turner, 1986; Turner, Hogg, Oakes, Reicher, & Wetherell, 1987).

It has been argued that continuity is vital within the process of forming an identification with the postmerger company (van Knippenberg & van Leeuwen, 2001; van Leeuwen, van Knippenberg, & Ellemers, 2003). Here we can see how such a situation can be created if the change has little effect on the employees' daily work, and the sense of continuity helps translate the premerger identification into a newly-formed identification with the postmerger entity (van Dick, Wagner, & Lemmer, 2004). These individuals are more likely to perceive the postmerger organization as a common in-group, experiencing the lowest negative emotions and most positive job satisfaction levels. This field of research has identified three key factors that will have a significant influence on postmerger identification. These consist of the level of premerger identification, perceived continuity, or in-group typicality (Bartels, Douwes, de Jong, & Pruyn, 2006) and the influence of perceived fair treatment of the individual (Amiot, Terry et al., 2007; Lipponen et al., 2004).

6.2 Antecedents of Identity Integration

A principal aim of managing employees through the transition of an organizational merger is to encourage an environment where a new superordinate identity can be enabled. Amiot, Terry et al. (2007) recognized this process as one of the key mechanisms of change and that the emerging or superordinate employee identity will develop as a cycle throughout this period. Of significant importance through the cycle will be the environment or social context of change, which will act as a mediator in its capacity to be either a facilitator or an inhibitor.

6.2.1 Facilitators of Social Identity Integration

The Similarity Effect

Any commonalities or similarities that exist between the merging social groups may facilitate the formation of a monadic identity, particularly if these associations can be identified at a cognitive level (Amiot, de la Sablonniere et al., 2007). It is acknowledged that this recognition of similarity between different subgroups (e.g. merging social groups) draws comparisons with the conceptual approach related to identity continuity. If a cognitive perception exists of similarities between the two premerger organizational groups, then this will help those individuals to facilitate the development of a new social identity over the period of merger integration. Also, a greater awareness of their identity will occur where the assimilating groups are able to resemble characteristics of an in-group at an early stage in this process. Such an approach recognizes that despite the social changes taking place around them there is still a camaraderie shared between groups that maintains the characteristics of the in-group over time (Jetten, Iyer, Tsivrikos, & Young, 2008; Sani, Bowe, & Herrera, 2008; Ullrich, Wieseke, & Van Dick, 2005).

While similarity has its advocates, several studies have challenged the principle that this has positive undertones for promoting cohesion between groups. Identified as the "similarity differentiation hypothesis" (Hewstone & Brown, 1986; Spears, Doosje, & Ellemers, 1997), findings within the context of these studies argued that similarities between the in-group and the out-group lead to antagonistic responses being engendered in members' behavior rather than the cooperation sought from a merger situation. However, the context of a merger is often more nuanced, attracting conditions that necessitate employee cooperation at multiple levels within the emerging organization, particularly if they are to overcome challenges and potential barriers to successful integration. While merging groups may perceive that similarities exist at a more interpersonal level, the need to overcome disparities between operational functionality and the integration of systems can also generate a mind-set of solidarity leading to cohesive working practices. This reduces the prospect of similarity being recognized as threatening because it becomes more critical in these circumstances to forge unity in a situation of adversity and help to compensate for the potential barriers arising from the integration at multiple levels in organizations. With empirical support, there is evidence that if such similarities are perceived to exist between merging subgroups, this will enhance the notion of a merged superordinate identity (Amiot, Terry, & McKimmie, 2012).

Based on the principles of similarity/attraction theory that are manifest within social identity theory, there is a bias toward both discrimination and prejudice of members of the out-group compared to those associated with the in-group. Therefore, we can assume when identification with a superordinate group is developed, it will help to eradicate such tendencies toward discrimination and in-group bias. There is empirical evidence to support this proposition with studies that have focused on the identity-discrimination relationship, confirming a negative association between increasing levels of identity that form an inclusive, superordinate merged entity and the existence of bias in favor of the premerger in-group (e.g. Lipponen et al., 2004; Terry, Carey, & Callan, 2001; Terry & O'Brien, 2001).

Coping Strategies

In more general terms, coping strategies may be aligned to a range of contexts and so any related activity will be dependent on the environment that the individual is placed within. Identified by Folkman (1984) as an effort to manage both the internal and external demands of the individual who finds themselves in a troubled person-environment (P-E) transaction, there are also connotations with the process of self-development (Skinner & Edge, 2002) and the construction of self-developmental mechanisms (see Brandtstadter, 1998; Heckhausen & Schulz, 1995). These are also designed to manage the P-E transactions. Within the context of a merger one of the key P-E transactions encountered will involve the forces of change that demand a transition to forming new social identities. If a merger transition is considered as a form of P-E transaction, then the transitional rituals and associated routinized behavior discussed in Chap. 5 may become an important form of coping mechanism. This is analogous to work in other contexts, such as career transitions (Heppner, Cook, Strozier, & Heppner, 1991) and transition to parenthood (Terry, 1991), which will also generate their own forms of coping mechanism.

If we reflect on the examples given earlier of P-E transactions and coping mechanisms, then a commonality that exists in relation to the transitions is the presence of stress from the perceived threat of a change to the unknown. How well members can adjust to the change when engaging with coping strategies, particularly in the early phases when the threats from readjustment are at their strongest, will have an influence on the level of perceived threat and subsequent stress encountered. Indeed, there is considerable support across a variety of studies that the implementation of coping strategies will act as a mediator in the relationship between appraisals of stress or threat and different outcomes for the individuals concerned (e.g. Lazarus & Folkman, 1984). There is also evidence that individuals can identify with a new social group and forge a stronger form of identification with the newly-formed superordinate organization when coping actions are used by members going through the process of change (Amiot, Terry, Jimmieson, & Callan, 2006). There is also substantive evidence to predict that during change such as that relating to organizational mergers, attaching oneself to the new superordinate identity that has been created not only has a positive impact on adjusting to the newly-developed workplace environment, but also creates a sense of well-being (Terry et al., 2001; Terry & O'Brien, 2001; van Dick et al., 2004).

A variety of studies have corroborated a link between the development of coping strategies and individual well-being. Research substantiates the causal links between psychological well-being and the development of coping strategies (e.g. see Moghaddam, Taylor, Ditto, Jacobs, & Bianchi, 2002; Cross, 1995). In support of these studies, Kosic (2004) demonstrated that the proximity of an individual's new cultural group could be enhanced by the active use of coping strategies in the process of acculturation and that these feelings are negatively affected by avoiding the use of coping strategies through disengagement and denial. In support of this proposition, it has been reported that where the level of cultural integration has been strengthened and there is a reduction in the likelihood of conflict erupting, it is predicted there will be greater psychological well-being experienced by those organizational members (Downie, Koestner, ElGeledi, & Cree, 2004).

Therefore, when taking into consideration the influence of successful social identity integration within the process of managing and potentially reducing intra-individual conflict, we should also reflect on the likely consequences of psychological adjustment and well-being for those involved. Research points us toward social identity (including ethnic identity) enabling prediction of enhanced well-being (e.g. Cameron, 1999; Phinney, 1995; Roberts et al., 1999) and an association with reducing discrimination for those who find themselves feeling stigmatized within a newly-formed group (e.g. Crocker, Luhtanen, Blaine, & Broadnax, 1994). These findings have important connotations for organizational justice theory and its development in the workplace during the radical change processes attached to M&A.

Support and Recognition

The impact of social support in the process of identity development has been discussed within several different contexts including support provided by friends, teachers, colleagues, and family members. As part of the identity development process, support has been recognized as a critical element (e.g. Phinney & Rosenthal, 1992; Ruble et al., 2004), and, indeed, at group level the involvement of notable others forming part of that environment has also been predicted to be important. The role of social support in the development of cultural identity leads to a much shorter lead time toward establishing meaningful relationships within these contexts (Bettencourt & Sheldon, 2001), creating the opportunity for a positive influence on identity creation and integration on an intergroup basis. Critically, the support from in-groups, particularly informational support, has been found to have a positive impact on attenuating stress (Haslam, Jetten, O'Brien, & Jacobs, 2004; Haslam, O'Brien, Jetten, Vormedal, & Penna, 2005). Another positive outcome of this enhanced interaction and identification with a more inclusive social group is the recognition of strengthening the individual's well-being at work (see Cross, 1995).

Managing the transition from premerger entities to a single, encompassing superordinate group consisting of the newly-merged organization is the challenge, and if this is conducted effectively, then the outcome is one common in-group identity. Behavioral outcomes relating to a propensity to identify with the superordinate group have been found to demonstrate lower in-group bias and better intergroup tolerance (Gaertner & Dovidio, 2000). Unfortunately, there is no magic formula to create this scenario, but if the creation of a common superordinate group is to be developed effectively, then at very least there needs to be a recognition of the premerger subgroups' particularities and characteristics (Amiot et al., 2012).

There are other pointers that draw on the need to maintain subgroup identity and that group members must perceive that their subgroup identity is recognized and respected in the newly-developed superordinate group (e.g. see Hornsey & Hogg, 2000a). Discrimination and prejudice is increased when there is a feeling that distinctiveness of the premerger subgroup is threatened or neglected to be considered within the new superordinate identity. Such triggers of perceived threat interrupt attempts to form intergroup harmony, and there is recognition that subgroup identities need to be inclusively encapsulated within the context of the newly-formed superordinate identity (Gonzalez & Brown, 2003; Hornsey & Hogg, 2000b).

The level of diversity should be acknowledged rather than an attempt to override such a critical element of human integration, ensuring that this incorporates the things that matter. These can appear trivial on the surface, which is why those change agents involved in the process of integration of systems and people need to be fully aware of the nuances and prototypical behavior type encountered in each of the premerger groups before integration occurred. It is imperative that the characteristics of both organizations are captured and that they are not prototypical of the higher-status group, which will then encourage more positive intergroup outcomes, such as increased tolerance (Mummendey & Wenzel, 1999; Waldzus, Mummendey, & Wenzel, 2005; Waldzus, Mummendey, Wenzel, & Weber, 2003). The argument to take into consideration the particularities of existing premerger subgroup identities and incorporate in the newly-developed superordinate identity is supported elsewhere (see Hewstone & Brown, 1986; Hornsey & Hogg, 2000a). This set of literature argues that preserving the premerger subgroup identities will also reduce the sense of identity threat experienced by organizational members, resulting in an increased rate of acceptance of the newly-created superordinate group (Gaertner & Dovidio, 2000).

Identity Is Developmental

However, personal, and social identities are dynamic, not static, entities, and their development over time becomes much more of a complex process than a simple acceptance or rejection of changing circumstances and situations. This becomes a process where different social identities are integrated into the self-concept over a period of time (Harter, 1999). While environmental and situational factors will impact an individual's acceptance of change, there is no evidence to suggest that circumstances will prevail where we are simply deemed to be either acceptors or rejectors of change or different social identities. The cognitive-developmental model of social identity integration (Amiot et al., 2007) acknowledges the variety of social identities that will be apparent in a changing intergroup context, with each group member subjectively representing a different social identity (Amiot et al., 2012). The model allows for the proposition that new social identities develop and change over periods of time drawing on an individual's specific developmental and cognitive processes. The model professes that there will be an increase in social identification with the new superordinate group over time as this new identity is incorporated in an individual's sense of self.

Another important element of increasing social identification over this time is that perceived similarities and commonalties between the premerger groupings are developed alongside an enhanced familiarity with one another (Gaertner, Dovidio, Bachman, & Rust, 1993). The framework also recognizes that each individual's social identity can be integrated into the larger model superordinate identity via a cognitive process of binding different subgroup (premerger) identities into the overall self. During this process, any new social identities that are generated and become integrated in the overall self are subject to new cognitive links helping to associate those identities that already existed (i.e. premerger group identity) and the new identity (superordinate identity) that has been created. This opportunity to develop an identification with the newly-merged organization is beneficial to intergroup relations, although we can see it involves an intricate and complex process of binding different identities into the overall self. A process that also draws benefits for intergroup relations, including those subgroups that have been identified as potentially diverse and even conflictual in nature (Amiot, de la Sablonniere et al., 2007).

It should also be noted that for some organizational members the opportunity to develop new social groupings resulting in a new superordinate identity may be more appealing compared to a continuation of social identity with the premerger subgroup. Social Categorization Theory (SCT) attempts to demonstrate the psychological accentuation of differences that develop between categories of different groups compared to the attenuation of differences between elements within categories (Turner et al., 1987). Drawing on this theory we can propose that the social category an individual will identify with in a postmerger situation will be dependent on whether the intergroup differences are greater than the intragroup differences. If intergroup differences can be perceived as minimal or even nonexistent, then we can propose social identification with the superordinate group will be more accessible and easer to facilitate.

6.2.2 Inhibitors of Social Identity Integration

Feeling Threatened

In contrast, different circumstances will emerge for employees who perceive the changing or transition of identity as a threat to their status or continued existence in the workplace. Those different outcomes will be more liable to form barriers toward, rather than facilitating, the development of a new superordinate identity (Hornsey & Hogg, 2000a). Evidence points toward identity threat being the cause of increased stress in organizational members, which will then tend to inhibit rather than enhance the integration process. The course of adjusting to the new social structures instigated by a merging of organizations means that different coping strategies need to be developed as the need to manage the transition of change arises (Roccas & Brewer, 2002).

To form some understanding of what this means, it is helpful to outline the different types of threat that may hinder the cognitive process of identity formation during this period of merger activity. Van Dick et al. (2006) recognize several key characteristics that are associated with identity threat, which include a perceived threat to the distinctiveness, influence, and representation of the premerger organization within the structures of the newly-amalgamated entity. In some of the more extreme cases, the entire existence of the member's in-group could be under threat within this new structure. However, the tendency for some to overemphasize the negative impacts from merging may lead to self-anchoring and a subsequent initial decrease in identification (Amiot et al., 2012). It is commonplace for subgroup members about to transition into a superordinate unit to form a sense of identification based on their expectations of life within the new social group. This abstract sense of identification can be generated even if the group members have very little information about the subgroup they will be amalgamating with (e.g. see Amiot, Terry, Wirawan, & Grice, 2010). Much akin to the principles of the psychological contract, these expectations will be revised upon encounter with the new situation and reactions may vary according to the evaluation of reality versus expectation. Again, this will also be subject to revision as time passes and the anticipated new social identity is impacted by reality and both the pros and cons of this are considered. The cultural integration of each subgroup will play an essential role as important factors such as pre-existing values and status of members are contested and contrasted with their counterparts in their new environment. The impact of self-anchoring via the encounter between idealization and reality may raise the potential for disidentification with the new social group (Sussman, 2000).

Different situational factors will elevate the level of perceived threat experienced by those organizational members transitioning through the merger process, and perhaps it is worth dwelling on individuals joining from what is perceived as the "low-status group". For those members, the status of threat they experience is escalated due to a potential confrontation of their in-group being entirely eradicated within the structures of the newly-merged superordinate group (van Leeuwen et al., 2003). In this case, due to the elevated presence of perceived threat, there could be a tendency for this group of individuals to form barriers toward the newly-developing superordinate in-group and, subsequently, experience lower identification because of these increased pressures.

Any perceived change to social identity that results from social change may be the source catalyst that instigates group members to feel threatened, which, in turn, slows down the development of a much-desired integrated identity (Ethier & Deaux, 1994). The facilitation of negative emotion among employees can work to inhibit the development of a common identity by slowing down the adjustment process (e.g. Kiefer, 2002). Terry et al. (2001) recognize how feelings of threat impact organizational member attitudes by impeding the adjustment process to organizational change through merger and, indeed, go on to reduce levels of identification with the newly-merged organization (Terry, 2003; Terry & O'Brien, 2001). The concept of perceived threat to an individual's social identity following dramatic social change has been related to important behavioral outcomes, such as predicting lower collective esteem (de la Sablonnière, Tougas, & Lortie-Lussier, 2009).

As witnessed, there is a multitude of diverse studies supporting the notion that a perceived threat to the existence of a social entity is a predicator of whether superordinate identification is achievable (see also Hornsey & Hogg, 2000a; Waldzus et al., 2005). Identity representations become increasingly complex and much less inclusive at times of uncertainty and stress (Roccas & Brewer, 2002). These studies support the proposition that the relationship between those going through dramatic social change of some form and collective esteem is mediated by feelings of threat to social entity (see also de la Sablonnière & Tougas, 2008).

The Interaction with Status and Power

When two entities combine, there will always be some presence of disparity, dependent on the characteristics and context of each premerger organization. Even though two organizations may be broadly recognized as being equals in terms of a range of aspects (e.g. size, turnover, share of market, or even the number of employees), nuances materialize that will distinguish each merger partner in one form or other. In fact, it is a rarity that the premerger organizations will be regarded as equal in terms of status. We may view this on several differing dimensions, but let us consider examples such as productivity, competence, prestige (in the eye of the beholder), access to resources, or perhaps economic competitiveness. From an employee perspective, each dimension will bear its own significance dependent on which premerger entity you are aligned to. Regarding the discussion about stress and threat, the asymmetry of the situation leads to a very different experience for those from the high-status group in comparison to those coming from the low-status group where higher levels of both are often reported (Terry, 2003; Terry & O'Brien, 2001). Other important attitudes and behaviors that are experienced very differently by those from the low-status group are an increased sense of unfairness (Amiot, Terry, et al., 2007; Gleibs, Mummendey, & Noack, 2008), increased difficulty in adjusting to the new job (Terry et al., 2001), and, importantly, a lower sense of identification with the newly-merged organization (Gleibs, Noack, & Mummendey, 2010; Terry et al., 2001).

It has been suggested that an individual's commitment to overseeing a successful organizational change process is impacted by their emotional or affective experiences during it (Huy, 2002). Although, there is evidence that those from the low status group who are motivated to search for alternatives to the status quo and improve their social identity may be the more likely to respond positively to conditions of increased social mobility into a higher-status group (Tajfel & Turner, 1979). Consequently, status can have a mixed impact on the facilitation of transcending to the position of a superordinate integrated state of identity and the role of intergroup structure will be one of the crucial factors recognized as either inhibiting or facilitating its development. For example, where groups share similar levels of power and status, facilitation of a new identity is more likely to be encouraged. However, where groups differ in their status and power, this environment of highly stratified intergroup entities are more likely to demonstrate and react to the conflicts and asymmetries that exist. This will tend to result in the emergence of a single dominant identity, which will negate all efforts to overcome the barriers to the identity development process (Phinney, 1995).

An important distinction needs to be drawn here between contexts where a change in one's identity is through freedom of choice and very different contexts where the change in identity is imposed on the individual or group. Amiot et al. (2012) recognize similarities where colonized countries had their new identity imposed on them, threatening the existence of their precolonial identity. Taylor's (1997, 2002) work recognized the confusion in identity status that can arise in such a situation where members of the colonized group lost their original identity, which was replaced incompletely with only elements of the colonizer's social identity. This, in turn, led to loss of direction and confusion among members of the colonized country. We can also consider this situation in an organizational merger and the potential complications that will emerge from a confusion of pre- and postmerger identities (i.e. to avoid a situation of maintaining separate corporate identities the dominant partner needs to ensure there is a consolidation of identity and this is clearly incorporated within the newly integrated entity. Status and power differentials are fundamental in determining which elements of identity are retained and those that are rejected and providing a shared sense of direction.

Further research also recognizes that premerger partners who experience the low-status are found consistently to experience lower identity with the newly-formed organization group than those emanating from the high-status premerger organization, and less likely to display tendencies of a common in-group identity (e.g. Terry, 2003; Terry & O'Brien, 2001; Terry et al., 2001). Another crucial consideration is the tendency for those employees from the dominated premerger organization to have much less involvement in shaping the formation, structure, and direction of the newly-merged entity. This also shapes a tendency for those employees to forge weaker links between their identity in its previous existence and their identity to emerge with the newly-formed entity (e.g. van Knippenberg, van Knippenberg, Monden, & de Lima, 2002; see also van Leeuwen et al., 2003). This has also been discussed as the level of identity continuity (e.g. Dackert, Jackson, Brenner, & Johansson, 2003; Ullrich et al., 2005).

6.3 Case in Question

6.3.1 The Importance of Organizational Justice

A primary aim of the case study from the outset was to compare the importance of organizational justice with the phenomena of both culture and organizational identity. A proposition to emerge was that in its role as one of the key factors affecting and influencing successful postmerger identification, perceived fair treatment of the individual shares the limelight as one of the essentially important dimensions of the merger process. Indeed, perceived justice has been recognized in its role to influence and determine employee attitudes and behaviors that ensue. However, academic evidence to support the impact of organizational justice within this context is relatively scarce, and a better understanding of the dynamic forces formed from its relationship with other important variables, including social and organizational identity, is needed. Therefore, pitching justice as not only important to employees involved with the process of merging, but comprehensively more important than the disruptions to identity and culture, was a major finding of the current study. The most significant difference was between the importance of organizational justice and the importance of identity, which was measured over two dimensions, team identity and organizational identity. In contrast to team identity, there was a lower value placed on organizational identity, which, although was noticeable at both campuses, was particularly pronounced for staff at the university. This outcome is not a surprise because, generally, staff at both campuses had indicated a strong attachment to the values of each of their pre-existing organizations, and, subsequently, there was a reluctance to accept the identity of the new organization values. There were also signs from the conversations conducted with employees from the premerger business school that they were less likely to identify with their employing organization than staff from the premerger management college. There was evidence that rather than organizational commitment, occupational commitment was more prevalent among those at the premerger business school. This can also be demonstrated from other results conducted during the investigation, which examined an individual's actual experiences of the merger. Staff at the university indicated a lower level of affective commitment to the new organization than those originating from the management college.

6.3.2 The Relationship Between Identity, Culture, and Organizational Justice

Evidence in existing research supports the proposition that threats to identity and culture influence attitudes, such as commitment and self-esteem (Bartels et al., 2006; van Dick et al., 2006), as transitions from a past state to a future state are being interpreted by employees besetting potential divisions between staff from the merging organizations (Cartwright & Cooper, 1996). The positive results to emerge from the first phase of research in the business school merger were indicative of the significance attributed within a merger to the two variables identity and culture, and supportive of previous research (see for example, Hubbard, 2001; Lipponen et al., 2004; van Knippenberg et al., 2002). Past research has also identified a close relationship between commitment and identity (Meyer & Allen, 1997; Mowday, Steers, & Porter, 1979), and results from Phase 2 of the study would suggest a consistency with this. However, within a merger context identity and culture have not previously been identified for their influential relationships with the dimensions of organizational justice. A major contribution of the current study was clear evidence of a dynamic relationship existing between these variables that has the capability to influence and impact the employee evaluation process and their attitudes and behaviors.

There was a considerable amount of emotion attached to certain aspects of the culture and identity that had been seriously affected by the harmonization of terms and conditions between the two merging organizations. This raises the effect of common fate and access to rewards for the high-status organization within a merger and a perception among those staff that where the same decision rules or the rule of equality has been applied during decision-making, there is a perceived threat upon their identity status (Brewer, 2000; Hornsey, van Leeuwen, & van Santen, 2003). The dominant merger partner in terms of organization size was undoubtedly the university, and on this measurement the subordinate group were the management college. Employees from the subordinate merger partner have been recognized as being more likely to consider the merger as more threatening because in such situations they are less likely to hold the balance of power (Gleibs et al., 2008). However, although it may be recognized that the premerger management college became the subordinate merger partner in terms of size, there was the distinct impression to emerge from Phase 2 of the study that staff at the management college believed they were from the higher-status group, borne, at least in part, from their perceived heritage as an elite business college. This was exemplified in some of the staff comments who proposed that the merger had resulted in a diminution of the management college brand and this was visually presented in the new business school logo which now also included the university's name. As discussed earlier in the chapter, in a merger or acquisition members of the high-status group will be motivated to maintain their identity (Amiot et al., 2007), which may also account for the higher level of importance indicated toward identity for this group. Again, this alludes to the relationship between identity and fairness in a merger context.

It is clear that both identity and organizational culture were fundamental to employees from the premerger management college in forming their perceptions of fairness. It is also evident, given the fundamentality of both culture and identity, that the results obtained from Phase 1 provide substantial evidence of how important organizational justice is to the employee in their evaluation of events during a merger or acquisition.

The Impact of Values on Perceived Justice

The importance of culture and identity was supported in Phase 1 of the study, and these two factors then became a central theme within Phase 2, identified as a principal part of the employee and organizational value systems. Changes motivated by the merger that were to have a disrupting effect on social interaction and relationships at the premerger management college, challenged employee and organizational values that went to the very heart of the social structure and ethos of the campus. The rituals of free lunches and coffee lounge drinks with both colleagues and clients formed part of the shared purpose and values that were described by some members as the social glue of the organization. These rituals were also recognized as unique experiences that made them feel part of a very special "family." The removal of these benefits through harmonization of terms and conditions was perceived by those employees as the destruction of the shared value system that formed part of the social and organizational identities, so important to the organization's culture. The anxiety that this caused had led to an emotionally charged atmosphere among some members of staff, and a seemingly just process using the rule of equality to harmonize terms and conditions was perceived as unjust by those individuals. This draws upon Mayer, Greenbaum, Kuenz, and Shteynberg's (2009) assertion that when an individual's personal or social identity is violated by a decision outcome, then objectively fair procedures used in determining that decision will have a weaker influence on justice perceptions. It also seems to support the value protection model proposed by Skitka (2002), which professes that an attack on an individual's personal values cannot be overcome by fair procedures or allocations.

A confrontation of values was also evident at the premerger business school where a change in the publishing culture caused anxiety among many of the academic staff. For some individuals there were indications that the change in strategy was a step too far, because goals that they valued were now in conflict with those of the new organization. It is evident that this incongruence between the goals and values of the employee and those of the organization leads to increased levels of uncertainty and anxiety over the future direction of the publishing strategy. Both examples engendered high emotions among employees across the new business school and, as discussed, seemed to go to the heart of the struggle for control between authorities and their staff. Skitka talks about the attachment to *moral mandates* having a possible effect of undermining group stability and threatening institutional control when individuals feel that their sense of personal identity is under threat. Distinct similarities can be drawn to the compromise of publishing strategy and the damage to social structure, of which both events were perceived to challenge employee rights from which personal, social, and organizational identities formed a common cultural bond of values. Emotions to emerge from these events further eroded trust in authorities and, consequentially, were recognized as unfair distributions to result from the merger process.

Further support for Skitka's (2002) value protection model materialized during interview discussions with employees from the premerger management college and relates to their attachment to brand identity. Although among these members of staff emotion ran high about the causes of the merger, considering their situation they were generally in favor of forming part of the new business school and securing their future. Even so, their brand name was to be transferred to the new business school and some staff appeared reluctant to share their brand identity with the premerger business school. As discussed previously, employees of the premerger management college considered their organizational identity to be more important than their colleagues from the premerger business school, and it was recognized that this could be related to the impression presented by those from the college that they belonged to the higher-order status group. Those employees who displayed this trait were also those who most wanted to protect their values and identity and seemed reluctant to share them with the new organization. Skitka's discussion about moral mandates indicated that they are selective expressions of values central to people's sense of personal identity and that the strength of these predicted perceived procedural justice and perceived distributive justice. Again, support for this assertion can be provided from the conversations held during Phase 2 when staff discussed the unfairness of sharing what they perceived to be their brand. Although much of the emotion stressed by employees over a brand with which they had shared their personal identity was because the circumstances in which they perceived their merger to be enforced had left them with the impression that this was more akin to a demise of the brand.

In further consideration of the relationship between organizational identity and association with the brand, it is evident that the basis of perceived fairness was rooted in the values of identity shared by employees at the premerger management college. It would also appear for those employees finding difficulty sharing their brand that this had been more influential than fair procedures in the determination of distributive justice. Organizational identity is encouraged by the individual's desire to fulfill social needs and the social group individuals belong to form a significant part of their own self-concept (Tajfel & Turner, 1986). There is evidence that a group's influence over an individual's attitudes and behaviors is promoted by their identification with that group (Hogg & Abrams, 1988), and in this case group values have had a significant influence among employees at the management college. For these employees it became a barrier to change at a time when, as it is acknowledged, employees need to disidentify with the previous organization (Chreim, 2002) and accept the new practices and processes.

At this point it is appropriate to return to the integration management framework provided by Birkinshaw, Bresman, and Hakanson (2000) and reported in Chap. 2. In this framework it is discussed that during the merger of organizations there should be an equal consideration of both hard and soft issues delineating the process of task integration and human integration. For merger or acquisition success to be achieved, the postacquisition integration strategy must take into account that both dimensions need to be realized and a situation where one is achieved at the expense of the other could impede this objective. Since employees had been left in situ at campuses 12 miles apart, unless there was a concerted effort to integrate the two sets of employees they would remain largely detached. There were isolated examples of where individuals had been involved with cross-site working, and their attitude toward the success of the new venture seemed to be much more positive. Indeed, this proposition was also supported in the findings from the Phase 4 survey conducted in the NHS Trust where employees who worked across sites appeared to avoid the issues with identity and culture that had so troubled some of their colleagues.

Each of these three events—brand identity, social interaction, and publishing strategy—was perceived as an attack on the shared values between the employee and their premerger organization. The journey to transfer identity from the preexistence to the new organization was contingent upon an acceptance of the changing nature in values and subsequently overcoming a potential identity crisis. There was evidence that this situation could have been at least partly mitigated if the quality of communication offered by the leadership had been more effective. It was proposed that a clear justification for these changes had not been provided and subsequently this promoted a sense of unjust behavior that challenged the rights of the employee. These clear indications provided during the Phase 2 interviews were supported within the Phase 3 and Phase 4 surveys by the establishment of a significant relationship between justification of the communicated message and psychological contract breach.

References

Amiot, C. E., de la Sablonniere, R., Terry, D. J., & Smith, J. R. (2007). Development and integration of social identities in the self: Toward a cognitive-developmental model. *Personality and Social Psychology Review, 11*, 364–388.

Amiot, C. E., Terry, D. J., & Callan, V. J. (2007). Status, fairness, and social identification during an intergroup merger: A longitudinal study. *British Journal of Social Psychology, 46*, 557–577.

Amiot, C. E., Terry, D. J., Jimmieson, N. L., & Callan, V. J. (2006). A longitudinal investigation of coping processes during a merger: Implications for job satisfaction and organizational identification. *Journal of Management, 32*, 552–574.

Amiot, C. E., Terry, D. J., & McKimmie, B. M. (2012). Social identity change during an intergroup merger: The role of status, similarity, and identity threat. *Basic and Applied Social Psychology, 34*, 443–455.

Amiot, C. E., Terry, D. J., Wirawan, D., & Grice, T. (2010). Changes in social identities over time: The role of coping and adaptation processes. *British Journal of Social Psychology, 49*, 803–826.

Bartels, J., Douwes, R., de Jong, M., & Pruyn, A. (2006). Organizational identification during a merger: Determinants of employees' expected identification with the new organization. *British Journal of Management, 17*, S49–S67.

Bettencourt, B. A., & Sheldon, K. (2001). Social roles as mechanisms for psychological need satisfaction within social groups. *Journal of Personality and Social Psychology, 81*, 1131–1143.

Birkinshaw, J., Bresman, H., & Hakanson, L. (2000). Managing the post-acquisition integration process: How the human integration and task integration processes interact to foster value creation. *Journal of Management Studies, 37*, 395–425.

Brandtstadter, J. (1998). Action perspectives on human development. In W. Damon (Series Ed.) & R. M. Lerner (Vol. Ed.), *Handbook of child psychology: Vol. 1. Theoretical models of human development* (5th ed., pp. 807–863). New York: Wiley.

Brewer, M. B. (2000). Superordinate goals versus superordinate identity as the bases of intergroup cooperation. In D. Capozzo & R. Brown (Eds.), *Social identity processes: Trends in theory and research* (pp. 117–132). London: Sage.

Cameron, J. E. (1999). Social identity and the pursuit of possible selves: Implications for the psychological well-being of university students. *Group Dynamics: Theory, Research, and Practice, 3*, 179–189.

Cartwright, S., & Cooper, C. L. (1993). The psychological impact of merger and acquisition on the individual: A study of building society managers. *Human Relations, 46*, 327–347.

Cartwright, S., & Cooper, C. L. (1996). *Managing mergers, acquisitions and strategic alliances: Integrating people and cultures*. Oxford, UK: Butterworth-Heinmann.

Chreim, S. (2002). Influencing organizational identification during a merger: A communication-based perspective. *Human Relations, 55*, 1117–1137.

Crocker, J., Luhtanen, R., Blaine, B., & Broadnax, S. (1994). Collective self-esteem and psychological well-being among White, Black, and Asian college students. *Personality and Social Psychology Bulletin, 20*, 503–513.

Cross, S. (1995). Self-construals, coping, and stress in cross-cultural adaptation. *Journal of Cross-Cultural Psychology, 26*, 673–697.

Dackert, I., Jackson, P. R., Brenner, S.-O., & Johansson, C. R. (2003). Eliciting and analysing employees' expectations of a merger. *Human Relations, 56*, 705–725.

de la Sablonnière, R., & Tougas, F. (2008). Relative deprivation and social identity in times of dramatic social change: The case of nurses. *Journal of Applied Social Psychology, 38*(9), 2293–2314.

de la Sablonnière, R., Tougas, F., & Lortie-Lussier, M. (2009). Dramatic social change in Russia and Mongolia: Connecting relative deprivation to social identity. *Journal of Cross-Cultural Psychology, 40*(3), 327–348.

Downie, M., Koestner, R., ElGeledi, S., & Cree, K. (2004). The impact of cultural internalization and integration on well-being among tricultural individuals. *Personality and Social Psychology Bulletin, 30*, 305–314.

Ethier, K. A., & Deaux, K. (1994). Negotiating social identity when contexts change: Maintaining identification and responding to threat. *Journal of Personality and Social Psychology, 67*(2), 243–251.

Folkman, S. (1984). Personal control and stress and coping processes: A theoretical analysis. *Journal of Personality and Social Psychology, 46*, 839–852.

Gaertner, S. L., & Dovidio, J. F. (2000). *Reducing intergroup bias: The common ingroup identification model.* Philadelphia: Psychology Press/Taylor & Francis.

Gaertner, S. L., Dovidio, J. F., Bachman, B. A., & Rust, M. C. (1993). The common ingroup identity model: Recategorization and the reduction of intergroup bias. *European Review of Social Psychology, 4*, 1–26.

Gleibs, I. H., Mummendey, A., & Noack, P. (2008). Predictors of change in postmerger identification during a merger process: A longitudinal study. *Journal of Personality and Social Psychology, 95*(5), 1095–1112.

Gleibs, I. H., Noack, P., & Mummendey, A. (2010). We are still better than them: A longitudinal field study of in group favouritism during a merger. *European Journal of Social Psychology, 40*, 819–836.

Gonzalez, R., & Brown, R. (2003). Generalization of positive attitude as a function of subgroup and superordinate group identifications in intergroup contact. *European Journal of Social Psychology, 33*, 195–214.

Harter, S. (1999). *The construction of the self: A developmental perspective.* New York: Guilford.

Haslam, S. A., Jetten, J., O'Brien, A., & Jacobs, E. (2004). Social identity, social influence and reactions to potentially stressful tasks: Support for the self-categorization model of stress. *Stress and Health: Journal of the International Society for the Investigation of Stress, 20*, 3–9.

Haslam, S. A., O'Brien, A., Jetten, J., Vormedal, K., & Penna, S. (2005). Taking the strain: Social identity, social support, and the experience of stress. *British Journal of Social Psychology, 44*, 355–370.

Heckhausen, J., & Schulz, R. (1995). A life-span theory of control. *Psychological Review, 102*, 284–304.

Heppner, P. P., Cook, S. W., Strozier, A. L., & Heppner, M. J. (1991). An investigation of coping styles and gender differences with farmers in career transition. *Journal of Counseling Psychology, 38*, 167–174.

Hewstone, M., & Brown, R. (1986). Contact is not enough: An intergroup perspective on the "contact hypothesis". In M. Hewstone & R. Brown (Eds.), *Contact and conflict in intergroup encounters* (pp. 1–44). Cambridge, MA: Blackwell.

Hogg, M. A., & Abrams, D. (1988). *Social identifications: A social psychology of intergroup relations and group processes*. London: Routledge.

Hornsey, M. J., & Hogg, M. A. (2000a). Assimilation and diversity: An integrative model of subgroup relations. *Personality and Social Psychology Review, 4*, 143–156.

Hornsey, M. J., & Hogg, M. A. (2000b). Intergroup similarity and subgroup relations: Some implications for assimilation. *Personality and Social Psychology Bulletin, 26*, 948–958.

Hornsey, M. J., van Leeuwen, E., & van Santen, W. (2003). Dragging down and dragging up: How relative group status affects responses to common fate. *Group Dynamics: Theory, Research and Practices, 7*, 275–288.

Hubbard, N. (2001). *Acquisition strategy and implementation*. Basingstoke, UK: Palgrave.

Huy, Q. N. (2002). Emotional balancing of organizational continuity and radical change: The contribution of middle managers. *Administrative Science Quarterly, 47*, 31–69.

Jetten, J., Iyer, A., Tsivrikos, D., & Young, B. M. (2008). When is individual mobility costly? The role of economic and social identity factors. *European Journal of Social Psychology, 38*, 866–879.

Kiefer, T. (2002). Understanding the emotional experience of organizational change: Evidence from a merger. *Advances in Developing Human Resources, 4*(1), 39–61.

Kosic, A. (2004). Acculturation strategies, coping process and acculturative stress. *Scandinavian Journal of Psychology, 45*, 269–278.

Lazarus, R. S., & Folkman, S. (1984). *Stress, appraisal, and coping*. New York: Springer.

Lipponen, J., Olkkonen, M. E., & Moilanen, M. (2004). Perceived procedural justice and employee responses to an organizational merger. *European Journal of Work and Organizational Psychology, 13*, 391–413.

Mael, F., & Ashforth, B. E. (1992). Alumni and their alma mater: A partial test of the reformulated model of organizational identification. *Journal of Organizational Behavior, 13*(2), 103–123.

Mayer, D. M., Greenbaum, R. L., Kuenz, M., & Shteynberg, G. (2009). When do fair procedures not matter? A test of the identity violation effect. *Journal of Applied Psychology, 94*(1), 142–161.

Meyer, J. P., & Allen, N. J. (1997). *Commitment in the workplace: Theory, research and application*. Thousand Oaks, CA: Sage.

Moghaddam, F. M., Taylor, D. M., Ditto, B., Jacobs, K., & Bianchi, E. (2002). Psychological distress and perceived discrimination: A study of women from India. *Journal of Intercultural Relations, 26*, 381–390.

Mottola, G. R., Gaertner, S. L., Bachman, B. A., & Dovidio, J. F. (1997). How groups merge: The effects of merger integration patterns on anticipated commitment to the merged organization. *Journal of Applied Social Psychology, 27*, 1335–1358.

Mowday, R. T., Steers, R. M., & Porter, L. W. (1979). Measurement of organizational commitment. *Journal of Vocational Behavior, 14*(2), 224–247.

Mummendey, A., & Wenzel, M. (1999). Social discrimination and tolerance in intergroup relations: Reactions to intergroup difference. *Personality and Social Psychology Review, 3*, 158–174.

Phinney, J. S. (1995). Ethnic identity and self-esteem: A review and integration. In A. M. Padilla (Ed.), *Hispanic psychology: Critical issues in theory and research* (pp. 57–70). Thousand Oaks, CA: Sage.

Phinney, J. S., & Rosenthal, D. A. (1992). Ethnic identity in adolescence: Process, context, and outcome. In G. R. Adams, T. P. Gullotta, & R. Montemayor (Eds.), *Adolescent identity formation: Advances in adolescent development* (Vol. 4, pp. 145–172). Newbury Park, CA: Sage.

Roberts, R. E., Phinney, J. S., Masse, L. C., Chen, Y. R., Roberts, C. R., & Romero, A. (1999). The structure of ethnic identity of young adolescents from diverse ethnocultural groups. *Journal of Early Adolescence, 19*, 301–322.

Roccas, S., & Brewer, M. B. (2002). Social identity complexity. *Personality and Social Psychology Review, 6*, 88–106.

Ruble, D. N., Alvarez, J., Bachman, M., Cameron, J., Fuligni, A., Garcia Coll, C., et al. (2004). The development of a sense of "we": The emergence and implications of children's collective identity. In M. Bennett & F. Sani (Eds.), *The development of the social self* (pp. 29–76). New York: Psychology Press.

Sani, F., Bowe, M., & Herrera, M. (2008). Perceived collective continuity and social well-being: Exploring the connections. *European Journal of Social Psychology, 38*, 365–374.

Skinner, E. A., & Edge, K. (2002). Self-determination, coping, and development. In E. L. Deci & R. M. Ryan (Eds.), *Handbook of self-determination research* (pp. 297–337). Rochester, NY: University of Rochester Press.

Skitka, L. J. (2002). Do the means always justify the ends, or do the ends sometimes justify the means? A value protection model of justice reasoning. *Personality and Social Psychology Bulletin, 28*, 588–597.

Spears, R., Doosje, B., & Ellemers, N. (1997). Self-stereotyping in the face of threats to group status and distinctiveness: The role of group identification. *Personality and Social Psychology Bulletin, 23*, 538–553.

Sussman, N. M. (2000). The dynamic nature of cultural identity throughout cultural transitions: Why home is not so sweet. *Personality and Social Psychology Review, 4*, 355–373.

Tajfel, H., & Turner, J. C. (1979). An integrative theory of intergroup conflict. In W. G. Austin & S. Worchel (Eds.), *The social psychology of intergroup relations* (pp. 94–109). Monterey, CA: Brooks-Cole.

Tajfel, H., & Turner, J. C. (1986). The social identity theory of intergroup behaviour. In S. Worchel & W. G. Austin (Eds.), *Psychology of intergroup relations* (2nd ed., pp. 7–24). Chicago: Nelson-Hall.

Taylor, D. M. (1997). The quest for collective identity: The plight of disadvantaged ethnic minorities. *Canadian Psychology, 38*, 174–190.

Taylor, D. M. (2002). *The quest for identity*. New York: Praeger.

Terry, D. J. (1991). Stress, coping and adaptation to new parenthood. *Journal of Social and Personal Relationships, 8*, 527–547.

Terry, D. J. (2003). A social identity perspective on organizational mergers: The role of group status, permeability, and similarity. In S. A. Haslam, D. van Knippenberg, M. J. Platow, & N. Ellemers (Eds.), *Social identity at work: Developing theory for organizational practice* (pp. 223–240). New York: Psychology Press.

Terry, D. J., Callan, V. J., & Sartori, G. (1996). Employees' adjustment to an organizational merger: Stress, coping and inter group differences. *Stress Medicine, 12*, 105–122.

Terry, D. J., Carey, C. J., & Callan, V. J. (2001). Employee adjustment to an organizational merger: An intergroup perspective. *Personality and Social Psychology Bulletin, 27*, 267–280.

Terry, D. J., & O'Brien, A. T. (2001). Status, legitimacy, and ingroup bias in the context of an organizational merger. *Group Processes and Intergroup Relations, 4*, 271–289.

Turner, J. C., Hogg, M. A., Oakes, P. J., Reicher, S. D., & Wetherell, M. S. (1987). Rediscovering the social group: A self-categorization theory. Oxford, UK: Blackwell.

Ullrich, J., Wieseke, J., & Van Dick, R. (2005). Continuity and change in mergers and acquisitions: A social identity case study of a German industrial merger. *Journal of Management Studies, 42*, 1549–1569.

van Dick, R., Ullrich, J., & Tissington, P. A. (2006). Working under a black cloud: How to sustain organizational identification after a merger. *British Journal of Management, 17*, S69–S79.

van Dick, R., Wagner, U., & Lemmer, G. (2004). The winds of change: Multiple identifications in the case of organizational mergers. *European Journal of Work and Organizational Psychology, 13*(2), 121–138.

van Knippenberg, D., van Knippenberg, B., Monden, L., & de Lima, F. (2002). Organizational identification after a merger: A social identity perspective. *British Journal of Social Psychology, 41*, 233–252.

van Knippenberg, D., & van Leeuwen, E. (2001). Organizational identity after a merger: Sense of continuity as the key to postmerger identification. In M. A. Hog & D. J. Terry (Eds.), *Social identity processes in organizational contexts* (pp. 249–264). Philadelphia: Psychology Press.

van Leeuwen, E., van Knippenberg, D., & Ellemers, N. (2003). Continuing and changing group identities: The effects of merging on social identification and ingroup bias. *Personality and Social Psychology Bulletin, 29*, 679–690.

Waldzus, S., Mummendey, A., & Wenzel, M. (2005). When "different" means "worse": In-group prototypicality in changing intergroup contexts. *Journal of Experimental Social Psychology, 41*, 76–83.

Waldzus, S., Mummendey, A., Wenzel, M., & Weber, U. (2003). Towards tolerance: Representations of superordinate categories and perceived ingroup prototypicality. *Journal of Experimental Social Psychology, 39*, 31–47.

7

Organization Communication

7.1 Introduction

From a structural perspective, organizational communication has been described via a number of different frameworks, but one of the most useful is proposed by Goldhaber (1999), who has recognized three common features. Firstly, organizational communication both influences its environment and, in a reciprocal relationship, is also influenced itself by the environment. It can therefore be described as operating within a complex, open system. Secondly, encapsulated within the auspices of organizational communication are the features we would associate with a message (flow, purpose, direction, and media). Thirdly, it involves people interacting directly or indirectly with their skills, relationships, attitudes, and feelings. This points toward organizational communication being dependent on a network of interdependent relationships. To further illuminate our perception of organizational communication, Tukiainen (2001) also recognized that communication needs to be regular, organized, and equal in status and that this may be exacerbated where separate communication channels exist for leadership and employees.

N. Jackson, *Organizational Justice in Mergers and Acquisitions*,
https://doi.org/10.1007/978-3-319-92636-0_7

Hostile and friendly mergers tend to generate dissimilar communication dynamics, which consequently result in a very different type of organizational behavior. Friendly acquisitions promote the environment of cooperation and joint planning from those companies involved as the acceptance of integration becomes a formality once the threat of other potentially interested parties has been removed (Hubbard, 2001). This will not happen in a hostile takeover where the environment often develops into a very different climate. Communication, which is so vital at every stage, is impeded as barriers more akin to this aggressive form of integration begin to develop, making the situation one of increased uncertainty for employees. Compared to a friendly acquisition, cooperation between acquiring and target management is unlikely in a hostile bid (Sudarsanam & Mahate, 2006). Generally, a hostile bidder will seek to take over underperforming targets and will look to make improvements as a primary source of value creation, using the disciplinary nature of the acquisition to either remove incumbent management in the target company or direct them in an expected turnaround in the company's fortunes. Adding to their uncertainty, acquiring management has no automatic entitlement to directly access target company employees. As an alternative form of communicating their messages, they may attempt to gain some influence and begin to set their agenda through access to the media.

One of the biggest barriers to acceptance of change for those going through the process is a cynicism about the causes and intended outcomes of the event. This leads to feelings of job insecurity, which can be reduced if effective communication processes are designed at a strategic level in the organization. The architecture of change processes need to include some planning on communication, particularly at significant points in the process, and frameworks need to be cognizant of the need to build in an efficient and effective communication process. Insufficient or, even worse, inferior information that may be incomplete or incorrect heightens these insecurities. Studies support the notion that such psychological insecurities can be reduced by effective communication, working to increase acceptance, openness, and commitment to change (Bordia, Hunt, Paulsen, Tourish, & DiFonzo, 2004; Schweiger & DeNisi, 1991; Wanberg & Banas, 2000).

7.2 Change and Communication

Galpin (1996) argues that within the process of change, organizations tend to focus on the technical, financial, and operational features at a strategic level and the significance of communication as a key input is relegated and not given the same prominence. The architecture created by formal communication including its channels, dissemination techniques, and regularity is often ignored and not considered with the same focal disposition when it comes to the formulation of strategy during integration. Efforts to establish communication as an important element of change at a strategic level need to include a diagnosis of its status within the process. This should then be followed by a systematic analysis of the procedures of communication, which will need to be profiled as one of the early outline stages during the design of change strategy.

A fundamental element of strategic planning is an acknowledgment that any approach to developing a successful change process involves both good-quality communication and information strategies. There needs to be understanding that these must be established within the organization so that reliable messages can be disseminated with clarity to all while the change is being implemented. Communication is recognized as instrumental to organizational survival and growth (Bordia, Hobman, Jones, Gallois, & Callan, 2004; Schweiger & DeNisi, 1991; Wanberg & Banas, 2000). This fact has served as a driving force in the development of efficient instruments for the measurement and analysis of communication in organizations (Downs, DeWine, & Greenbaum, 1994). The basic idea is that a communication audit creates a foundation for diagnosing the quality of its transmission in practice. Auditing communication involves the assessment of current communication practices to determine what steps are required for improvement.

7.2.1 The Strategic Importance of Communication

The relationship between formalizing and orchestrating a successful change program and the development of an effective communication strategy in the workplace has been recognized as inextricable. It would seem imperative that there needs to be a deeper understanding of how various forms and practices of communication will influence the quality of the initiative. The significance of implementing effective communication processes is emphasized if we consider their influence in helping to develop essential provisions, such as linking and binding different elements of the organization together, a crucial activity during the disquiet aroused by the uncertainties of change. Opening effective communication channels is essential for the gathering of feedback to all parties involved, whether this relates to those disseminating the information about change or receiving it. Reliable information about the mood of employees and their main concerns will be vital if those responsible for organizing and implementing the change are able to contain resistance and encourage participation. Therefore, communication needs to be considered from the outset as part of the strategic plans for the change program.

In this state of organizational flux, communication has been described as a tool used in preparing those going through the change by helping to announce, explain, and prepare those individuals for either the positive or negative outcomes to processes, systems, and routines (Spike and Lesser, 1995). From the outset, the rationale and the likely consequences of change need to be confronted and explained to those individuals affected by it, regardless of the impending outcomes (Galpin, 1996). For this to occur, communication and its critical contribution need to be visible in every step of the change process (Spike and Lesser, 1995; Galpin, 1996). To ensure that this is the case, the nature of any change process and the nuances associated with it need to be clearly defined at the early planning stage. For example, any forms and instruments that are utilized to value and measure the effectiveness of communication within this process of change need to be recognized as a strategic tool. Their role is to help those responsible for designing and implementing the change to detect different developments and fluctuations in the process as it evolves, so that communication flow and strategy can be adjusted accordingly. An example we can draw on here is how an organization should plan to adapt its interconnectivity strategies dependent on the different staging posts of a change initiative.

If the change is deemed to be more episodic in nature, this may mean a very different form of interconnectivity with employees at the start when the initiative or event is announced compared to later stages when organization members are fully engaged and may be more accepting of its outcomes. Consequently, dependent on the situation, we need to ask, when does a change process begin and end? The early stages can be seen as the preparatory phases of change where the planners and implementers will be organizing for release of information that is effective and efficient in distribution to all parties. Consistency of the communicated message should be recognized as imperative if trust is to be established in these early phases, setting the terms of reference for the relationship between the strategists who will be responsible for implementing the conditions of change and those that will be affected by it. However, this may not be so easy in situations that are represented by continuous change, where linearity of the process is not obvious and different stages of change are harder to delineate. Different mechanisms and strategies will need to be considered dependent on the idiosyncrasies of the situation.

7.3 Uncertainty Avoidance

Within the context of organizational change, one of the major consequences is a tendency to promote employee uncertainty (Ashford, 1988; Schweiger and Denisi, 1991). The uncertainty that is aroused by the employee's perceived outcomes from the change may be in relation to several ensuing issues. These may include misunderstandings (or no understanding) of the rationale for change, and the processes through which the change has been implemented (Jackson et al., 1987; Buono and Bowditch, 1989). Process, and how this is perceived, is an essential ingredient of employee attitude development. Subsequently, these processes are an important function of employee resolve toward accepting the change and other mechanisms that will intervene in this relationship, such as perceived fairness of the outcomes and trust in the intentions of management in their justifications for their purported rationale. Inevitably, there is an air of uncertainty about employees regarding future interference with elements of their current environment in the workplace, such as security of their status and how the change will impact roles and responsibilities going forward (Bordia, Hobman et al., 2004).

7.3.1 The Role of Disseminating Information

Predictability in the immediate social system is so important because change in an uncertain environment can become a major stressor for those who will eventually be impacted by the consequences of this current state of flux. Uncertainty has been identified as a stressful psychological state (Berger & Calabrese, 1975; Schweiger & Denisi, 1991; Kramer, 1993), and in these situations the seeking of information to relieve conditions of ambiguity becomes a primary objective. Activities and events that will minimize uncertainty will therefore need to be identified and their impact recognized if the more acceptable face of change is to predominate. The dissemination of information needs to be recognized as central to these processes, and it is in this capacity that we investigate the significance of communication at the organizational level. Of course, within these contexts we can also perceive uncertainty as a motivational force. Uncertainty reduction theory, initially developed by Berger and Calabrese (1975) and later adapted by Kramer (1999), perceives individuals as driven to seek further information when confronted by a situation of uncertainty. Their aim is that the state of aversion to change may, in part, be addressed by the additional information they are able to obtain.

The Quality of Information

Naturally, any state of uncertainty reduction that is to remain permanent and develop trust in those who provide it will be contingent on the accuracy and pertinence of the information, which may be an unknown quantity at the point of data exchange. While it is accepted that communication is a vital ingredient of the implementation of a successful change program (Schweiger & Denisi, 1991; Lewis & Seibold, 1998), it is also recognized that the success of strategies developed to impart information through these channels will be dependent on the quality of the information and how effectively this is disseminated to employees (Smeltzer, 1991; Armenakis and Harris, 2002). Hence, it is recognized that quality of information rather than its mere presentation is imperative if it is to bear influence on employee appraisal of that change and have a chance of reducing uncertainty and facilitating openness and positive attitudes toward the change (Bordia, Hobman et al., 2004).

Sources of Information

In addition to the relationship between quality and pertinence of information, another important factor is to have an awareness about the range of sources employees seek out for further information during their attempts to counteract situations of uncertainty. The context of where the uncertainty has been derived may be critical in this process, and a clear understanding of the source of this information will help those in a position that are able to counteract the uncertainty. For example, it would be most appropriate and effective if change communication to counteract uncertainty about strategic activity was disseminated by a member, or members, of senior management. Even so, merger and acquisition (M&A)-related change can create unique circumstances in which the key figures within the newly-appointed senior board are alien to those who are the lesser partner in a merger or those who are being acquired within the partnership. A known and trusted member of management may appear to be a more dependable source of communication, even if they are not part of the strategic decision-making team. More local sources of information, including supervisors and team leaders can address concerns over structural and job-related uncertainty, drawing on appropriate forums, such as team or departmental meetings, which tend to be more participative (Bordia, Hobman et al., 2004). The significance of the source and their perceived authority to provide quality information will be influential in this process. Their ability and opportunity to communicate effectively is paramount otherwise employees will seek to reduce uncertainty via alternative sources, including those internal (e.g. grapevine) and external (e.g. media) to the organization (Hargie & Tourish, 2000).

7.4 Interpretation and Employee Involvement

We can see the argument for effective communication between the organization and employee during times of change, and this involves a more considered approach to information sharing with subjects from both integrating organizations. The process communication model offered by Larsson, Brousseau, Driver, and Sweet (2004) concentrates on three elements of the M&A process. At a time of great uncertainty for employees, this is a period when communication is considered as integral to enhancing their perceptions of feeling valued by the organization. Larsson et al. state, "One of the few easy things in M&A is to actualize positive surprise in acquired employees with two-way communication, career development, opportunities to influence, and organizational investments, given their prevalent negative expectations, fears, and rumors" (p. 16). Indeed, the rumor mill undoubtedly provides an opportunity to escalate uncertainty among individuals, and, as discussed, honest communication will play a significant role in helping to alleviate this issue. Two-way communication develops a relationship that offers opportunity for the workforce to buy into the process as it develops; a buy-in process aimed at turning employee resistance into cooperation. Details of their proposed model are displayed in Table 7.1.

The VIP model projects the message that employees will feel more valued if engaged in two-way communication involving the process of change as it develops. A case that is particularly pertinent for acquired employees because of their additional uncertainties. The framework characterizes communication as two-way because there is an emphasis on both feedback and involvement from the employee within the decision-making process.

The significance of employee participation is renowned, and there is much discussion formed around the "participation climate" and its influence in shaping behaviors of individuals going through the change process. It has been emphasized during development of change processes and reorganization caused by change that employees need to recognize they have an influence and are able to participate in the decision-making

Table 7.1 The VIP model

Characteristic	Interpretation
Voice	Timely, honest communication that reduces employee uncertainty, actively listening to their thoughts and feelings to learn how to best integrate the combining companies.
Involvement	Involvement in the integration process by retaining as much of the acquired corporate values as possible and by seeking ideas and suggestions from employees about their integration and improvement solutions.
Precision	Precision in two-way communication and integration because people process information in different ways, have different career motives, experience threats in different ways, and therefore need different information and solutions.

Note: Based on "The secrets of merger and acquisition success: A co-competence and motivational approach to synergy realization," by R. Larsson, K.R. Brousseau, M.J. Driver and P.L. Sweet, 2004. In A.L. Pablo and M. Javidan (Eds). *Organization development: A process of learning and changing*, (2nd Edn.). Oxford, UK: Blackwell Publishing

process. In this sense, participation has been defined as the notion that employees have a key role in planning and control of their own work (Wilson & Peel, 1991), and the ability to achieve their workplace goals. They will need to secure enough knowledge and power to influence the organizational processes and outcomes that the achievement of these goals will be dependent upon. Content, quality, timing, and structure of information dissemination are particularly critical (Christensen, 2014). Managers feeding back to employees is an integral part of this process and has implications for influencing employee commitment (Van Vuuren, de Jong, & Seydel, 2007). This climate of communication, as defined by Rafferty and Jimmieson (2010), is positively related to the quality of work life and has a negative correlation with role ambiguity, distress, and work overload. Job satisfaction, a key indicator of positive employee attitudes toward their work environment, is also affected by the level and quality of the information communicated throughout the organization. Indeed, this has been described as essential (De Nobile & McCormick, 2008). It is acknowledged that forms of employee participation during periods of change can empower them, perhaps leading to become a predictor of change acceptance (Gagne, Koestner, & Zuckerman, 2000; Wanberg & Banas, 2000). Alternatively, communication problems often become symptoms of more deeply rooted problems, such as lack of understanding, poor planning, a lack of common goals, and so on (Koontz, 2001). To try and understand the source of these problems, communication of information needs to be understood for its potential impact on organizational processes and assessed on its merit. Similarly, the effectiveness of communication on team functioning will be dictated by available resources, rules, procedures, policies, and the relationships formed within those teams. In addition to communication becoming a barrier to effective operations and implementation of change procedures, in turn these also become obstacles to the development of effective communication processes.

7.4.1 Process Control

To this point I have discussed the potential impact on behavior and how important it is that quality information is disseminated to employees via effective communication. This information will also need to be updated on a regular basis, and to make sure this occurs, there will need to be strategies in place to ensure that the process of dissemination is designed to reach those who need this at the right time points. One of the crucial elements to consider when building a communication strategy is involvement of employees in the process of planning and implementation of change and the preceding collection of information and ideas (Christensen, 2014). Buying into this process involves securing a stake for the employee and some form of responsibility toward the success of outcomes. As the employee becomes a stakeholder, they will naturally form a common interest with others who are also stakeholders including management and, perhaps, senior managers of the organization. This will be the case even if the outcomes are not always favorable for the individual and other colleagues of theirs in the organization. An understanding of the reasoning behind decision-making may make the medicine more bearable because the employee can gain visibility of the often less desirable consequences if this course of action is not followed.

Supporting Academic Arguments

The relationship between perceived fairness and levels of control in the decision-making process (process control) was originally discussed by Thibaut and Walker (1975) in their seminal work, which, at the time, expanded on the notion of distributive justice. Their argument is founded on the principle that procedures are perceived as fairer by affected individuals if they are allowed to become involved in the decision-making process via input or influence. In a decision-making situation, individuals will seek a level of control over the process through such influence in an attempt to maximize their outcomes within the exchange relationship (Kickul, Lester, & Finkl, 2002). Leventhal, Karuza, and Fry (1980) carried this concept into an organizational setting and their work on procedural justice centered on perceptions of fairness.

Meyer, Becker, and Vandenberghe (2004) also discuss the proposal that employee participation in the decision-making, or goal-setting process will increase their commitment to achieving the desired outcome. In a similar vein they also warn that

> Using a 'tell' strategy to assign a goal, combined with a public statement of acceptance, is likely to, at best, instill continuance commitment [commitment due only to the perceived cost of leaving the organization]. As a result, employees might do what is required to achieve the goal but nothing more. (p. 1004)

The opportunity for the individual to exercise a level of control in the process has been linked to a number of other behavioral and attitudinal outcomes. For example, as well as positively influencing perceptions of fairness in the decision-making process there is also evidence of an increase in job satisfaction and subsequent increase in levels of commitment from the employee (Davy, Kinicki, & Scheck, 1991). Increased trust in management has also been evidenced where process control has been exercised, along with some support for an increase in job performance (Cropanzano & Greenberg, 1997).

Therefore, within the procedural justice framework there is the opportunity for the organization to alleviate negatively held perceptions about outcomes through effectively communicating explanations for the decisions that underpin those outcomes (Saunders, Thornhill, & Lewis, 2002). In fact, effectively transmitted organizational communication can remove some of the experience of powerlessness associated with change and the ensuing feelings of threat that result (Brockner, DeWitt, Grover, & Reed, 1990; Greenhalgh, 1983; Greenhalgh & Rosenblat, 1984; Shaw & Barrett-Power, 1997). An example is the positive relationship of procedural fairness and the employee's subsequent intentions to stay (Daly & Geyer, 1994).

7.5 Case in Question

7.5.1 The Business School

During the merger implementation, the role of involvement in procedure setting (voice) materialized as one of the main concerns among premerger management college employees. The general feeling was that although a mechanism for two-way interaction between members of staff and the senior management team existed in the form of a representative committee, any benefits of this were undermined by the belief that their comments and concerns would be disregarded. This perception by employees of *disingenuous voice* was a major critique of the merger implementation process. Support for this view was presented by remarks such as "You got the impression they were allowing us the chance to say what we wanted to say because they have to by law" (MC-PT 8) and "I felt that the communication was one-way and that one's own views weren't really considered" (MC-PT 24).

There was a sense of emotion portrayed by staff who detected a sense of betrayal from the organization in what they perceived to be a reciprocal relationship of trust. One individual remarked, "There was no belief in what we were being told by the [premerger management college] and that lack of trust pre-dates the merger" (MC-PT 15). Perhaps the fear that acting as an individual would have little influence in their new environment led one person to comment, "Lots of people have joined the union because that's the only way we feel we have a voice against [the premerger business school]" (MC-PT 1).

In addition to the relationship developed with involvement, there were also indications of a prominent relationship between communication and trust, another of the *a priori* Level 1 themes identified within the study during the development of the qualitative thematic analysis. This was revealed in statements such as "If there had been more openness about the communication and rationale for it, I think, yes, honesty about what was in prospect, there would have been less of an issue" (MC-PT 7). Another member of staff commented, "I was feeling distrustful of the information that was coming from the top... I felt unsure about the exact message" (MC-PT 13). Again, relating to perceived honesty of the communication, one participant commented, "It sometimes felt as though the truth wasn't always being told" and they went on to add that the effect was, "there has been a massive dip in morale here" (MC-PT 12).

Cartwright and Cooper (1992) inform that if employee uncertainty is to be addressed, one of the most important parts of the management process following the announcement of a merger is consistent communication, which will have a considerable impact on the individual's assessment of their psychological contract. Honest and direct communication is imperative toward helping build employee confidence in the process during the renegotiation and assessment of the psychological contract (Hubbard, 2001; Schweiger & DeNisi, 1991). The disruptive nature of a merger will have a negative impact on employees, and the effectiveness of organizational communication will directly affect how they cope with the changing organizational environment. Morrison and Robinson (1997) discuss the two factors in the employee-employer exchange relationship that may give rise to contract breach as *reneging* and *incongruence*. They assert that the facilitation of ongoing communication is an effective method of minimizing incongruence of promises made and therefore any employee interpretation of their breach. Justification through the use of social accounts offered by management has been found to reduce the assignment of blame (Walster, 1966) and alter the employee's perception of causality, control, and intentionality (Bies, 1987).

7.5.2 The NHS Trust

In the NHS Trust merger study, communication was one of the main themes that materialized. Again, this also supported results obtained from earlier questions in the survey emphasizing the relationship between interactional justice and psychological contract breach. Emotions were revealed, and a sense of anger was displayed by one employee who protested, "The merger was fought for several years with two lots of public consultation, which we were left feeling was a paper exercise, that the decisions had been made regardless of public outcry, and professional opinions" (S1-PT 216). This was added to by a sense of anguish by one member of staff who commented, "Everything was quite distressing in the department at one time as we were losing members, not being informed as to what was going to happen" (SS-PT 78). There were other remarks in support of this feeling that came from employees across the Trust, highlighting the poor level of consultation with members of staff or inadequate use of social accounts by management to justify and explain their actions and likely consequences.

7.5.3 Discussion

If knowledge certainty is considered as an antonym of uncertainty, then it is fair to predict that in the employee-employer relationship an increase in knowledge may influence a reduction in the level of uncertainty experienced by the individual. As previously recognized, there is evidence that uncertainty in a change environment has the potential to be reduced through communication with authorities and, subsequently, as the level of control increases for the individual in that relationship. With this in mind, it is evident that the level of detachment between the leadership and employees of the new business school was partially responsible for the poor communications and an increase in the levels of uncertainty among members of staff.

However, it is proposed that the strategy of communication at the new business school is also highly related to the problem of control. It is purported that effectively transmitted organizational communication can remove some of the experience of powerlessness associated with change and the ensuing feelings of threat that result (Shaw & Barrett-Power, 1997). This is of great importance because, under normal circumstances, power within the employee-employer relationship normally resides with the employer (Blau, 1964). The problem for employees of the premerger management college was not necessarily the dissemination of information through regular communication but, perhaps befitting of an authoritarian leadership, the communication was perceived as a one-way process. This was evident in the lack of genuine voice offered to employees, which resulted in increasing the levels of distrust in the leadership and portrayed a lack of respect for the opinions of staff (interactional justice). Interactional justice is the construct of organizational justice concerned with the social exchange of the superior-subordinate relationship (Bies & Moag, 1986). It is proposed that an individual's relationship with the organization is based on the social exchange framework, which will continue until unfairness is evidenced, at which point the individual will reinterpret the relationship (Organ, 1990). The communication strategy employed by the leadership returns the emphasis to a concern over the impact from a perceived breakdown in the expectations of a successful social exchange between employee and employer. This pattern of behavior seems to support previous research conducted into employee-employer exchange relationships during times of significant change. It has been reported that the relationship between manager and employee becomes increasingly pertinent during times of organizational instability (Hubbard & Purcell, 2001) at a time when employees become concerned about their changing environment.

Marks and Mirvis (1998) reported that the methods engaged by senior management when handling a merger affect both employees' feelings about their jobs and their sense of personal stability. Trust among employees is increased when there is presence of good communication before and after a change in addition to good employee relations during that change (Nikandrou, Papalexandris, & Dimitris, 2000). In part, because of the deep levels of distrust felt toward the authorities, the relationship between the leadership and employees of the premerger management college, and increasingly for those of the premerger business school, was dysfunctional. Ineffective communication provided for a further erosion of trust and a deepening of employee uncertainty and ambiguity, leaving them to explore the gaps in their knowledge and try to complete these through social cues provided by their external environment. As employees tried to search for their answers, grapevine interaction was left to fill the gaps.

A further issue with communication was an apparent breakdown in the employer-employee feedback mechanisms, which were crucial if the changes to terms and conditions and strategic focus were to be justified. A distinct lack of justification for the communicated message was a major cause of uncertainty among employees because, again, a major element of the consultation process was not being addressed by the leadership, encouraging misunderstanding through the shortfall of information. It would appear that social accounts (explanation or justification of an action) used by senior management were inadequate when used to justify decisions taken as part of the integration process. These are an integral part of the wider issues already discussed relating to control and uncertainty. Insufficient explanation of reasons for change are defined by Cobb, Wooten, and Folger (1995) as *causal accounts*, but in this case a broader perspective was necessary to present a vision of where the new organization was being positioned and subsequently, the goals that it wished to achieve. Had such a global vision been clearly articulated across the workforce, binding in the changes being implemented as a series of objectives to achieve this vision, and therefore presenting a sense-making account at a more local level, this may have alleviated the uncertainties and subsequent outcomes of employees. The use of *reframing accounts* is discussed by Sitkin and Bies (1993) and involves an attempt to change employee perceptions of unfair treatment by persuading them to accept a new standard of comparison. During many of the discussions with employees from the premerger management college, whether realistically viable or not, alternative options to a merger with the university were raised. Merger or acquisition is a strategic choice and alternative strategies and their implications for the management college could have been presented, eliminating each for its comparable deficiencies. These comparisons, or referent alternatives, had not been clearly articulated leaving the individual, once again, in a state of knowledge deficiency and uncertainty.

As discussed, it became evident during the Phase 2 interviews that issues of trust in management were largely confined to the leadership of the business school. The other two dimensions of interactional justice that received such prominence were justification of the communicated message and the management's respectful treatment of the employee. Again, these were aspects of the relationship between the leadership and employee with no indications of anger exhibited toward the employee's supervisor or other forms of line management, which appears to shed new light on the assertion that interactional justice is confined to the leader-member exchange relationship (see Cropanzano, Prehar, & Chen, 2002). Supported by results of the survey, interactional injustice was a significantly greater issue for employees of the premerger management college compared to their colleagues from the premerger business school. Although certainly not the case with the current leadership, historical relationships between the leadership and employee had experienced few barriers, and a closeness depicting a "family relationship" was portrayed during the interviews. This is emphasized in the special bond that existed between management and staff of all levels across the organization and characterized through the cultural rituals and the development of a thriving social cohesion that had become part of the foundations of the organization. It would appear that interactional justice is dependent on the proximity of the relationship, and where this has developed as a characteristic between employees and their leader, interactional justice may also be a preserve of that relationship and is therefore not confined to more local relationships between employees and their supervisors and line managers. The dynamics of this proposition may be particularly pertinent to the structure of an organization and style of leadership (i.e. organic structure vs. bureaucratic structure, democratic leadership vs. autocratic leadership).

The important connotations of these findings are if employees can experience interactional justice between themselves and their leadership, then it is possible that this perception becomes a personification of the organization itself. There is support for the proposition that the actions of senior management become a personification of the employee's perceptions toward the organization and its policies, not least from evidence that associates procedural justice with the actions of senior management and the organization itself (Folger & Konovsky, 1989; Sweeney & McFarlin, 1993).

As discussed earlier, an outcome of this situation of information-uncertainty was the impression it left on an individual's trust in the leadership and their decision-making during the merger implementation. Another consequence of receiving either insufficient information or information that wasn't trusted was the effect on the individual's judgment and their method of evaluating fairness as a consequence of information-uncertainty. Van den Bos (2003) maintained that in situations where directly relevant information is not available individuals are more likely to base their justice evaluation on affect, thereby increasing the possibility of making irrational judgments. There was evidence of this being a major problem among staff at both campuses, due partly to actions without justification, and also as a consequence of the untrusting relationship between employees and the senior management. There was also evidence of a grapevine effect where employees circulate their own discussion, which may, inevitably, lead to rumor and misinterpretation.

Organizational trust is discussed at greater length in the next chapter.

References

Armenakis, A. A., & Harris, S. G. (2002). Crafting a change message to create transformational readiness. *Journal of Organizational Change Management, 15*(2), 169–183.

Ashford, S. J. (1988). Individual strategies for coping with stress during organizational transitions. *Journal of Applied Behavioral Science, 24*(1), 19–36.

Berger, C., & Calabrese, R. J. (1975). Some explorations in initial interaction and beyond: Toward a developmental theory of interpersonal communication. *Human Communication Research, 1*(2), 99–112.

Bies, R. (1987). The predicament of injustice: The management of moral outrage. In L. L. Cummings & B. M. Stow (Eds.), *Research in organizational behavior* (Vol. 9). Greenwich, CT: JAI Press.

Bies, R. J., & Moag, J. F. (1986). Interactional justice: Communication criteria of fairness. In R. J. Lewicki, B. H. Sheppard, & M. H. Bazerman (Eds.), *Research on negotiations in organizations* (Vol. 1, pp. 43–55). Greenwich, CT: JAI Press.

Blau, P. (1964). *Exchange and power in social life*. New York: Wiley.

Bordia, P., Hobman, E., Jones, E., Gallois, C., & Callan, V. J. (2004). Uncertainty during organizational change: Types, consequences, and management strategies. *Journal of Business and Psychology, 18*(4), 507–532.

Bordia, P., Hunt, E., Paulsen, N., Tourish, D., & DiFonzo, N. (2004). Uncertainty during organizational change: Is it all about control? *European Journal of Work and Organizational Psychology, 134*, 345–365.

Brockner, J., DeWitt, R. L., Grover, S., & Reed, T. (1990). When it is especially important to explain why: Factors affecting the relationship between managers' explanations of a layoff and survivors' reactions to the layoff. *Journal of Experimental Social Psychology, 26*, 389–407.

Buono, A. F., & Bowditch, J. L. (1989). *The human side of mergers and acquisitions*. San Francisco, CA: Jossey-Bass.

Cartwright, S., & Cooper, C. L. (1992). *Mergers and acquisitions: The human factor*. Oxford, UK: Butterworth-Heinmann Ltd.

Christensen, M. (2014). Communication as a strategic tool in change processes. *International Journal of Business Communication, 51*(4), 359–385.

Cobb, A. T., Wooten, K. C., & Folger, R. (1995). Justice in the making: Toward understanding the theory and practice of justice in organizational change and development. *Research in Organizational Change and Development, 8*, 243–295.

Cropanzano, R., & Greenberg, J. (1997). Progress in organizational justice: Tunneling through the maze. In C. Cooper & I. Robertson (Eds.), *International review of industrial and organizational psychology* (pp. 317–372). New York: Wiley.

Cropanzano, R., Prehar, C. A., & Chen, P. Y. (2002). Using social exchange theory to distinguish procedural justice from interactional justice. *Group and Organizational Management, 27*, 324–351.

Daly, J. P., & Geyer, P. D. (1994). The role of fairness in implementing largescale change: Employee evaluations of process and outcome in seven facility relocations. *Journal of Organizational Behaviour, 15*, 623–638.

Davy, J. A., Kinicki, A. J., & Scheck, C. L. (1991). Developing and testing a model of survivor responses to layoffs. *Journal of Vocational Behaviour, 38*, 302–317.

De Nobile, J. J., & McCormick, J. (2008). Organizational communication and job satisfaction in Australian Catholic primary schools. *Educational Management Administration & Leadership, 36*(1), 101–122.

Downs, C. W., DeWine, S., & Greenbaum, H. H. (1994). Measures of organizational communication. In R. B. Rubin, P. Palmgreen, H.-E. Sypher, et al. (Eds.), *Communication research measures: A sourcebook* (pp. 57–78). New York: Guilford Press.

Folger, R., & Konovsky, M. A. (1989). Effects of procedural and distributive justice on reactions to pay raise decisions. *Academy of Management Journal, 32*(1), 115–130.

Gagne, M., Koestner, R., & Zuckerman, M. (2000). Facilitating acceptance of organizational change: The importance of self-determination. *Journal of Applied Social Psychology, 30*(9), 1843–1852.

Galpin, T. J. (1996). *The human side of change: A practical guide to organizational redesign*. San Francisco, CA: Jossey-Bass.

Goldhaber, G. M. (1999). Organizational communication in 1976: Present domain and future directions. In P. Salem (Ed.), *Organizational communication and change* (pp. 4–30). Cresskill, NJ: Hampton Press.

Greenhalgh, L. (1983). Managing the job insecurity crisis. *Human Resource Management, 22*, 431–444.

Greenhalgh, L., & Rosenblatt, Z. (1984). Job insecurity: Toward conceptual clarity. *Academy of Management Review, 9*, 438–448.

Hargie, O., & Tourish, D. (2000). Charting communication performance in a healthcare organization. In O. Hargie & D. Tourish (Eds.), *Handbook of communication audits for organizations* (pp. 195–209). London: Routledge.

Hubbard, N. (2001). *Acquisition strategy and implementation*. Basingstoke, UK: Palgrave.

Hubbard, N., & Purcell, J. (2001). Managing employee expectations during acquisitions. *Human Resource Management Journal, 11*(2), 17–33.

Jackson, S., et al. (1987). Managing stress in turbulent times. In A. Riley & S. Zaccaro (Eds.), *Occupational stress and organizational effectiveness* (pp. 141–166). New York: Praeger.

Kickul, J., Lester, S. W., & Finkl, J. (2002). Promise breaking during radical organizational change: Do justice interventions make a difference? *Journal of Organizational Behavior, 23*(Special Issue S1), 469–488.

Koontz, H. (2001). *Management: A global perspective* (10th ed.). New York: McGraw-Hill.

Kramer, M. W. (1993). Communication and uncertainty reduction during job transfers: Leaving and joining processes. *Communication Monographs, 60*(2), 178–198.

Kramer, M. W. (1999). Motivation to reduce uncertainty: A reconceptualization of uncertainty reduction theory. *Management Communication Quarterly, 13*(2), 305–316.

Larsson, R., Brousseau, K. R., Driver, M. J., & Sweet, P. L. (2004). The secrets of merger and acquisition success: A co-competence and motivational approach to synergy realization. In A. L. Pablo & M. Javidan (Eds.), *Mergers and acquisitions: Creating integrative knowledge*. Oxford, UK: Blackwell Publishing.

Leventhal, G. S., Karuza, J., & Fry, W. R. (1980). Beyond fairness: A theory of allocation preferences. In G. Mikula (Ed.), *Justice and social interaction* (pp. 167–218). New York: Springer-Verlag.

Lewis, L., & Seibold, D. (1998). Reconceptualizing organizational change implementation as a communication problem: A review of literature and research agenda. In M. E. Roloff (Ed.), *Communication yearbook* (Vol. 21, pp. 93–151). Thousand Oaks, CA: Sage.

Marks, M. L., & Mirvis, P. H. (1998). Rebuilding after a merger: Dealing with survivor sickness. *Organizational Dynamics, 21*(2), 18–32.

Meyer, J. P., Becker, T. E., & Vandenberghe, C. (2004). Employee commitment and motivation: A conceptual analysis and integrative model. *Journal of Applied Psychology, 89*, 991–1007.

Morrison, E. W., & Robinson, S. L. (1997). When employees feel betrayed: A model of how psychological contract violation develops. *The Academy of Management Review, 22*(1), 226–256.

Nikandrou, I., Papalexandris, N., & Dimitris, B. (2000). Gaining employee trust after acquisitions: Implications for managerial action. *Employee Relations, 22*(4), 334–348.

Organ, D. W. (1990). The motivational basis of organizational citizenship behavior. *Research in Organizational Behavior, 12*(1), 43–72.

Rafferty, A. E., & Jimmieson, N. L. (2010). Team change climate: A group-level analysis of the relationships among change information and change participation, role stressors, and well-being. *European Journal of Work and Organizational Psychology, 19*(5), 551–586.

Saunders, M. N. K., Thornhill, A., & Lewis, P. (2002). Understanding employees' reactions to the management of change: An exploration through an organizational justice framework. *Irish Journal of Management, 23*(1), 85–108.

Schweiger, D. M., & DeNisi, A. S. (1991). Communication with employees following a merger: A longitudinal field experiment. *Academy of Management Journal, 34*, 110–135.

Shaw, J. B., & Barrett-Power, E. (1997). A conceptual framework for assessing organization, work groups and individual effectiveness during and after downsizing. *Human Relations, 50*(2), 109–127.

Sitkin, S. B., & Bies, R. J. (1993). Social accounts in conflict situations: Using explanations to manage conflict. *Human Relations, 46*, 349–370.

Smeltzer, L. R. (1991). An analysis of strategies for announcing organization-wide change. *Group & Organization Studies, 16*(1), 5–24.

Spike, B. K., & Lesser, K. (1995). We have met the enemy. *Journal of Business Strategy, 16*(2), 17–23.

Sudarsanam, S., & Mahate, A. A. (2006). Are friendly acquisitions too bad for shareholders and managers? Long-term value creation and top management turnover in hostile and friendly acquirers. *British Journal of Management, 17*, S7–S30.

Sweeney, P. D., & McFarlin, D. B. (1993). Workers evaluation' of the "ends" and the "means": An examination of four models of distributive and procedural justice. *Organizational Behavior and Human Decision Processes, 55*, 23–40.

Thibaut, J., & Walker, L. (1975). *Procedural justice: A psychological analysis.* Hillsdale, NJ: Erlbaum.

Tukiainen, T. (2001). An agenda model of organizational communication. *Corporate Communications: An International Journal, 6*(1), 47–52.

van den Bos, K. (2003). On the subjective quality of social justice: The role of affect as information in the psychology of justice judgments. *Journal of Personality and Social Psychology, 85*, 482–498.

Van Vuuren, M., de Jong, M., & Seydel, E. (2007). Direct and indirect effects of supervisor communication on organizational commitment. *Corporate Communications: An International Journal, 12*(2), 116–128.

Walster, E. (1966). Assignment of responsibility for an accident. *Journal of Personality and Social Psychology, 3*, 73–79.

Wanberg, C. R., & Banas, J. (2000). Predictors and outcomes of openness to change in a reorganizing workplace. *Journal of Applied Psychology, 20*(1), 132–142.

Wilson, N., & Peel, M. J. (1991). The impact on absenteeism and quits of profit sharing and other forms of employee participation. *Industrial and Labor Relations Review, 44*(3), 454–468.

Part III

The Employee

8

Trust

8.1 Introduction

To this point we have considered the discussions formed around the characteristics of mergers and acquisitions (M&A) and how these may impact the individual at work, their attitudes, and their behaviors. As discussed in Chap. 7, the dissemination of information and quality of communication is recognized for the influence it will bear on how organizations perform during the period of M&A integration. Hubbard (2001) identifies and discusses the intricate relationship between employee trust and effective communication from the acquiring organization. The context of a merger provides a situation for employees that is unpredictable and easy to misinterpret, arousing a likelihood for them to react by feeling vulnerable and therefore creating an environment of distrust (Krug & Nigh, 2001; Stahl & Sitkin, 2010). It is likely that any existing psychological contract with the employer will be perceived by the employee to be in a state of renegotiation due to potential breach or, in more extreme cases, a perceived violation of that trust (Buono & Bowditch, 1989; Cartwright & Cooper, 1996). Within this context a period of intense vulnerability and risk assessment is often aroused, particularly in the interlude following a merger announcement (Stahl, Larsson, Kremershof, & Sitkin, 2011).

N. Jackson, *Organizational Justice in Mergers and Acquisitions*,
https://doi.org/10.1007/978-3-319-92636-0_8

In their case survey study into the antecedents and consequences of trust in acquired organizations, Stahl, et al. (2011) analyzed results from 50 previous qualifying studies investigating trust-related issues during the postacquisition integration period. The authors proclaimed, "Despite a large body of anecdotal evidence supporting the critical role of trust in M&A, little is known about the factors that influence how trust develops in acquired organizations and the effects of that trust on post-acquisition integration outcomes and performance" (p. 593). Significant findings from the study include support for a relationship between target firm member trust and quality of communication, perceived employee benefits, as well as attitudinal and behavioral outcomes including job satisfaction and commitment, acceptance of change, intentions to stay, and willingness to cooperate. Such outcomes have also been associated with perceived fairness (organizational justice) in decision-making and resource allocations, a concept that is widely associated with trust in organization environments (e.g. see Colquitt & Rodell, 2011).

Encouraged by research conducted by Stahl and colleagues (2011) there is an argument that it is time for a more nuanced approach to the role of trust in leadership during a period of organization integration to understand better the dynamics of this multifaceted concept. Although more akin to acquisitions, an idiosyncratic feature of M&A change is the proximal and distal relationships that develop between organization members and their change leaders. The impact from the nature of the exchange relationship between trustor and trustee is fundamental to the development of trust, and this is an important omission from current research into impact of leadership in M&A change.

8.2 Trust Defined

Trust has been recognized as a social mechanism by which society keeps moral order and avoids chaos and is identified as multifaceted, comprising cognitive, emotional, and behavioral dimensions (Cummings & Bromiley, 1996). From an organizational perspective, it has been identified as a critical ingredient of mechanisms designed to motivate members to successfully share knowledge. Therefore, it makes an important contribution toward the effective functioning of an organization's human resource operation and, in turn, the overall architecture of the organization system. It can also work as an enabler for people who work in uncertain environments and where risk is a key component of their everyday lives. Consequently, trust between organization members can provide the backbone of any successful enterprise and its ability to strive toward that golden objective of developing a sustainable competitive advantage.

Although there have been various interpretations of how trust can be defined (e.g. Cook & Wall, 1980; Gabarro & Athos, 1976; Lewicki & Bunker, 1995), one of the more commonly accepted approaches is offered by Mayer, Davis, and Schoorman (1995) as a willingness of one party to be vulnerable to the actions of another party. Rousseau, Sitkin, Burt, and Camerer (1998) concurred defining the concept as "a psychological state comprising the intention to accept vulnerability based upon positive expectations of the intentions or behavior of another" (p. 395). Drawing on these broad definitions of trust, Gillespie and Deitz (2009) offered two other factors that should also be recognized within the shape of interactions between two or more parties in the process that may either impede or enhance the development of trust. One of these factors is risk, which, to some extent, is an element that is present within any interpersonal relationship when there is uncertainty for either party regarding how the other will act. Another factor that may be present is interdependence, which will become a concern when there is a reliance on the other party's input for goal attainment to be achieved (e.g. Zucker, 1986). Interdependence within the employee relationship may be a critical aspect in supporting their employer to achieve corporate goals, which may be particularly coveted if it relates to a perception that the organization will reciprocate these efforts in return. There is a payback that is dependent on this relationship, and trust will become a vital element in a pursuit to achieve these goals.

Rather than understanding trust and distrust as concepts that can be measured on a single spectrum, Lewicki, Tomlinson, and Gillespie (2006) recognize both trust and distrust as two distinct, but related, constructs. Taking this perspective, the relationship of trust between the trustor and the trustee should be understood as multifaceted in that the trustee may be trusted in some ways by the trustor but not others. To understand this and other aspects of the relationship in greater depth, we now move on to look at how trust is developed between entities.

8.3 Developing Organizational Trust

It has already been identified that due to the idiosyncrasies of M&A, change in this context can prompt different forms of attitude and behavioral reactions to similar scenarios in other environments. There is an acceptance that interpreting the attitude of trust in the context of M&A encourages the need for a more nuanced approach to better understand the interplay between the dimensions of trustworthiness and the significance of each within differing contexts. For example, in this process of determining trust with the trustor, is the ability or competence of the trustee to perform a task more important than the openness or willingness to share thoughts, feelings, and information? If so, is this affected by temporality of the integration process (i.e. the stage of the process)? In other contexts, these arguments have been developed. For instance, there is evidence that individuals emphasize positive information relating to competence (ability of the trustee) more generously than negative information, and in contrast they will place greater emphasis on negative information about integrity more profoundly than positive information. Furthermore, as Rousseau et al. (1998) have identified, trust is not static phenomena where a situation of complete trust or distrust may arise. There is indeed a case to suggest that trust changes over time and may develop or decrease, or even resurface, particularly where long-standing relationships are prevalent. Given these alternative perceptions, it seems fair to predict that the dimensions of trustworthiness and their antecedents will also develop multifaceted relationships and interpretations between different groups of employees in a merger context.

8.3.1 Trust Formation

As Rousseau et al. (1998) acknowledge, trust is a psychological state and there is an increasing acceptance that as it evolves this is not solely based on a cognitive process. There are also emotional and social influences (Kramer, 1999). Cognitive-based trust is the result of a careful, methodical procedure an individual will go through to determine whether another individual, group or organization is trustworthy. Affective-based trust may be developed in the absence of evidence in the trustee to cognitively evaluate (McAlister, 1995). Another form of affective-based trust, defined as *relational trust*, is developed from repeated interactions between the trustor and trustee over a period, and therefore information that is available to the trustor from within the relationship itself forms the basis of the trust (Rousseau et al., 1998). In contrast, calculus-based trust is built on rational choice and is therefore more akin to the cognitive form of trust development. It is characteristic of interactions built on economic exchange rather than the social exchange transactions of relational trust. In contrast willingness to trust is limited to exchanges of a specific nature (e.g. financial transactions) but not formed through the same mechanisms as the relational form of trust.

Influence of the Interaction

Whichever form of trust exists (e.g. cognitively- or emotionally formed), it is widely accepted that whether trust is to be developed or diminished will be dependent on the quality of interaction between the trustor and trustee. In example cases of organizational activity where there are restricted levels of interaction (e.g. M&A), it has been acknowledged that the development of trust among team members will be hampered. The willingness of the trustor to be vulnerable in an exchange relationship with the trustee is seen to be an act of willingness to take risk, and therefore trust should not be identified as taking risk per se, but the actual willingness to take risk. Without this element of risk, trust becomes irrelevant because there is no vulnerability (Lewicki & Bunker, 1996; Mayer et al., 1995; Rousseau et al., 1998).

The act of trustworthiness is important because it is the perceived level of this dimension that will lead to trust in the trustee. In Mayer et al.'s (1995) model of trust development, three common characteristics of the trustee, believed to explain a major portion of trustworthiness, are identified as being of primary importance: *ability*, *benevolence*, and *integrity*. Ability is defined as the skills, characteristics, or competencies attributed to the trustee that enables them to bear influence within a specific domain. Benevolence relates specifically to the social exchange relationship between the trustee and the trustor and accounts for the level of welfare the former has for the latter as perceived by the trustor. Principles found to be acceptable to the trustor and whether the trustee adheres to those principles determine the level of integrity upon which the trustee will be judged and form a relationship with the third characteristic of trustworthiness as perceived by the trustor. In addition, within their model Stahl et al. (2011) raise two further dimensions of *openness* (openly sharing thoughts, feelings, and information with another person) and *value congruence* (extent to which individuals, groups, or organizations share values helps to establish trust within those relationships). They inform that these dimensions have been recognized by several scholars as important elements of trustworthiness (Gabarro, 1978; Mishra, 1996; Sitkin & Roth, 1993; Whitener, Brodt, Korsgaard & Werner, 1998), and they considered all five dimensions worthy of inclusion in their investigation. In addition to openness, accuracy of the communication (Muchinsky, 1977) and adequate explanations and timely feedback (Folger & Konovsky, 1989; Konovsky & Cropanzano, 1991) have also been identified as important aspects of communication in the relationship with perceived trustworthiness. Stahl and colleagues also consider other antecedents of trustworthiness in their model and identify both status variables (relationship history and interfirm distance) and process variables. The process variables include aspects from two of the three dimensions of organizational justice, perceived benefits of the merger (distributive justice) and communication quality (interactional justice).

8.3.2 Sense-making

Lewis and Weigert (1985) recognized trust as a socially constructed phenomenon that aids sense-making in both relationship development and decision-making and therefore playing a key role in the cognitive process of understanding our world around us (Weick, 1995). This sense-making process can be influenced by those who operate within our environment and each new action they may provide helps us to add information that will assist in either developing or diminishing our levels of trust toward an activity or event (Adabor, 2005). Magala (2009) sums this up neatly by referring to the act of sense-making being encouraged by a context whereby "communication, interaction, feedback and self-reflection combine and recombine in fluid networked, evolving social worlds" (p. 46).

Of course, the processes of relationship development and decision-making are interpreted as important ongoing activities in the day-to-day routines of organizational life that draw heavily on the concept of sense-making, and something we come to take for granted in the role of management and leadership. The interaction between these managerial activities and how they are perceived through the lens of justice is critical, being identified by scholars as one of the important elements during either the development or decline of trust in management (e.g. Chory & Hubbell, 2008; Colquitt & Rodell, 2011). Employees have expectations that management decision making is both unbiased and honest and anything else will challenge their integrity (Colquitt & Rodell, 2011) and sense-making will play an essential role in these circumstances. For example, applying the consistency rule to acts of decision-making is one comparison that employees will reflect on to determine the fairness of the outcome (Leventhal, 1980). In addition, a common bond of trust should be supported by evidence that those with the capacity to determine outcomes will evaluate, communicate, and apply these in a fair and just manner. If there is insufficient evidence that managers are to be trusted, then employees will use rules of thumb or proxies to develop their own subjective perceptions of fairness. Scholars have identified this as fairness heuristic theory (see Lind, 2001; Van den Bos, 2001), indicating that employees will apply the type of justice (e.g. distributive, procedural, and interactional) and develop their own circumstantial rules as appropriate at the time dependent on how they perceive the actions or events that have occurred.

An important contribution to this process of employee perception is the proximity of the relationship between the leader and member, and this may well be dependent on the level and regularity of interaction. This is often guided by the seniority of the manager in question and the relationship between their role and that of the subordinate and so it may be helpful to categorize these at three different levels of engagement: i) the employee's immediate supervisor (Chory & Hubbell, 2008; Colquitt & Rodell, 2011), ii) subsequent higher tiers of management (Frazier, Johnson, Gavin, Gooty, & Snow, 2010) and, iii) senior levels of organizational management (Vanhala, Puumalainen, & Blomqvist, 2011). The impact on employee behavior is worth considering at each of these levels as we gain a greater understanding of how trust, fairness and employee expectations synchronize in their powers to change the nature of the psychological contract with their employer. We need to bear in mind that trust should not only be considered as an act of honesty or dishonesty, but also in relation to the competence of others and their reliability to perform (ability). This may be influenced by the proximity of the relationship and subsequent interaction between leader and member, or the seniority of the manager and employee expectations of that individual (e.g. autonomy to perform). For example, the proximal relationship formed between employees and their supervisor is less likely to raise issues of procedural justice, which tends to be system driven and therefore more likely to impact between employees and their senior management. Our understanding of procedural justice is vital because there is evidence that its role in determining employee's levels of trust is greater than that of distributive justice (Tyler, 1990). A study by Neves and Caetano (2009) showed the relationship here between these variables and the attitude of affective, or emotional, commitment to the organization as well as behaviors, such as reducing turnover intentions, improved performance, and organizational citizenship.

Emotion and Trust

It is worth returning briefly to the discussion earlier in this chapter and remind ourselves that, similarly to other attitudes, trust is multifaceted and comprises cognitive, emotional, and behavioral dimensions. Therefore, in addition to its cognitive capacities, trust may also encourage affective and behavioral reactions (for examples of scholarly studies see Lewicki et al., 2006; McAlister, 1995). To illuminate this proposition, we need to consider that any emotional component of trust will be advanced with varying intensity and the context of this will, in part, be dependent on the process of sense-making and how this develops. Weick (1995) recognizes the interruptions of events, such as change that can trigger various feelings in an emotional response to the event itself. In these situations, trust is recognized as having a major impact on both employee commitment and resistance to organizational change because of its ability to cause an emotional reaction to either the process or outcome of change (Piderit, 2000; Smollan, 2011). Because of the more radical form of change associated with M&A (e.g. downsizing), employee anxiety will often have negative repercussions in the trusting relationship formed between the employee and the employer (Paterson & Cary, 2002). Even so, the quality of interactions within this relationship can have a significant role in helping to maintain levels of trust via the mechanisms of interactional justice.

Because trust within the employer-employee relationship is such an important element of an employee's emotional response to change, we now return to consider the discussion about how managers and leaders of change are perceived within the overall context of trust. In part, the psychological contract is formed around employee expectations of their managers and we now turn to investigate the impact of failing to meet expectations and any implications for trust from a perceived breach of the psychological contract.

8.3.3 Expectations

As discussed in Chap. 7, the quality and volume of organizational communication during times of change can be pivotal to alleviate uncertainty, helping to encourage positive attitudes, such as commitment, and quell negative responses, such as different forms of resistance. While there are several factors that will be at play here, the source of the communication and the perceived levels of trust that employees are willing to commit to that source will be fundamental. Uncertainty has a greater chance of being addressed and reduced. Strategies to include employees in the decision-making process and add voice to that process are examples of organization practices where open communication forms part of the culture, and expectations may be forged around these existing practices. The difficulty in a merger situation is that, for various reasons, existing practice may need to be adapted or even curtailed in the short- to medium term due to confidentiality surrounding certain aspects of the deal at points in time. There is also the merger partner to consider who may not have been used to operating in such an open climate, and therefore it is highly likely that business as usual will be disrupted.

Other management practices that have become embedded as part of the culture include the levels of employee support offered by the organization and, in a similar vein to the act of participative decision-making, expectations that this will continue may have an impact on perceived trust (Robinson, 1996). These prior expectations, influenced by management practice, will permeate employee mind-sets across the newly-formed organization as it begins to forge the culture and climate. Subsequently, this will have a substantial influence on early levels of trust development and employee perceptions of the change communication, which is clearly important while avoiding resistance to a change event. Supported by the empirical findings from a study by Rousseau and Tijoriwala (1999), in climates where high trust prevails over low trust, there is a much stronger alliance between the reasoning used by managers to justify the change and the perceived legitimacy among employees of those reasons. These findings also support the persuasive tendency for preconceived ideas of trust in management to influence either the formation or diminution of trust for those encountering change in the future. They also encourage the development of effective management practices to build a climate of trust, inspiring trustees to be more open and accepting of future change processes when they are introduced.

Within the newly-integrated organization, the proximity of the relationships forged between organization members and change leaders (i.e. proximal vs. distal) will influence the level of trust and how this is developed (e.g. cognitive- or affective-based trust). Evidently, it will have major implications for founding the bases from which trust will be formed between organization members and authorities. Research suggests that in the initial stages of a relationship, trust is more likely to be exhibited on the basis that it will be warranted if there is no evidence to the contrary (McKnight, Cummings, & Chervany, 1998). In comparison, in cases where individuals base their perceptions of trust on previous experiences, the trustee who is mistrusted will not only have to reestablish positive expectations but also overcome any negative expectations (Kim, Ferrin, Cooper, & Dirks, 2004). Hence, parties to a merger who find their existing relationship with the leadership or organization is differentiated on a proximal versus distal basis may find their early perceptions of trustworthiness differ considerably.

Psychological Contract

When drawing on the constructs of trust and fairness, we can see their influence within the employee-employer relationship and the perceived expectations of each other within the working partnership. This has been identified in the academic literature as a psychological contract that exists between the two parties. Although I discuss the psychological contract in much greater depth in Chap. 11, its relevance to the current discussion cannot be ignored and we should consider the implications while discussing a presence of trust within the concept of fairness. While definitions of the theory underpinning the psychological contract will be investigated later in the text, the core principle is based on an employee's perception of mutual obligations (Chaudhry, Coyle-Shapiro, & Wayne, 2011; Robinson & Rousseau, 1994), which inevitably depend on the expectations of each party involved. When asked to consider the psychological contract and those factors that are more likely to influence employee perceptions, trust was identified as one the key factors valued most along with respect, open and honest communication, and fair treatment (Lester & Kickul, 2001). In the case where employees feel their trust in management has been disregarded, emotional reactions associated with feelings of betrayal including anger, fear, frustration, and shock may be expected (Smollan, 2012). To define the term "betrayal" in this context, we turn to Elangovan and Shapiro (1998), who defined it as a "voluntary violation of mutually known pivotal expectations of the trustor by the trusted party (trustee), which has the potential to threaten the well-being of the trustor" (p. 546). Once this has occurred, it is recognized that the relationship with the employee is tarnished by this betrayal of trust and the emotional outrage that may pursue (Lewis & Weigert, 1985). Such negative reactions are experienced when perceived promises are not adhered to by either management or the organization (Robinson, 1996; Robinson & Rousseau, 1994). Subsequently, this lack of adherence to perceived promises is viewed by the employees as a breach or violation of their psychological contract with the organization and therefore deemed to be unfair (Kickul, Lester, & Finkl, 2002).

Trust in management becomes much more of a pertinent issue when organizations are experiencing periods of change (Lines, Selart, Espedal,

& Johansen, 2005) and during times when the psychological contract comes under greater scrutiny. Indeed, the two activities are often aligned. Understandably, when these circumstances occur, organizations will be challenged to meet the previous norms and expectations of employees as the change begins to take shape. During such periods, previous environments and routines are disrupted, at very least in the short- to medium term, which may not arouse the purely negative connotations that would be expected. It is difficult to gauge whether employees will react by forming more flexible attitudes during this period, enabling them to adapt their expectations to correspond with the changing environment that they encounter. This will be largely dependent on the level of uncertainty associated with the change and any insecurities that emerge. Trust is not necessarily both developed and diminished in a consistent and uniform pattern. Whereas trust is developed incrementally over a period, there may be a sudden disappearance of its presence rather than a steady erosion due to several events or activities (Atkinson & Butcher, 2003).

8.4 Case in Question

At the business school merger, it became apparent during interviews with employees from the premerger management college that their experiences of what they perceived to be an authoritarian leadership predated the merger. Their experiences encouraged those employees to form preconceptions about the expected behavior of their leadership during and after the merger. In addition to other expectations this appeared to influence their attitude of trust. Conversely, employees from the premerger business school had become accustomed to a more democratic style of leadership that had encouraged inclusivity. These individuals were less likely to experience similar preconceptions. The struggle for an element of control in the workplace between the employee and authorities had become an everyday expectation for staff at the premerger management college. We can infer from this that an autocratic leadership style will lead to employee preconceptions that they will have little or no control during a period of likely uncertainty where unknown outcomes will act as an intensifier of increased anxiety.

Evidence of the effect this had on employee attitudes was presented as issues of trust, which took form in two distinct, but related, ways. First, there was an inherent disbelief among employees from the premerger management college of the leadership's stated intentions, and this was manifest in criticisms that they were secretive and uncommunicative. The second example of trust is related to an employee perception that leadership suffered from flawed judgment and irrational decision-making. These employee perceptions of leadership were significant in determining their *a priori* expectations of fair process in the merger, and perhaps led to a distortion of views through a preconceived lens. Folger (1993) claimed that people compare change situations to referent others, which he went on to explicate through the mechanism of *referent cognitions theory*. This, he said, provided reason why individuals will attempt to compare their environment and all the uncertain connotations that will evolve along with this move in situations. The past not only serves as a referent for current expectations and certainty, but it is also more familiar to them, leading to a reduction in uncertainty and greater control. An anchor then for employees at the premerger management college came in the form of expectations derived from the past behavior of their leadership. Although this may have been a method of providing more certainty to their environment, it appears from the conversations in Phase 2 of the study that this was mitigated by the high level of uncertainty to emerge from their ineffective communications strategy.

This was not the case for employees based at the premerger business school, who had no prior experience of the new leadership and, therefore, in the initial stages were more likely to form a balanced perspective that hadn't been influenced by preconceptions. However, there were some expressions from those employees during the interviews that their interpretation of the leadership changed as the merger progressed and similar issues of control and related uncertainty had also started to develop. Previous studies conducted in a similar climate have found that a loss of trust leading toward uncertainty of authorities tends to increase the prospect of negative perceptions being formed about procedural fairness (van den Bos, Wilke, & Lind, 1998). This was also supported in the current study where procedural justice became a prominent factor among employees of the new business school in their evaluations of fairness. As we have discussed in earlier sections, perceived fairness in the process (procedural justice) is greatly enhanced by employee participation, which is also dependent on knowledge transfer and the part it plays in helping to reduce uncertainty. Procedural fairness matters more when an individual is uncertain whether they can or cannot trust the authority. This is especially so in situations of information-uncertainty where they are more likely to base their overall opinions of fairness on procedures used in the determination of outcomes (van den Bos, 2001).

Expectations based on previous behaviors shaped employees' early merger perceptions from the premerger management college, and those relating to fair outcomes from the integration. Therefore, how did future expectations based on organizational life beyond the merger affect employee perceptions of fairness in the current process? It has been discussed how an individual's positive and negative trait affect can influence their perception of fairness, and it may be considered that future expectations will be an important factor in these judgments. On this basis there was a divide between assessments from employees of the two premerger organizations, motivated in part by the merger objectives of each organization. In conversations conducted with employees from the premerger business school, they appeared to be reticent about the merger because they could see little, if any, benefit for themselves from the integration. The outcome for those employees was a change of name to that of the premerger management college, and, more divisively, a change in publication strategy for the business school. From some of the comments articulated by these employees, occupational commitment was of greater consideration to them than organizational commitment, and this was borne out in their declarations that publishing strategy was a personal goal.

Also, the results from the first and second surveys provided evidence that they were less committed to the new organization than employees from the premerger management college. In each of the values measured for organizational identity, team identity, and affective commitment, they returned a significantly lower value than their counterparts at the premerger management college. Their expectations looking forward were of becoming part of a mainstream business school with a changed identity and purpose and a shift in business objectives that were increasingly moving out of alignment with their own personal objectives. These were their biggest concerns, and what they deemed to be unfair was that there had been very little justification or consultation and as a result had been shown little respect for their position in the organization.

In comparison, future expectations for employees from the premerger management college appeared to provide them with more hope and therefore fairness for these staff members was more in relation to previous and current events. As discussed, the reasons for merger were distinct for each organization and each can be related to the type of change being undertaken. Weick and Quinn's (1999) continuous change model befitted the radical change to business strategy that was part of the planning and objectives of the premerger business school before the merger was announced. The integration with the premerger management college offered an ideal opportunity to assist in the progress with this continuous change by providing an instantaneous transformation of identity. The merger enabled the radical change program to be implemented and became the object of blame for the employees of the premerger business school for the changes being undertaken to the publishing strategy that they so vehemently opposed.

The episodic change being experienced at the premerger management college was more of a necessity due to financial constraints and was much more acceptable to staff who largely welcomed the relief of removing an ever-increasing concern of retaining their jobs. The main concern of these employees was with the leadership with whom they had experience, and the unfair process and distribution of outcomes from the merger that they had delivered. Discussions with these employees also revealed the opportunities they envisaged may occur within the new business school, and therefore there were many reasons to believe that their outlook had been greatly improved. Opportunities for self-development in a new learning environment that offered job training and the chance to learn skills from a change in culture and practice, in addition to the possible boost to their career prospects from an increase in the range of internal positions, were, for some, another reason why, over the long term, the merger appeared to be a personally uplifting experience.

However, the singularly predominant event that united the employees of the premerger management college in their belief that better times may lie ahead was the change in leadership that would take place once the merger implementation was largely complete. New leadership for these members of staff presented the prospect of overcoming anxieties they held toward the current leadership and a possible move toward openness and clarity in decision-making and relationships between authority and employee. This point was emphasized emphatically by the belief that by joining forces with the premerger business school and becoming a member of the newly-formed organization with a new leadership raised the prospect of a relationship of trust developing and forming a more trusting environment. From evidence such as this, the results infer that employee expectations form an important role in their perceptions of fair treatment, and the perspective of whether their referent of comparison is based on experience or future predictions will have an influential contribution.

These were the factors of expectation that were most influential to employees across the new business school, and their impact on the individual's evaluation of fairness within the process differed considerably.

8.5 The Relationship with Justice

The dynamic interaction of trust and organizational justice has been recognized as having important connotations to employee outcomes. The seeds of a meaningful relationship between justice and trust are supported in various studies. In their model Stahl et al. (2011) recognize aspects of both distributive justice and interactional justice as antecedents of perceived trustworthiness. Colquitt and Rodell (2011) found some particularly interesting outcomes that supported a reciprocal relationship between procedural and interpersonal justice (a dimension of interactional justice) and the benevolence and integrity dimensions of trustworthiness. This argument is strengthened in research conducted by Whitener et al. (1998), who identified *sharing and delegation of control* (integral to procedural justice) as one of the main dimensions of trustworthy behavior. They highlight that allowing for employee involvement increases their likelihood of favorable outcomes and reduces the chance of managerial opportunism purporting that "the extent to which managers involve employees influences the development of trust" (p. 517).

The relationship between aspects of procedural justice and trust has already been alluded to in the current study, which confirms other supporting evidence that where procedural justice levels are high, the perceptions of trust in general management will increase (e.g. see Korsgaard, Brodt, & Whitener, 2002; Ferres, Connell, & Travaglione, 2005). This is particularly so when employees can become involved in the decision-making process (Lines et al., 2005), which encourages factors of enhancement, such as increased transparency and the matter that those involved have taken on some of the burden of responsibility for the ensuing outcomes. Involvement has been identified in several studies to be positively associated with trust even when the employee is simply allowed to voice opinions (not necessarily being engaged in any formal decision-making process) during the process of decision-making (e.g. see Folger & Konovsky, 1989; Korsgaard & Roberson, 1995).

8.5.1 Case in Question

One of the most important issues to emerge from the newly-combined business school was how employees perceived the establishment of procedures that were applied to determine merger outcomes and instrumental activity, such as the dissemination of accurate and reliable information. This had a central role in the development of trust within the decision-making process. Communication mechanisms activated to set up dialogue between organizational members and their leaders to warn of any change to procedures and employee outcomes, were to have a major bearing on how they evaluated fair treatment. A critical element that exerted influence in this process was the level of control employees experienced during these activities.

As discussed in Chap. 3, procedural justice is one of the principal components of organizational justice and may even lead to a mitigation of perceived fairness or unfairness of outcomes. Looking forward to the newly-integrated organization, staff at the premerger management college provided the distinct impression that adopting the university's procedures led them to conclude that, in future, they would have an increased level of trust in the operational process. One member of staff from the old management college who preferred the rigor of the university's procedures commented about the new expense system and getting used to questions such as "What project code does it come under? Whose authority is it under? There's a sort of sign-off trail that wasn't there before" (MC-PT 8). Another individual commented: "At least there is a clear process to go through" (MC-PT 1). Emphasizing the relationship between setting procedures that exuded a sense of clarity and promoting an environment of honesty, one participant declared, "There is trust in there that [the pre-merger business school] have got these procedures in place, and that can help [develop a trusting relationship]" (MC-PT 11).

For the new business school employees, trust could be broadly defined as consisting of two categories, delineated by each cohort from the two premerger organizations. Because the leadership team from the premerger management college also had responsibility for implementing the merger, there was a general experience of *distrust* that emanated from *a priori* expectations of those employees. A commonality of thought for this group was a disbelief in their leaders' intentions and their abilities to make rational decisions. In contrast, employees from the premerger business school had been used to the possession of a more *relational* form of trust in their leadership team. For this group, a concern was an element of uncertainty impelled by either a sense of unfamiliarity with the new leadership team, or because of the change in leadership style from a close democratic system to a more authoritative and distant relationship.

8.5.2 Case in Question: Trust and Uncertainty

Evidence emerged from the interviews in Phase 2 of the business school merger that the anxiety created by uncertainty in a merger or acquisition is intensified when employees are not offered voice in the decision-making process, a notion supported by contrasting examples. Employees who had been asked to participate in some of the decisions that affected their remit of work spoke about how encouraged they were with the behavior of authorities and how this had increased their level of trust in them in both a personal sense and a relational sense. Conversely, employees who stated they were not given voice in the process were more likely to portray a negative view of their leadership's behavior and demonstrate lower levels of trust in their intentions or ability to make rational decisions. The act of inviting an individual to become involved in the merger process sends a signal that their abilities are recognized by the authority and enhances a relationship of mutual respect. It should be noted how the action of giving voice bares similarities to the development of an effective communication strategy. There is evidence that this relationship is dependent on the mechanisms of social exchange, governed by the norms of reciprocity between the parties involved.

Therefore, action taken by authorities to either offer control or increase current levels of control had a positive effect on the employee's perception of their leadership. In addition to improving levels of commitment to change, an increase in control reduced employee uncertainty and, subsequently, increased their level of trust in the leadership, whereas the offer of control where it had previously been neglected promoted feelings of respect and self-efficacy. Problems with some members of staff from the premerger management college arose because it was felt that the voice they were being offered was disingenuous when compared with their *a priori* expectations. This then appeared to have the adverse effect of increasing their levels of uncertainty and decreasing levels of trust in the leadership.

8.5.3 The Role of Leadership

To summarize, we can assert that concerns over trust in the leadership were partly related to employee experience and a subsequent expectation that leadership behavior would follow previous characteristics and that this would lead to an unfair merger process. Trust was one of the *a priori* Level 1 themes to emerge from previous research, and in the case of the business school merger it had several representations. The first of two exemplars is the distrust of senior management activity, which was largely a preserve of the premerger management college employees' expectations of their leadership. This first example can be broken down further into two subdimensions: (i) a disbelief in their stated actions and intentions and (ii) a disbelief in their capacity to make rational judgments and decisions. There were deeply held convictions that the leadership of the premerger management college were self-indulgent and that their actions were not necessarily motivated with the college's best intentions at heart.

The second of these two reasons for distrust in management activity was a comprehensive belief among those interviewed at the college that the leadership's judgment had been called into question in relation to several major decisions that had been financially unrewarding in the years immediately preceding the merger. There was the impression that these financial misdemeanors had made a significant contribution to the decline of the college and the subsequent position that a merger was enforced to save financial catastrophe. The effect of either of these two factors on the employee was to reduce the level of trust they held in the leadership, which may be construed as having legitimacy, or wholly inappropriate. Either way, the message communicated during the conversations was assured and the true effect was dependent upon the interpretation by the employee and not in the legitimacy of their belief. In these cases, their convictions established the mind-set of the employee, which appeared to play a crucial role in how they determined trust in the process of decision-making during the merger implementation.

The second exemplar of trust was largely related to employees from the premerger business school that had not previously been acquainted with the leadership team. The issue here was relational, partly concerning employee unfamiliarity with the senior management team, and therefore the need to build trust through familiarity and forming relationships with the leadership. The second relational issue was concerning the difficulties employees were facing building that relationship due to a change they were encountering in leadership style. As previously alluded to, senior management from the premerger business school were recognized for their democratic and consultative leadership style, unlike the new leadership team, which was described as autocratic and remaining generally detached from the employees. Such barriers had created a distance between the staff and leadership and that gap was filled with uncertainty as any knowledge about the senior management was limited to hearsay.

This problem with detachment also compounded the issues with trust experienced by employees from the premerger management college as they made their judgments based largely on expectations about the quality of decision-making. Events such as these that arise where information is either limited or nonexistent may leave the individual to make their evaluations based on other material, which is what Salancik and Pfeffer (1978) refer to when discussing *social information processing theory*. They discuss the situation where individuals will fill the gaps left by ambiguity of the communicated message (*heuristic substitute*) through social influence and obtain information from "relevant others" upon which to base their perceptions and evaluations. Situations of information-uncertainty that reduce the level of trust in the authority responsible for disseminating that information will result in the increased need for the individual to draw on the procedures used when evaluating a decision outcome, intensifying the requirement for fair procedures (van den Bos, 2001). Therefore, even in situations where communication between authority and employee is good, if the sincerity or the quality of that information is not convincing, then that erosion of trust will also lead to situations of information uncertainty.

It is also accepted that in situations where information- uncertainty exists, an individual's affective state will become more prominent in judgments, further increasing the subjectivity of their perceptions of fairness and reducing levels of logicality and objectivity in the process. Furthermore, because they tend to focus on the negative aspects of the situation, employees who experience negative trait affectivity are more likely to perceive unfair treatment than those experiencing low negative trait affectivity (Wanberg, Bunce, & Gavin, 1999). There was considerable evidence of the subjective-affective evaluation process during conversations with employees from both campuses, and cases could be determined from the four different rationales provided of effecting trust. Figure 8.1 depicts the situation emerging from the current study and proposes a two-dimensional framework of trust leading to similar outcomes of uncertainty and an increase on the emphasis of fair procedures.

Forming part of the framework of organizational justice antecedents, trust is one of the most dynamic variables. Authority's embodiment of trust in their decisions and actions during the M&A process proved to be a pivotal factor in employee perceptions of justice, and this was exemplified by contrasting profiles of their leadership. Those members of staff that had been able to develop a working relationship with the leadership

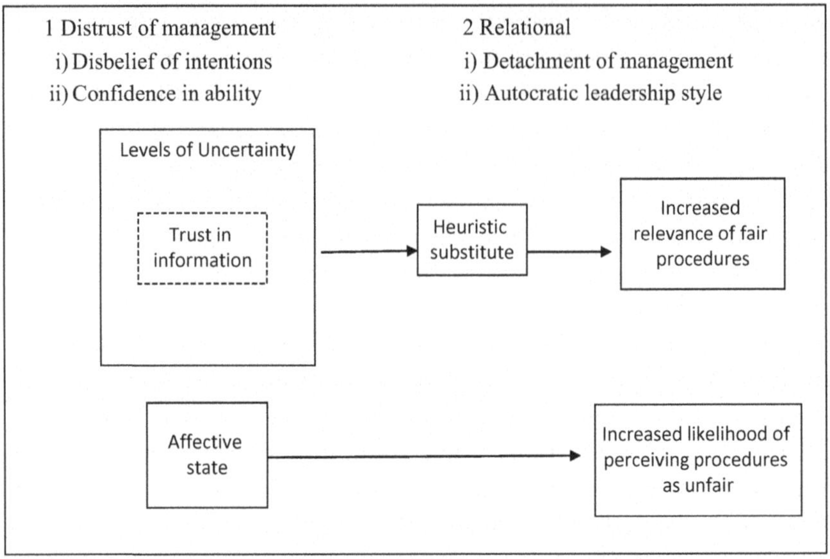

Fig. 8.1 The effect of trust on the perceived fairness of procedures

and had gained their support were more positive in their personal appraisal of those authorities and the merger process that they were leading. During the Phase 2 interviews, it was found that so many of the variables upon which organizational justice is dependent were reliant on a reciprocated exchange relationship of trust. For instance, as well as influencing employee preconceptions of their leadership and subsequently the perception of their expected behavior during the merger, building trust was also effective in developing new relationships with employees from the premerger business school. Within both roles trust was found to influence both the uncertainty of the employee and their perceived fairness of the communicated message. In addition, from the results of the Phase 3 and 4 surveys, levels of trust were also found to influence the belief that promises made during implementation have been kept and will therefore help to reduce any doubts an individual may harbor that their psychological contract with the organization has been breached.

With such an impact on the individual it is therefore important to identify the main reasons for an employee to experience feelings of distrust for authorities in a merger. There is clear evidence from research conducted at the business school that the characteristics of trust in this situation can be identified as two dimensional. The two dimensions and their subdimensions are presented in Table 8.1.

From the Phase 2 interviews it would appear that levels of trust may be increased through careful consideration of building interpersonal relationships where they do not exist. Where they do exist, ensuring that strong communication mechanisms are developed that not only provide an explanatory function but also provide the option of genuine voice. For the employee, being offered genuine voice is imperative for creating a level of control in the process and reducing some of their uncertainty. It is also necessary to recognize the role of perceived organizational support (POS) in the exchange relationship and the dynamics of this variable in a trusting relationship built on the norms of reciprocity.

Table 8.1 Relationships with authorities and their influence on trust

Personal The distrust is attributed to characteristics of the individuals acting as authority	**Intentions**	The intentions of those individuals acting as authority are perceived by the employee as potentially damaging to the employee's interests (e.g. authority's actions are perceived to be self-serving rather than in the interests of the organization; authority's actions are perceived to be in the interests of the organization but a threat toward the interests of the employee).
	Ability	The ability of those in authority to make rational decisions that will benefit the organization.
Relational The distrust is an attribute of the proximity of the relationship between the authority and the employee.	**Distance**	The authority makes little or no effort to remove the barriers between them and the employee to develop a working relationship.
	Unfamiliarity	The authority is new and unfamiliar to the employee because they have not had time to develop a working relationship.

References

Adabor, H. (2005). Trust as sensemaking: The microdynamics of trust in interfirm alliances. *Journal of Business Research, 58*(3), 330–337.

Atkinson, S., & Butcher, D. (2003). Trust in managerial relationships. *Journal of Managerial Psychology, 18*(4), 282–304.

Buono, A. F., & Bowditch, J. L. (1989). *The human side of mergers and acquisitions*. San Francisco: Jossey-Bass.

Cartwright, S., & Cooper, C. L. (1996). *Managing mergers, acquisitions and strategic alliances: Integrating people and cultures*. Oxford, UK: Butterworth-Heinmann.

Chaudhry, A., Coyle-Shapiro, J. A.-M., & Wayne, S. J. (2011). Psychological contracts: A longitudinal study of the impact of organizational change on transactional, relational, and psychological contracts. *Journal of Leadership and Organizational Studies, 18*(2), 247–259.

Chory, R. M., & Hubbell, A. P. (2008). Organizational justice and managerial trust as predictors of antisocial employee responses. *Communication Quarterly, 56*(4), 357–375.

Colquitt, J. A., & Rodell, J. B. (2011). Justice, trust and trustworthiness: A longitudinal analysis integrating three theoretical perspectives. *Academy of Management Journal, 54*(6), 1183–1206.

Cook, J., & Wall, T. D. (1980). New work attitude measures of trust, organizational commitment, and personal need non-fulfillment. *Journal of Occupational Psychology, 53*, 39–52.

Cummings, L. L., & Bromiley, P. (1996). The organizational trust inventory (OTI): Development and validation. In R. M. Kramer & T. R. Tyler (Eds.), *Trust in organizations: Frontiers of theory and research* (pp. 302–330). Thousand Oaks, CA: Sage.

Elangovan, A. R., & Shapiro, D. L. (1998). Betrayal of trust in organizations. *Academy of Management Review, 23*(3), 547–566.

Ferres, N., Connell, J., & Travaglione, A. (2005). The effect on future redeployment on organizational trust. *Strategic Change, 14*(2), 77–91.

Folger, R. (1993). Reactions to mistreatment at work. In J. K. Murnighan (Ed.), *Social psychology in organizations: Advances in theory and research* (pp. 161–183). Englewood Cliffs, NJ: Prentice Hall.

Folger, R., & Konovsky, M. A. (1989). Effects of procedural and distributive justice on reactions to pay raise decisions. *Academy of Management Journal, 32*(1), 115–130.

Frazier, M. L., Johnson, P. D., Gavin, M., Gooty, J., & Snow, D. B. (2010). Organizational justice, trustworthiness, and trust: A multifoci examination. *Group and Organization Management, 35*(1), 39–76.

Gabarro, J. J. (1978). The development of trust, influence and expectations. In A. G. Athos & J. J. Gabarro (Eds.), *Interpersonal behaviour: Communication and understanding in relationships* (pp. 290–303). Englewood Cliffs, NJ: Prentice Hall.

Gabarro, J. J., & Athos, J. (1976). *Interpersonal relations and communications.* Englewood Cliffs, NJ: Prentice-Hall.

Gillespie, N., & Deitz, G. (2009). Trust repair after an organization-level failure. *Academy of Management Review, 34*(1), 127–145.

Hubbard, N. (2001). *Acquisition strategy and implementation.* Basingstoke, UK: Palgrave.

Kickul, J., Lester, S. W., & Finkl, J. (2002). Promise breaking during radical organizational change: Do justice interventions make a difference? *Journal of Organizational Behavior, 23*(4), 469–488.

Kim, P. H., Ferrin, D. L., Cooper, C. D., & Dirks, K. T. (2004). Removing the shadow of suspicion: The effects of apology versus denial for repairing competence versus integrity-based trust violations. *Journal of Applied Psychology, 89*, 104–118.

Konovsky, M., & Cropanzano, R. (1991). Perceived fairness of employee drug testing as a predictor of employee attitudes and job performance. *Journal of Applied Psychology, 76*, 698–707.

Korsgaard, M. A., Brodt, S. E., & Whitener, E. M. (2002). Trust in the Face of conflict: The role of managerial trustworthy behavior and organizational context. *Journal of Applied Psychology, 87*, 312–319.

Korsgaard, M. A., & Roberson, L. (1995). Procedural justice in performance evaluation: The role of instrumental and non-instrumental voice in performance appraisal discussions. *Journal of Management, 21*, 657–669.

Kramer, R. M. (1999). Trust and distrust in organizations: Emerging perspectives, enduring questions. *Annual Review of Psychology, 50*, 569–598.

Krug, J. A., & Nigh, D. (2001). Executive perceptions in foreign and domestic acquisitions: An analysis of foreign ownership and its effect on executive fate. *Journal of World Business, 36*, 85–105.

Lester, S. W., & Kickul, J. (2001). Psychological contracts in the twenty-first century: What employees value most and how well organizations are responding to these expectations. *Human Resource Planning, 24*(1), 10–21.

Leventhal, G. S. (1980). What should be done with equity theory? New approaches to the study of fairness in social relationships. In K. J. Gergen, M. S. Greenberg, & R. H. Willis (Eds.), *Social exchange, advances in theory and research* (pp. 27–55). New York: Plenum.

Lewicki, R. J., & Bunker, B. B. (1995). Trust in relationships: A model of development and decline. In B. B. Banker & J. Z. Rubin (Eds.), *Conflict, cooperation, and justice* (pp. 133–173). San Francisco: Jossey-Bass.

Lewicki, R. J., & Bunker, B. B. (1996). Developing and maintaining trust in work relationships. In R. M. Kramer & T. R. Tyler (Eds.), *Trust in organizations: Frontiers of theory and research* (pp. 114–139). Thousand Oaks, CA: Sage.

Lewicki, R. J., Tomlinson, E., & Gillespie, N. (2006). Models of interpersonal trust development: Theoretical approaches, empirical evidence, and future directions. *Journal of Management, 32*, 991–1022.

Lewis, J. D., & Weigert, A. (1985). Trust as a social reality. *Social Forces, 63*(4), 967–985.

Lind, E. A. (2001). Fairness heuristic theory: Justice judgments as pivotal cognitions in organizational relations. In J. Greenberg & R. Cropanzano (Eds.), *Advances in organizational justice* (pp. 57–88). Stanford, CA: Stanford University Press.

Lines, R., Selart, M., Espedal, B., & Johansen, S. T. (2005). The production of trust during organizational change. *Journal of Change Management, 5*(2), 221–245.

Magala, S. (2009). *The management of meaning in organizations*. London: Palgrave Macmillan.

Mayer, R. C., Davis, J. H., & Schoorman, F. D. (1995). An integrative model of organizational trust. *Academy of Management Review, 20*, 709–734.

McAlister, D. J. (1995). Affect- and cognition-based trust as foundations for interpersonal cooperation in organizations. *Academy of Management Journal, 38*, 24–59.

McKnight, H., Cummings, L. L., & Chervany, N. (1998). Initial trust formation in new organizational relationships. *Academy of Management Review, 23*, 473–490.

Mishra, A. K. (1996). Organizational responses to crisis: The centrality of trust. In R. M. Kramer & T. R. Tyler (Eds.), *Trust in organizations: Frontiers of theory and research* (pp. 261–287). Thousand Oaks, CA: Sage.

Muchinsky, P. M. (1977). Organizational communication: Relationships to organizational climate and job satisfaction. *Academy of Management Journal, 20*(4), 592–607.

Neves, P., & Caetano, A. (2009). Commitment to change: Contributions to trust in the supervisor and work outcomes. *Group and Organization Management, 34*(6), 623–644.

Paterson, J. M., & Cary, J. (2002). Organizational justice, change anxiety, and acceptance of downsizing: Preliminary tests of an AET-based model. *Motivation and Emotion, 26*(1), 83–103.

Piderit, S. K. (2000). Rethinking resistance and recognizing ambivalence: A multi-dimensional view of attitudes towards organizational change. *Academy of Management Review, 25*(4), 783–794.

Robinson, S. L. (1996). Trust and the breach of the psychological contract. *Administrative Science Quarterly, 41*, 574–599.

Robinson, S. L., & Rousseau, D. M. (1994). Violating the psychological contract, not the exception but the norm. *Journal of Organizational Behavior, 15*(3), 245–259.

Rousseau, D. M., Sitkin, S. B., Burt, R. S., & Camerer, C. (1998). Not so different after all: A cross-discipline view of trust. *Academy of Management Review, 23*, 393–404.

Rousseau, D. M., & Tijoriwala, S. A. (1999). What's a good reason to change? Motivated reasoning and social accounts in promoting organizational change. *Journal of Applied Psycholgy, 84*(4), 514–528.

Salancik, G. R., & Pfeffer, J. (1978). A social information processing approach to job attitudes and task design. *Administrative Science Quarterly, 23*, 224–253.

Sitkin, S. B., & Roth, N. L. (1993). Explaining the limited effectiveness of legalistic "remedies" for trust/distrust. *Organization Science, 4*, 367–392.

Smollan, R. K. (2011). The multi-dimensional nature of resistance to change. *Journal of Management and Organization, 17*(6), 828–849.

Smollan, R. K. (2012). Emotional responses to the injustice of organizational change: A qualitative study. In N. M. Ashkanasy, C. E. J. Hartel, & W. J. Zerbe (Eds.), *Research on emotion in organizations* (Vol. 8, pp. 175–202). Bingley, UK: Emerald Insight.

Stahl, G. K., Larsson, R., Kremershof, I., & Sitkin, S. B. (2011). Trust dynamics in acquisitions: A case survey. *Human Resource Management, 50*(5), 575–603.

Stahl, G. K., & Sitkin, S. (2010). Trust dynamics in acquisitions: The role of relationship history, interfirm distance, and acquirer's integration approach. *Advances in Mergers and Acquisitions, 9*, 51–82.

Tyler, T. R. (1990). *Why people obey the law: Procedural justice, legitimacy, and compliance.* New Haven, CT: Yale University Press.

van den Bos, K. (2001). Uncertainty management: The influence of uncertainty salience on reactions to perceived procedural fairness. *Journal of Personality and Social Psychology, 80*, 931–941.

van den Bos, K., Wilke, H. A. M., & Lind, E. A. (1998). When do we need procedural fairness? The role of trust in authority. *Journal of Personality and Social Psychology, 75*, 1449–1458.

Vanhala, M., Puumalainen, K., & Blomqvist, K. (2011). Impersonal trust: The development of the construct and the scale. *Personnel Review, 40*(4), 485–513.

Wanberg, C. R., Bunce, L. W., & Gavin, M. B. (1999). Perceived fairness of layoffs among individuals who have been laid off: A longitudinal study. *Personnel Psychology, 52*, 59–84.

Weick, K. E. (1995). *Sensemaking in organizations*. Thousand Oaks, CA: Sage Publications.

Weick, K. E., & Quinn, R. E. (1999). Organizational change and development. *Annual Review of Psychology, 50*, 361–386.

Whitener, E. M., Brodt, S. E., Korsgaard, M. A., & Werner, J. M. (1998). Managers as initiators of trust: An exchange relationship framework for understanding managerial trustworthy behavior. *Academy of Management Review, 23*, 513–539.

Zucker, L. G. (1986). Production of trust: Institutional sources of economic structure, 1840–1920. *Research in Organizational Behavior, 8*, 53–111.

9

Organizational Commitment

9.1 Introduction

Organizational commitment has received a lot of consideration from attitudinal researchers over several years and is the focus of ongoing research attention (Reichers, 1985). In addition to its positive relationship with job performance, organizational citizenship behavior, and a willingness to share knowledge, it has been found to have a negative relationship with a number of important withdrawal behavior outcomes in a workplace setting, such as employee turnover, absenteeism, and tardiness (e.g. Becker, Billings, Eveleth, & Gilbert, 1996; Maertz, Mosley, & Alford, 2002; Mowday, Steers, & Porter, 1979). Importantly, organizational commitment has been identified in the reciprocal exchange relationship with perceived organizational fairness (see Cobb, Vest, Hills, Frey, & Tamoff, 1991; Lind & Tyler, 1988). Lower commitment from inequities in procedural justice (e.g. Folger & Cropanzano, 1998) and distributive justice (e.g. Sweeney & McFarlin, 1993) have been reported as important relationships that bear impact on employee behaviors such as intentions to leave the organization (Liao & Rupp, 2005; Shapiro & Kirkman, 1999).

N. Jackson, *Organizational Justice in Mergers and Acquisitions*,
https://doi.org/10.1007/978-3-319-92636-0_9

9.2 A Three-Tier Framework

Evidence is overwhelming that most organizational change negatively impacts employee commitment in some form. Therefore, it is not surprising that many questions are raised about the true value of mergers and acquisitions, particularly when lower commitment levels of employees have been identified as a central instigator for missing the intended long-term outcomes of such change (van Dierendonck & Jacobs, 2012). This is at a time when organizations need to rely on the commitment levels of their employees to drive through the changes that are necessary. Dependence on their support to rebuild and reform is essential (van Dierendonck & Jacobs, 2012).

Early studies recognized two streams of research. One focused on the emotional attachment an individual has with their organization and was developed among others by Porter, Steers, Mowday, and Boulian (1974), while the other stream considered the cost of leaving the organization compared to remaining in situ. Over time this dual-factor framework has been further developed into a three-tier framework, initially identified by Meyer and Allen (1991) and Allen and Meyer (1990) and entitled the three-component model. In addition to analyzing the impact from each of the three components (unidimensional), this model offers the prospect of a multidimensional approach to each of the single dimensions of commitment. As well as offering the opportunity to recognize similarities and differences of each dimension, the framework also offers the benefit of being able to compare an individual's level of commitment for each of the dimensions (e.g. high affective commitment vs. low normative and continuous levels of commitment). At the same time, there is recognition that each dimension will always be present to some extent. These propose that an employee will simultaneously experience commitment enshrined in: i) an emotional attachment, known as affective commitment (Porter, et al., 1974); ii) feelings of obligation to the organization, recognized as normative commitment (Meyer, Paunonen, Gellatly, Goffin, & Jackson, 1989); and, finally, iii) a perception that leaving the organization would bear an economic and/or social cost to the employee that is unacceptably high, known as continuance commitment. Studies have established that each of the three components are independent of each other and are unanimous in finding that affective commitment has the strongest and most consistent relationship to workplace behaviors (Mathieu & Zajac, 1990). If we consider the impact of these outcomes in light of an organization in the situation of planning and implementing a program of significant change within the organizational context, then it is helpful to consider the model of commitment proposed in the study by Herscovitch and Meyer (2002). They describe the interaction with each of the three components as follows: (i) the desire by employees to provide support for the program of change with a belief in its inherent benefits (an affective attachment to the change; (ii) a perception that there are costs attached to not supporting the change that will impact the employee and therefore nonsupport will impact the individual from this perspective (the formation of a continuance commitment to the change); and, finally, (iii) the employee feels a sense of obligation to support the organization through the program of change (a normative commitment to the change). Understandably, the first of these forms of commitment will be the strongest.

Studies that have focused on the employee (person-centered as opposed to criterion-centered) emphasize this combined influence from the three types of commitment on the individual. A range of scholars have undertaken a variety of work that concentrates on recognizing commitment profiles. For example, Meyer and Herscovitch (2001) were able to codify a series of patterns and captured these in a framework that derived an individual's commitment levels based on their relative levels of affective, normative, and continuance commitment. These ranged from the highly committed (high AC, NC, and CC) to relatively uncommitted (low AC, NC, and CC). More nuanced profiles have also been developed that consider a much deeper level of detail (i.e. affective-continuance dominant, affective-normative dominant, etc.). This notion of a combined influence from commitment factors at play enables us to develop profiles of likely behavioral outcomes. Evidence suggests that an affective dominant profile will have the greatest influence on work outcomes, such as employee retention and citizenship behaviors when compared to either continuance or normative dominant profiles. However, there is also a role for both continuous and normative commitment in this relationship as each have been found, either individually or in combination (conjointly), to attenuate the positive impact of affective commitment on both these outcome variables (Meyer & Herscovitch, 2001). This research raises the level of complexity toward our understanding of how commitment effects the employee and any outcomes that prevail and is documented in a study by Gellatly, Pilling, Cole, and Skarratt (2006), supporting the relationship with turnover intentions and citizenship behavior. Other research in this field supports the notion that an interaction between each profile will impact the strength of overall commitment but is less committal toward the direction of impact (see Gellatly et al., 2006; Wasti, 2003). While these complexities need further investigation, there is a body of research that agrees that the level of any one component will influence how the others are experienced, supporting the proposition that we need to understand commitment from a person-centered, profile perspective.

Investigations by Gellatly et al. (2006) recognized that patterns developed within the three tiers of commitment not only impacted work outcomes but may also explain why the presence of each other factor is experienced. For example, when high levels of affective commitment were detected, it was more likely that there would be a positive relationship existing between normative commitment and the outcome variables of intention to remain and citizenship behavior. However, when continuous commitment was high, there was a weaker relationship with these outcome variables. One explanation proffered that may account for this was that normative commitment could be recognized as a moral obligation when affective commitment is high and continuous commitment is low and becomes more of an indebted obligation when affective commitment is low and continuous commitment is low. Thereby these three commitment profiles are much more inextricably bound together than we may first imagine and cannot be considered in isolation. We can consider their infuence in light of M&As.

9.2.1 Affective Commitment

Considering each dimension of the Meyer and Allen (1991) framework in turn, affective commitment reflects the level of employee's feelings of belonging and attachment to the firm. Recognized as the strongest form of commitment, it is seen by those who can demonstrate an emotional attachment and the fulfillment of personal needs, this being a primary process in the development of affective commitment. Those employees who have a desire to stay with an organization are less likely to demonstrate withdrawal behaviors and will be more focused on attending work regularly, take on more discretionary acts (organizational citizenship behavior (OCB)), and stretch themselves to ensure they perform to the best of their ability (Herscovitch & Meyer, 2002). If we consider a merger context, it becomes evident that if employees can get a clear indicator that their experiences of the change that is occurring is fulfilling or rewarding, then it is more likely that their affective commitment will be positively impacted. If the individual has positive expectations of the newly-emerging organization that are subsequently fulfilled, then they are more likely to form an emotional attachment to that organization and identify with its goals and objectives (Chang, 1999). The potential disruption caused by a merger toward an employee's targets, goals, and objectives at work could be considerable, but these may be supported or, at very least, any damage may be mitigated if the employee can see a way for themselves to succeed within the newly-formed organization.

9.2.2 Normative Commitment

Normative and continuance forms of organizational commitment are less binding in their nature and, consequently, are identified as weaker forms of commitment than the affective form. An individual experiencing normative commitment would feel a strong sense of moral obligation to remaining with the firm (Meyer & Parfyonova, 2010). According to Meyer and Allen (1997), there are three conditions that promote the development of normative commitment: (i) the process of socialization (e.g. employee induction), which sets the marker that putting time aside in the early weeks of employment is important if the employing organization wants to develop commitment of this form in their newly-integrated employee; (ii) where employees feel the organization has invested in them and yet they are unable to reciprocate with parity (e.g. training and development); (iii) where there is an obligation perceived because of the perceived terms of a psychological contract developed with the employer.

9.2.3 Continuous Commitment

An example of the economic or social costs that would affect an individual's level of continuance commitment would include financial costs, such as accrued pension, and nonfinancial costs, such as high levels of unemployment impeding alternative forms of employment. So, the perceived cost of leaving the organization is greater than remaining in situ and any act or event that strengthens this case will increase levels of continuous commitment being experienced by the individual. The antecedents recognized as being most influential in any variation experienced are investments and alternatives (Meyer & Allen, 1991). Because these needs are more specific to circumstances that depend on being explicit and comparable (i.e. the cost of staying or leaving), they are not always as obvious to the individual as affective and normative commitment. It is conceivable that in a merger situation continuous commitment becomes the commitment profile of primary importance. For example, even if there is a reduction in affective commitment due to the circumstances of the merger (e.g. opportunities to achieve workplace objectives are impacted), the individual sees their investment in the organization being of more importance, or the alternatives elsewhere are even less favorable.

9.3 Referents of Commitment

When trying to understand the concept of organizational commitment, a better representation would be to consider it as an attachment to a workplace setting rather than to the organization itself. It is often conceptualized (in part because the term tends to lead us down this path) as an attachment to the organization in its entirety. However, this would be an incorrect interpretation in all cases because other referents, such as the business subunit, department, team, or even supervisor can promote attitude development toward commitment (Becker, 1992; Becker et al., 1996; Brockner, Tyler, & Cooper-Schneider, 1992; Herscovitch & Meyer, 2002). Meyer and Herscovitch (2001) highlight this by explaining that employees should not be merely perceived as having an attachment to the organization as an entity, but to other social systems that also operate within either its internal or external environment. Identifying these attachment objects as the target to which members profess their commitment (referred to in some studies as foci; for example, Becker & Kernan, 2003), they are perceived as anchors of attachment. In addition to the organization, these can include a supervisor (e.g. Stinglhamber & Vandenberghe, 2003), a team that the individual is affiliated to (e.g. Bishop, Scott, & Burroughs, 2000), the employee's peers or coworkers (e.g. Paille, 2009), the occupation itself (e.g. Meyer, Allen, & Smith, 1993), an organized union (e.g. Snape, Redman, & Chan, 2000), or even customers (e.g. Redman & Snape, 2005). This follows on from work conducted by scholars such as Burke and Litwin (1992) and Goodman and Rousseau (2004), who found in their respective studies that we need to establish the proximity of the impact from a change event before we consider evaluating its likely outcome for the individual. For example, changes that have a proximal impact (i.e. those changes effecting an employee's immediate working environment, such as their job requirements or their work group) will have a more salient impact on the change-commitment relationship than a more distal impact that only affects higher levels of the organization or other business units. In addition to the locus of the change for those involved, other factors that also need to be considered in their light are the favorableness of the change being considered and, inevitably, the magnitude of the impact. In all, this paints a complex picture when determining the effect on an individual's commitment levels.

There is sufficient evidence to indicate that a committed employee is a positive move for organizations, and the better our understanding of its antecedents and outcomes, the greater the chance for the corporate world to design workplaces that incorporate elements of positivity.

9.4 Organizational Commitment and Commitment to Change

A distinction needs to be drawn between a more general attitude toward organizational commitment and a commitment to change. Several studies have investigated the two and recognize an advantageous outcome is more likely (e.g. a successful change program) in an environment where employees are affectively engaged and feel a social identification with their workplace before the process begins (i.e. this is an initial condition). A distinction should be drawn between those with a commitment to help the organization to work toward the change itself (i.e. a willingness to exert effort on behalf of the change) and those that merely experience a lack of resistance to the change. The former is more likely to represent the opinions and attitudes of those who profess greater affective commitment to the organization in general (Kotter & Schlesinger, 1979; Piderit, 2000). Further verification was developed in a study conducted by Ford, Ford, and D'Amelio (2008), who concluded that commitment to a form of strategic change displays the signs of being empirically and conceptually different to organizational commitment and will be a better predictor of specific behaviors related to it, such as acceptance of the change.

While organizational commitment can be an important factor of change acceptance, outcome valence will also undoubtedly be a critical indicator of whether there is general acceptance of the change being implemented. Indeed, this may become a more relevant factor within this scenario than levels of employee commitment experienced before the occurrence of change (i.e. outcome valence takes over as the critical factor where perceptions of a major change event impact the daily working lives of employees and their broader context of commitment). While organizational-level impact is clearly important for members, it is more likely that individual outcomes will be more relevant in determining levels of commitment to the change (Novelli, Kirkman, & Shapiro, 1995), particularly in the near term. This is considered in light of the justice literature that professes outcomes of organizational events will impact those involved as outcome-related judgments are processed (Adams, 1965). These considerations of justice-related outcomes have been linked to several employee attitudes, including commitment (Ambrose, 2002). Such occurrences are frequently the result of recent past events, which can often be used as a referent in these judgmental cases (Oldham et al., 1982).

9.4.1 Short- and Long-Term Commitment Considerations

These propositions lead us to conclude that how working lives are changed for the better or worse can help determine levels of organizational commitment during and after the period of change and, subsequently, have a critical impact on employee reactions. On a broader perspective, change that helps to provoke a realization that the organization's values and goals are closely aligned with those of the individual can encourage a closer bond and sense of commitment within that working relationship. This may simply be due to recognition of existing organization values and goals, or invoked by changes introduced by the newly-formed organization and its key mission, goals, and emerging culture. Change that benefits individuals may be perceived as assisting them in achieving their personal goals and/or values (change for the greater good) in which case the organization is working in their best interests by introducing the change.

In respect of merger or acquisition change, there are considerable implications for the levels of commitment experienced by employees undergoing the transformation in their working lives, not least their level of commitment and support toward the implementation of the change itself. In these circumstances it is short-term commitment that comes under scrutiny. Although, often overlooked as a consideration in the early stages of a merger, the longer-term reciprocal relationship of commitment experienced by both employees and their organization needs to be carefully considered. Bearing in mind the first of these two aspects, short-term commitment, there is ample discussion in the organizational justice literature (e.g. Brockner et al., 1992) that points us toward how organizational members will react to the event in respect of both the outcomes and the process of change. This evaluation in terms of fairness of outcomes and process may also have an impact on how members perceive their longer-term commitments to the organization beyond the implementation of the change initiative. For example, one may consider their view of how the workplace and their daily routine of work will be impacted by the change once it has been embedded. This may include a summing up of what it all means for the relationship they experience with their immediate environment, including any association with processes, systems, and people that they currently interact with.

If the strategists and implementers of change are to acquire an understanding of how to manage employee reactions and any subsequent impact on their levels of commitment, then a more nuanced approach is required. This is the case for either short-term commitment (i.e. to the change itself) or longer-term commitment (toward the organization). This tailored assessment of needs following the introduction of change rather than a "one-size-fits-all" approach, enables those tasked with strategizing and implementing change to consider events more proximal to the working lives of employees, whether this is at an individual, team, or work unit level. Signs of organizational commitment are not necessarily a good predictor of change commitment. However, in the context of organizational change, even though it is acknowledged that commitment to change and organizational commitment may be empirically different, there should be an acceptance by change agents that their programs can enhance or reduce a more general inclination toward organizational commitment by individual members and vice versa. The fallout from a given change initiative may cause an individual to reconsider their relationship with the organization to an extent where the levels of affective commitment are realigned (Hui & Lee, 2000; Judge, Thoresen, Pucik, & Welbourne, 1999). This reexamination of commitment is an important aspect of the psychological concept of change that individuals will form and that change agents will need to be aware of.

9.4.2 Case in Question: Expectations of Justice

Expectations based on previous behaviors shaped employees' early merger perceptions from the premerger management college, and those relating to fair outcomes from the integration. Therefore, how did future expectations based on organizational life beyond the merger affect employee perceptions of fairness in the current process? It has been discussed how an individual's positive and negative trait affect can influence their perception of fairness, and it may be considered that future expectations will be an important factor in these judgments. On this basis there was a divide between assessments from employees of the two premerger organizations motivated in part by the merger objectives of each organization. In conversations conducted with employees from the premerger business school, they appeared to be reticent about the merger because they could see little, if any, benefit for themselves from the integration. The outcome for them was a change of name to that of the premerger management college, and, more divisively, a change in publication strategy for the business school. From some of the comments passed by these employees, occupational commitment was of greater consideration to them than organizational commitment, and this was borne out in their declarations that publishing strategy was a personal goal. Also, the results from the first and second surveys provided evidence that they were less committed to the new organization than employees from the premerger management college. In each measure of organizational identity, team identity, and affective commitment, they returned a significantly lower value than their counterparts at the premerger management college. Their expectations looking forward were of becoming part of a mainstream business school with a changed identity and purpose and a shift in business objectives that were increasingly moving out of alignment with their own personal objectives. These were their biggest concerns, and what they deemed to be unfair was that there had been very little justification or consultation and as a result had been shown little respect for their position in the organization.

9.5 Commitment and Its Reciprocal Relationships

9.5.1 Organizational Justice

The important employee attitude of commitment is, to some extent, governed by the level of *perceived organizational support* (POS) they receive in an ongoing two-way reciprocal relationship (Eisenberger, Huntington, Hutchison, & Sowa, 1986). A concept identified as closely related to organizational justice, POS is described as portraying caring, approval, and respect of the employee by the organization, which it is believed will fulfill socio-emotional needs, leading to incorporation into their social identity of role status and organizational membership. Indeed, it has been acknowledged that through the norms of reciprocity perceived fairness builds a relationship of positive outcomes that may be important to the organization and a potential direct impact upon the ability to achieve strategic objectives. For instance, a positive relationship has been developed between process control (level of control over the process of determining a decision outcome) and positive perceptions of fairness and job satisfaction (Davy, Kinicki, & Scheck, 1991).

Subsequently, this has a positive effect upon commitment levels of the employee and their intentions to stay (Saunders, Thornhill, & Lewis, 2002), as well as attitudes and behaviors that management may seek to inspire, particularly during the acquisition process. In addition, Rhoades, Eisenberger, and Armeli (2001) established a relationship between perceived organizational support, affective commitment, and voluntary employee turnover. Further support is provided by Allen, Shore, and Griffeth (1999), who also found evidence of a relationship between participation in decision-making, POS, and affective commitment.

The study of perceived justice should not only be applied at an individual level because the influence of decision outcomes at group level also has an important bearing upon evaluations by organizational members. The principle of equality between groups needs to be considered when combining employees from more than one organization and decision outcomes are not only being determined on an individual basis. Collectives or groups of employees from opposing factions will also have considerable influence. For example, when senior management allocate roles and status hierarchies are developed in the newly-merged entity, how do each of the premerger groups fair? In an acquisition, management groups from the premerger acquired organization are more likely to demonstrate commitment to the new entity if there is a principle of equality demonstrated between them and the acquiring group of managers when those newly-developed positions are allocated. However, this may not be the case for those groups within the acquiring organization who are more likely to expect the principle of merit to be applied in accordance with the balance of power in favour of their own organization.

For the discussed, it can therefore be determined that justice is an important factor in the relationship between the concept of change, how this is perceived by the employee and their reactions going forward. Considering other antecedents that may impact these relationships, we need to understand that attitudinal reactions to change, such as commitment, will be affected by feelings of failure relating to the change, as well as feelings of uncertainty and its associate, a loss of control (e.g. Ashford, Lee, & Bobko, 1989; Oreg, 2003). As previously discussed, these factors will provide a context for fairness perceptions to be evaluated and subsequently will bear impact on the individual's reactions and outcomes to the change (Caldwell, Herold, & Fedor, 2004).

9.5.2 Perceived Organizational Support

It is well known that where employees experience POS there is an important role forged with building their commitment toward the organization and its goals (Cropanzano & Mitchell, 2005). A meta-analysis conducted by Rhoades and Eisenberger (2002) found a strong positive correlation occurred between affective commitment and POS. We have already discussed the role of social exchange in building important relationships between the organization and employee, and how this interaction is interpreted will be critical toward the levels of commitment demonstrated by organizational members. For example, Rhoades, Eisenberger, and Armeli (2001) indicated that a positive relationship existed and that their findings were consistent with the premise of social exchange theory (SET). Those employees that show a high degree of affective commitment to their organization are engaged in employment where the employer shows a higher level of concern for their well-being at work.

The role of organizational support and how the employee interprets this also has a critical role to play in these interactions. A concept initially developed by Eisenberger et al. (1986), the intention was to help provide a better understanding of how employee commitment was instigated and developed in organizational life. If POS is perceived as an interpretation of how far the employee believes the employer is willing to go to support them in their performance of duties in the working environment, then it also demonstrates how much the employee is valued in this context for their efforts and contributions. An additional benefit is that it offers an opportunity to show concern for employee welfare and well-being. Of course, to some extent, this is dependent on where the basis of the decision lies if high levels of POS are to be experienced. For example, if support is deemed to have originated from pressures of other stakeholders, such as the government or trade unions, then it is less likely to be returned with positive outcomes such as high levels of commitment (Rhoades & Eisenberger, 2002). If employees are to reciprocate positively and build commitment with the organization, they need to perceive the support has originated from a voluntary action performed by the organization or with its patronage.

9.5.3 Case in Question: Perceived Organizational Support

In support of this developed theory, and converse to the general situation experienced among employees within the business school, an exception was presented by two individuals, one from the premerger business school and the other from the premerger management college. Circumstances had developed where both employees had been offered the opportunity to work with the leadership and develop a relationship that was cordial and interactive, leading to a very different perception of their senior management than that proposed from other accounts obtained during the period of interview. From the relationships that developed, it was asserted that they had enjoyed support within their respective roles from the senior leadership team. This coincided with a much more favorable impression of the senior leadership team's ability and the way in which the merger process had been implemented. For the individual from the premerger management college, it transpired that this very different perception of their leadership was based on a preconceived supporting relationship that had been developed over a period prior to the merger. The individual from the premerger business school had no preconceived perception of the leadership. This individual's evaluation had been developed during the period of merger implementation when the support they had received for their involvement in one of the project teams appeared to be a decisive factor.

So, what were the factors at play that helped to establish the contrast in how these employees assessed their senior leaders in comparison to their peers? A dismantling of individual barriers through interpersonal interaction appeared to be the critical factor in differentiating perceptions. A positive relationship of social exchange had been advanced through the norms of reciprocity cultivated, in part, from the support provided by authorities at a time when this was most needed by these members of staff. The outcome of this exchange for these employees was to form a positive attitude influencing how personable they perceived their leadership to be. A situation is then cultivated in which perceptions of leadership are developed partly through trust in that relationship, which, in turn, affects uncertainty at a time of significant change. This will have a crucial impact not only on the importance of fairness in the process, but also how the employee perceives it. This situation appears to have been influenced by the level of perceived support that they experienced, or is likely to be offered to the employee by those authorities. It should be recalled that POS is founded on the norms of reciprocity and is a critical element of the employee-organization relationship, encouraging employees to acquire a feeling of obligation to reciprocate. As a consequence they are more likely to assist the organization achieve its objectives and care about its welfare (Rhoades & Eisenberger, 2002).

Therefore, it would be correct to assume that employees who have experienced support from the leadership may be more accepting of the organization's merger objectives and more inclined to work toward achieving them than if they were working in an unsupportive environment. POS is described as portraying caring, approval, and respect of the employee by the organization, which it is believed will fulfill socioemotional needs, leading to incorporation into their social identity of role status and organizational membership. From an organizational perspective, a strengthening of employee perceptions that performance leads to rewards will have a positive relationship with affective commitment, performance, and reduced turnover. From an employee perspective, enhancing such beliefs will promote positive attitudes and job satisfaction (Rhoades & Eisenberger, 2002).

The relationship between affective commitment and organizational justice has already been emphasized in this study. There would also appear to be recognition of a close association between an individual's perceived support by the organization and the perspective on procedural justice; particularly relating to process control. This is asserted by Shore and Shore (1995), who state that "unfair procedures contribute to mistrust, which in turn undermines the social exchange relationship and associated feelings of employee obligation" (p. 159). Discussions with the employees who felt support from the organization raised the point that they had experienced little loss of control because they had been given continued autonomy in their role which had subsequently led to a feeling of control retention. They talked about a feeling that they were in possession of a freedom to control their own career and destiny, which was a very different conversation to those conducted with employees who had not experienced the same level of support.

9.5.4 The Relationship with Organization Socialization

Entering a new world of the merged organization can be challenging for its members, and therefore a period of socialization is often important to reidentify employees with their roles, teams, and the newly-integrated entity. Even if the coworkers and their roles within the newly-formed organization bears little, if any, change, there is a good chance that within their wider social systems they will encounter either new surroundings, procedures, systems, or people. Organization socialization (OS) has been defined as the "process by which an individual acquires social knowledge and skills necessary to assume an organizational role" (Van Maanen & Schein, 1979, p. 211). Socialization is connected to the level of affective commitment that new members will develop at different levels of their working environment, and it is therefore critical to developing positive attitudes that are going to impact the quality of the behaviors already discussed.

In a merger situation it is relatively easy to see how this aligns with OS theory, which goes on to explicate how new members are able to acquire this social knowledge to a level where they are able to perform effectively through internalization of the beliefs, values, skills, and behaviors (Cooper-Thomas & Anderson, 2006; Saks & Ashforth, 1997). In relation to values, the act of commitment is dependent on the psychological state experienced where an employee shares the values of the organization and agrees to adhere to its objectives (Mowday et al., 1979). At this point, the affective commitment or emotional attachment will occur. Where this is the case, an increased convergence between the values and objectives recognized as close to the heart of the employee and organization will lead to a higher level of employee commitment. Inversely, much weaker levels of employee commitment will be experienced when there are low levels of convergence between the values and objectives of both the employee and the organization. O'Reilly and Chatman (1986) discuss this by considering different forms of attachment being forged between an organization and its members. They recognize three common levels of attachment as: i) compliance (an instrumental form of behavior designed to gain rewards for the employee); ii) identification (occurring when an employee aims to maintain a relationship with an organization whose goals and/or values they find attractive and yet they may not be able to adopt personally); and, iii) internalization (reflecting the principles of affective commitment where an organizational member aligns their own internal values or goals with those proposed by the organization).

Any role change that can be conceived as "boundary crossing" necessitates the acquisition of new information about the position or the job (Louis, 1980). It is the effectiveness of learning that new information through successful management of the "how" and "what" questions that will impact the "oh so important" attitudes and behaviors of those individuals going through this process (Korte, 2009; Ostroff & Kozlowski, 1992; Saks, Uggerslev, & Fassina, 2007). Merger change can become a major passage for even the most experienced and senior employees, creating an environment of uncertainty and ambiguity as the status quo of the premerger world is disrupted (Seo & Hill, 2005; Shook & Roth, 2011). It is one of the primary aims for managers to focus on maintaining and increasing commitment among their employees during the merger period and immediately after because those employees who are committed to the change are more inclined to support organizational efforts and contribute to the success of the newly-merged organization (Nikolaou, Vakola, & Bourntas, 2011). During this period, levels of employee uncertainty can influence negative feelings and emotions, which, in turn, will impact the level of employee commitment, jeopardizing efforts to increase commitment levels (Michaela & Vena, 2012; Schweizer & Patzelt, 2012). Mergers are a notorious conduit to increase levels of anxiety and stress in an organization (Cartwright, Tytherleigh, & Robertson, 2007; Ozag, 2006).

Social and Economic Exchange

In this process of socialization and commitment building, the social exchange between the individual and the organization is fundamental. According to social exchange theory, evidence suggests that there is a feeling of obligation by employees to display positive attitudes and behaviors to reciprocate any exchange content from their organizations that they perceive to be valuable (Cropanzano & Mitchell, 2005). Positive attitudes to materialize from this reciprocation include organizational commitment and job satisfaction (Tekleab & Chiaburu, 2011). In a study conducted by Yalabik (2013), it was found that supervisors can play an influential role in disseminating this information, and training in the art of effective communication with employees may have valuable returns at this time.

Further support for these claims exist and provide theoretical and empirical support for the existence of strong exchange mechanisms in the process of building affective commitment to the organization (Shore, Coyle-Shapiro, Xiao-Ping, & Tetrick, 2009). There are a number of studies that we are able to draw from presenting this perspective (e.g. Millward & Hopkins, 1998; Gakovic & Tetrick, 2003; Hom et al., 2009; Loi, Mao, & Hang-yue, 2009; Shore, Bommer, Rao, & Seo, 2009), and I have already alluded to the positive relationship between the affective commitment of organizational members and perceptions of their exchange with the organization. In this relationship there are numerous intervening variables that need to be considered, and one is the quality of the relationship between the members and their immediate supervisor. The wider relationship with the organization, including the level of affective commitment experienced by individuals, will be influenced by this leader-member exchange (LMX) relationship. It is often the case that the wider organizational relationship may be more of a distal nature, particularly when we consider situations within large MNCs or where workers are operating on a remote basis and don't experience as much personal interaction with their colleagues. Or, for example, the relationship between member and organization is based on the premise of economic exchange as opposed to the characteristics of a more closely aligned social exchange. Where this is the case, research has supported the notion that economic exchange is negatively related to affective commitment (e.g. Shore, Bommer et al., 2009). In such examples, the supervisor and the quality of the relationship held with the individual may be crucial in ensuring that the employee carries out their obligations to the organization to good effect (Shore & Tetrick, 1994; Piccolo, Bardes, Mayer, & Judge, 2008). Therefore, we can gain insight of how important this one-to-one relationship will be in forging awareness that the organization will support the individual as they pursue their goals and objectives, and that they will trust and value them in the process of reciprocation. For their part, the employees reciprocate with a stronger level of affective commitment, and therefore this will be undermined or strengthened by the quality of the relationship with their immediate supervisor.

However, this may be dependent on the strength of LMX that predominates the relationship between the subordinate and supervisor. As purported by Buch (2015), if the nature of the relationship bears all the principles of an economic exchange (ELMX) rather than the more interactive and socially dependent social exchange (SLMX), then the relationship between organization social exchange and affective commitment of the individual is likely to be weakened rather than strengthened. If a positive influence is to be achieved, then an SLMX relationship with the supervisor needs to predominate. An ELMX relationship bears little more involvement than what is stipulated in the contract of employment (Liden & Graen, 1980), whereas SLMX is more likely to develop the trusting, long-term socioemotional bonds with the organization referred to earlier (Shore, Tetrick, Lynch, & Barksdale, 2006). In part, this has been found to exist because a higher level of SLMX, borne from the more integrated socially developed subordinate-supervisor relationship, reflects a situation in which the employee has access to more and better-quality information (Harris & Kacmar, 2005). This will encourage numerous benefits for the employee, such as raising awareness to opportunities for promotion and enhancing skill development, plus enhancing the clarity of procedures and outcomes for them (Yukl, O'Donnell, & Taber, 2009).

In addition to the benefits alluded to earlier, forming a relationship founded on SLMX encourages a more trusting relationship between individuals and their superiors. According to the principles of POS, this is behavior that is more likely to encourage a reciprocation of organizational exchanges, leading to increased affective commitment toward the organization due to the perception they are being valued and supported. An exchange relationship based on economic terms is more likely to be short-term and less likely to encourage reciprocal acts from the employee (Dysvik, Kuvaas, & Buch, 2010). As a consequence, a relationship of this nature, founded on the tenets of economic exchange, is less likely to enable the formation of strong bonds associated with affective organizational commitment (Buch, 2015). The emphasis on a short-term relationship means that employees will be more uncertain about any obligations the organization may have toward them in the long-term. As expected, this results in employees developing a focus on short-term, more narrowly defined benefits from the change initiative being introduced (Wong, Wong, Ngo, & Lui, 2005). In addition, the tendency to focus on short-term outcomes from the relationship takes precedence over any potential long-term commitments the organization may offer its employees, which increases their levels of uncertainty that those longer-term obligations will ever be fulfilled (Loi et al., 2009; Wong et al., 2005). The result is a workforce that is less psychologically and emotionally involved with the change because their priorities become more aligned to immediate and tangible benefits, causing less potential to either form or develop affective commitment with either the change initiative or the organization. With ELMX, the focus becomes more aligned to formal and contractual relations rather than the employee's needs or preferences (Shore, Bommer et al., 2009), which is particularly apt for consideration in the specific change environment of a merger or acquisition.

However, even when the relationship between the employee and organization is dominated by the auspices of an economic exchange, the outcomes may well be influenced by the employee's perceptions of their more immediate relationship with the supervisor (Purcell & Hutchinson, 2007). If we try to understand the combined outcome from an interaction of these two different levels of relationship, Buch (2015) proffers that where higher levels of SLMX exist with a supervisor, then, to some extent, this will counteract any negative outcomes from the more short-term partnership an employee will experience from a dominant economic relationship at organizational level. Where individuals are in a high-quality SLMX relationship with their supervisor, they are more likely to experience high interaction on a daily basis. In these cases, there is a probability that the immediate supervisor will aim to facilitate the longer-term benefits of organizational membership, including any socioemotional aspects of the employment relationship that are not evident otherwise. We can surmise from this that the reduction in affective commitment to the organization will be negated to some extent as well, and due to the promotion of social exchange outcomes, SLMX is likely to reduce the levels of uncertainty being experienced by the employee from the economic exchange relationship at organizational level (Buch, 2015). Another example of why the bonds formed within the employee-supervisor relationship can be critical toward behavioral outcomes including acceptance or rejection of change.

9.5.5 Turnover Intentions

While studies have traditionally focused on the antecedents of each component of the three-tier model, attention has also been given to the influence on work outcomes, including OCB, job performance, and withdrawal behaviors (e.g. absenteeism and intentions to leave) (Meyer & Allen, 1997). Although still an important indicator, a much less significant relationship exists with the outcome variables of OCB and job performance than intentions to leave. Consequently, those members with a strong sense of commitment are less likely to indicate they are seeking to leave the company and find employment elsewhere. In part, this is because of commitment's close relationship with organizational identity.

Traditionally, research has found a negative relationship between affective and normative commitment and intentions of employees to leave the organization, but no significant relationship between continuance commitment and intentions to leave (see Allen & Meyer, 1990; Meyer et al., 1993). Those employees demonstrating either affective or normative commitment are more likely to perform at their best, take up discretionary acts, and stress an intention to stay with the organization, particularly if this is perceived as a means of reciprocating other benefits they have received (Herscovitch & Meyer, 2002). However, these studies contrast to the findings of Hackett, Bycio, and Hausdorf (1994), who found the relationship between an intention to quit and all three components of commitment. Regarding higher-ranking managers going through the merger or acquisition process, there is evidence that maintaining an affective commitment is vital and is positively related to actual integration effectiveness and, with reference to acquisitions, the acquiring firms' financial performance.

A central outcome of these studies is that commitment shines through as the strongest predictor of both intentions to leave an organization and actual employee turnover. When compared to one of the other key predicting attitudes, job satisfaction, Peters, Bhagat, and O'Connor (1981) found commitment is more closely aligned with turnover intention. While both are predictors, each attitude works in tandem to strengthen one's intentions to quit their posts and leave the organization, forming both an independent and interactive force in this relationship.

Case in Question: Commitment and Behavioral Changes

At the premerger management college, the act of organizational citizenship behavior, demonstrated by additional hours worked on an evening and weekend, had been curtailed, and this coincided with an indication that affective commitment levels toward the organization had been reduced. There was also an indication by staff across both campuses of an intention to leave the organization in the near future. In a discussion with one interviewee who stressed that concern for the honesty of communication during the merger had changed the individual's perception of management and the organization, they commented, "You don't stop doing the things you were doing; I don't think the link between that and your commitment is that linear ... but for things that you do require a bit of extra effort ... you think, why should I do the extra stuff" (MC-PT 6). Another interviewee added, "I felt that I always had a strong organizational commitment to [the management college], and my commitment was severely tested, but I didn't stop my commitment to [the organization] even though I still don't have that sense of organizational commitment that I used to. What it made me do was to focus very much on my job and try and get as much engagement and satisfaction" (MC-PT 24). Here we see indications that to maintain job satisfaction the emphasis for this employee was a switch in commitment from the organization to the job itself.

The assertion that fair treatment breeds commitment has been supported in several studies (see Brockner et al., 2001; Folger & Cropanzano, 1998; Shapiro & Kirkman, 1999), and this relationship was detected in a noticeable amount of conversations conducted during Phase 2. A few of the interview discussions appeared to indicate a correlation between a reduction of affective commitment to the organization and a perception of unfair treatment during the merger process. Conversations alluded to the fact that concern for the honesty of communication during the merger had changed their perception of management and the organization. The general mood tended to support the notion that while "business as usual" or meeting role expectations was still an aspiration, the feeling among employees was that there was less commitment to exert extra effort above and beyond the call of duty. A move in commitment away from the organization coincided with an emphasis to switch from an affective attachment toward a predominance of either a normative or continuous form of commitment.

References

Adams, J. S. (1965). Inequity in social exchange. In L. Berkowitz (Ed.), *Advances in experimental social psychology* (pp. 267–229). New York: Academic Press.

Allen, D., Shore, L., & Griffeth, R. (1999). *A model of perceived organizational support.* Unpublished manuscript, University of Memphis and Georgia State University.

Allen, N. J., & Meyer, J. P. (1990). The measurement and antecedents of affective, continuance and normative commitment to the organization. *Journal of Occupational Psychology, 63*, 1–18.

Ambrose, M. L. (2002). Contemporary justice research: A new look at familiar questions. *Organizational Behavior & Human Decision Processes, 89*(1), 803–812.

Ashford, S. J., Lee, C., & Bobko, P. (1989). Content, cause, and consequences of job insecurity: A theory-based measure and substantive test. *Academy of Management Journal, 32*(4), 803–829.

Becker, T. E., Billings, R. S., Eveleth, D. M., & Gilbert, N. L. (1996). Foci and biases of employee commitment: Implications for job performance. *Academy of Management Journal, 39*(2), 464–482.

Becker, T. E., & Kernan, M. C. (2003). Matching commitment to supervisors and organizations to in-role and extra-role performance. *Human Performance, 16*(4), 327–348.

Becker, T. T. (1992). Foci and bases of commitment: Are they distinctions worth making. *Academy of Management Journal, 35*(1), 232.

Bishop, J. W., Scott, K. D., & Burroughs, S. M. (2000). Support, commitment and employee outcomes in a team environment. *Journal of Management, 26*(6), 1113–1132.

Brockner, J., Ackerman, G., Greenberg, J., Gelfand, M. J., Francesco, A. M., Chen, Z. X., et al. (2001). Culture and procedural justice: The influence of power distance on reactions to voice. *Journal of Experimental Social Psychology, 37*, 300–315.

Brockner, J., Tyler, T. R., & Cooper-Scheider, R. (1992). The influence of prior commitment to institution on reactions to perceived unfairness: The higher they are, the harder they fall. *Administrative Science Quarterly, 37*, 241–261.

Buch, R. (2015). Leader-member exchange as a moderator of the relationship between employee-organization exchange and affective commitment. *International Journal of Human Resource Management, 26*(1), 59–79.

Burke, W. W., & Litwin, G. H. (1992). A causal model of organizational performance and change. *Journal of Management, 18*(3), 523–545.

Caldwell, S. D., Herold, D. M., & Fedor, D. B. (2004). Toward and understanding of the relationships among organizational change, individual differences, and changes in person-environment fit: A cross-level study. *Journal of Applied Psychology, 89*(5), 868–882.

Cartwright, S., Tytherleigh, M., & Robertson, S. (2007). Are mergers always stressful? Some evidence from the higher education sector. *European Journal of Work and Organizational Psychology, 16*(4), 456–478.

Chang, E. (1999). Career commitment as a complex moderator of organizational commitment and turnover intentions. *Human Relations, 52*(10), 1257–1278.

Cobb, A. T., Vest, M., Hills, F., Frey, F. F., & Tamoff, K. (1991). *Procedural justice: Source attributions and group effects in performance evaluations.* Proceedings, Southern Management Association.

Cooper-Thomas, H. D., & Anderson, N. (2006). Organizational socialization: A new theoretical model and recommendations for future research and HRM practices in organizations. *Journal of Managerial Psychology, 21*(5), 492–516.

Cropanzano, R., & Mitchell, M. S. (2005). Social exchange theory: An interdisciplinary review. *Journal of Management, 31*(6), 874–900.

Davy, J. A., Kinicki, A. J., & Scheck, C. L. (1991). Developing and testing a model of survivor responses to layoffs. *Journal of Vocational Behaviour, 38*, 302–317.

Dysvik, A., Kuvaas, B., & Buch, R. (2010). Trainee programme reactions and work performance: The moderating role of intrinsic motivation. *Human Resource Development International, 13*(4), 409–423.

Eisenberger, R., Huntington, R., Hutchison, S., & Sowa, D. (1986). Perceived organizational support. *Journal of Applied Psychology, 71*, 500–507.

Folger, R., & Cropanzano, R. (1998). *Organizational justice and human resource management.* Thousand Oaks, CA: Sage.

Ford, J. D., Ford, L. W., & D'Amelio, A. (2008). Resistance to change: The rest of the story. *Academy of Management Review, 33*, 326–377.

Gakovic, A., & Tetrick, L. E. (2003). Psychological contract breach as a source of strain for employees. *Journal of Business & Psychology, 18*(2), 235–246.

Gellatly, A., Pilling, M., Cole, G., & Skarratt, P. (2006). What is being masked in object substitution masking? *Journal of Experimental Psychology, 32*(6), 1422–1435.

Goodman, P. S., & Rousseau, D. M. (2004). Organizational change that produces results: The linkage approach. *Academy of Management Executive, 18*(3), 7–19.

Hackett, R. D., Bycio, P., & Hausdorf, P. A. (1994). Further assessments of Meyer and Allen's (1991) three-component model of organizational commitment. *Journal of Applied Psychology, 79*(1), 15–23.

Harris, K., & Kacmar, K. M. (2005). Easing the strain: The buffer role of supervisors in the perceptions of politics-strain relationship. *Journal of Occupational & Organizational Psychology, 78*(3), 337–354.

Herscovitch, L., & Meyer, J. P. (2002). Commitment to organizational change: Extension of a three-component model. *Journal of Applied Psychology, 87*(3), 474–487.

Hom, P. W., Tsui, A. S., Lee, T. W., Fu, P. P., Wu, J. B., Zhang, A. Y., et al. (2009). Explaining employment relationships with social exchange and job embeddedness. *Journal of Applied Psychology, 94*(2), 277–297.

Hui, C., & Lee, C. (2000). Moderating effects of organization-based self-esteem on organizational uncertainty: Employee response relationships. *Journal of Management, 26*(2), 215–232.

Judge, T., Thoresen, C., Pucik, V., & Welbourne, T. (1999). Managerial coping with organizational change: A dispositional perspective. *Journal of Applied Psychology, 84*(1), 107–122.

Korte, R. F. (2009). How newcomers learn the social norms of an organization: A case study of the socialization of newly hired engineers. *Human Resource Development Quarterly, 20*(3), 285–306.

Kotter, J. P., & Schlesinger, L. A. (1979). Choosing strategies for change. *Harvard Business Review, 57*(2), 106–114.

Liao, H., & Rupp, D. E. (2005). The impact of justice climate and justice orientation on work outcomes: A cross-level multifoci framework. *Journal of Applied Psychology, 90*, 242–256.

Liden, R. C., & Graen, G. (1980). Generalizability of the vertical dyad linkage model of leadership. *Academy of Management Journal, 23*(3), 451–465.

Lind, E. A., & Tyler, T. R. (1988). *The social psychology of procedural justice.* New York: Plenum.

Loi, R., Mao, Y., & Hang-yue, N. (2009). Linking leader-member exchange and employee work outcomes: The mediating role of organizational social and economic exchange. *Management & Organization Review, 5*(3), 401–422.

Louis, M. R. (1980). Surprise and sense-making: What newcomers experience in entering unfamiliar organizational settings. *Administrative Science Quarterly, 25*, 226–251.

Maertz, C. P., Mosley, D. C., & Alford, B. L. (2002). Does organizational commitment fully mediate constituent commitment effects? A reassessment and clarification. *Journal of Applied Social Psychology, 32*(6), 1300–1313.

Mathieu, J. E., & Zajac, D. M. (1990). A review and meta-analysis of the antecedents, correlates, and consequences of organizational commitment. *Psychological Bulletin, 108*(2), 171–174.

Meyer, J. P., & Allen, N. J. (1991). A three-component conceptualization of organizational commitment. *Human Resource Management Review, 1*, 61–89.

Meyer, J. P., & Allen, N. J. (1997). *Commitment in the workplace: Theory, research and application*. Thousand Oaks, CA: Sage.

Meyer, J. P., Allen, N. J., & Smith, C. A. (1993). Commitment to organizations and occupations: Extensions and test of a three-component conceptualization. *Journal of Applied Psychology, 78*, 538–551.

Meyer, J. P., & Herscovitch, L. (2001). Commitment in the workplace: Toward a general model. *Human Resource Management Review, 11*, 299–326.

Meyer, J. P., & Parfyonova, N. M. (2010). Normative commitment in the workplace: A theoretical analysis and re-conceptualization. *Human Resource Management Review, 20*(4), 283–294.

Meyer, J. P., Paunonen, S. V., Gellatly, I. R., Goffin, R. D., & Jackson, D. N. (1989). Organizational commitment and job performance: It's the nature of the commitment that counts. *Journal of Applied Psychology, 74*(1), 152–156.

Michela, J. L., & Vena, J. (2012). A dependence-regulation account of psychological distancing in response to major organizational change. *Journal of Change Management, 12*(1), 77–94.

Millward, L. J., & Hopkins, L. J. (1998). Psychological contracts, organizational and job commitment. *Journal of Applied Psychology, 28*(16), 1530–1556.

Mowday, R. T., Steers, R. M., & Porter, L. W. (1979). Measurement of organizational commitment. *Journal of Vocational Behavior, 14*(2), 224–247.

Nikolaou, I., Vakola, M., & Bourantas, D. (2011). The role of silence on employees' attitudes "the day after" a merger. *Personnel Review, 40*(6), 723–741.

Novelli, L., Jr., Kirkman, B. L., & Shapiro, D. L. (1995). Effective implementation of organizational change: An organizational justice perspective. *Journal of Organizational Behavior, (1986–1998), 15*, 15–36.

O'Reilly, C., & Chatman, J. (1986). Organizational commitment and psychological attachment: The effects of compliance, identification, and internalization of prosocial behavior. *Journal of Applied Psychology, 71*(3), 492–499.

Oldham, G. R., Nottenburg, G., Kassner, M. W., Ferris, G., Fedor, D., & Masters, M. (1982). The selection and consequences of job comparisons. *Organizational Behavior & Human Performance, 29*(1), 84–111.

Oreg, S. (2003). Resistance to change: Developing an individual differences measure. *Journal of Applied Psychology, 88*(4), 680–693.

Ostroff, C., & Kozlowski, S. W. J. (1992). Organizational socialization as a learning process: The role of information acquisition. *Personnel Psychology, 45*(4), 849–874.

Ozag, D. (2006). The relationship between the trust, hope, and normative and continuance commitment of merger survivors. *The Journal of Management Development, 25*(9), 870–883.

Paille, P. (2009). Assessing organizational citizenship behavior in the French context: Evidence for the four-dimensional model. *Journal of Psychology, 143*(2), 133–146.

Peters, L. H., Bhagat, R. S., & O'Connor, E. J. (1981). An examination of the independent and joint contributions of organizational commitment and job satisfaction on employee intentions to quit. *Group & Organization Studies, 6*(1), 73–82.

Piccolo, R. F., Bardes, M., Mayer, D. M., & Judge, T. A. (2008). Does high quality leader-member exchange accentuate the effects of organizational justice? *European Journal of Work & Organizational Psychology, 17*(2), 273–298.

Piderit, S. K. (2000). Rethinking resistance and recognizing ambivalence: A multidimensional view of attitudes toward and organizational change. *Academy of Management Review, 25*(4), 783–794.

Porter, L. W., Steers, R. M., Mowday, R. T., & Boulian, P. V. (1974). Organizational commitment, job satisfaction, and turnover among psychiatric technicians. *Journal of Applied Psychology, 59*(5), 603–609.

Purcell, J., & Hutchinson, S. (2007). Front-line managers as agents in the HRM-performance causal chain; theory, analysis and evidence. *Human Resource Management Journal, 17*(1), 3–20.

Redman, T., & Snape, E. (2005). Unpacking commitment: Multiple loyalties and employee behaviour. *Journal of Management Studies, 42*(2), 301–328.

Reichers, A. E. (1985). A review and reconceptualization of organizational commitment. *Academy of Management Review, 10*(3), 465–476.

Rhoades, L., & Eisenberger, R. (2002). Perceived organizational support: A review of the literature. *Journal of Applied Psychology, 87*, 698–714.

Rhoades, L., Eisenberger, R., & Armeli, S. (2001). Affective commitment to the organization: The contribution of perceived organizational support. *Journal of Applied Psychology, 86*, 825–836.

Saks, A. M., & Ashforth, B. E. (1997). Socialization tactics and newcomer information acquisition. *International Journal of Selection & Assessment, 5*(1), 48–61.

Saks, A. M., Uggerslev, K. L., & Fassina, N. E. (2007). Socialization tactics and newcomer adjustment: A meta-analytic review and test of a model. *Journal of Vocational Behavior, 70*(3), 413.

Saunders, M. N. K., Thornhill, A., & Lewis, P. (2002). Understanding employees' reactions to the management of change: An exploration through an organizational justice framework. *Irish Journal of Management, 23*(1), 85–108.

Schweizer, L., & Patzelt, H. (2012). Employee commitment in the post-acquisition integration process: The effect of integration speed and leadership. *Scandinavian Journal of Management, 28*(4), 298–310.

Seo, M.-G., & Hill, N. S. (2005). Understanding the human side of merger and acquisition: An integrative framework. *Journal of Applied Behavioral Science, 41*, 422–443.

Shapiro, D. L., & Kirkman, B. L. (1999). Employees' reaction to the change to work teams: The influence of "anticipatory" injustice. *Journal of Organizational Change Management, 12*(1), 51–66.

Shook, L., & Roth, G. (2011). Downsizings, mergers, and acquisitions: Perspectives of human resource development practitioners. *Journal of European Industrial Training, 35*(2), 135–153.

Shore, L. M., Bommer, W. H., Rao, A. N., & Seo, J. (2009). Social and economic exchange in the employee-organization relationship: The moderating role of reciprocation wariness. *Journal of Managerial Psychology, 24*(8), 701–721.

Shore, L. M., Coyle-Shapiro, J. A.-M., Xiao-Ping, C., & Tetrick, L. E. (2009). Social exchange in work settings: Content, process, and mixed methods. *Management & Organization Review, 5*(3), 289–302.

Shore, L. M., & Shore, T. H. (1995). Perceived organizational support and organizational justice. In R. Cropanzano & K. M. Kacmar (Eds.), *Organizational politics, justice, and support: Managing social climate at work* (pp. 149–164). Westport, CT: Quorum Press.

Shore, L. M., & Tetrick, L. E. (1994). Validation of a measure of perceived union support. *Journal of Applied Psychology, 79*(6), 971–977.

Shore, L. M., Tetrick, L. E., Lynch, P., & Barksdale, K. (2006). Social and economic exchange: Construct development and validation. *Journal of Applied Psychology, 36*(4), 837–867.

Snape, E., Redman, T., & Chan, A. W. (2000). Commitment to the union: A survey of research and the implications for industrial relations and trade unions. *International Journal of Management Reviews, 2*(3), 205–230.

Stinglhamber, F., & Vandenberghe, C. (2003). Organizations and supervisors and sources of support and targets of commitment: A longitudinal study. *Journal of Organizational Behavior, 24*, 251–270.

Sweeney, P. D., & McFarlin, D. B. (1993). Workers evaluation' of the "ends" and the "means": An examination of four models of distributive and procedural justice. *Organizational Behavior and Human Decision Processes, 55*, 23–40.

Tekleab, A. G., & Chiaburu, D. S. (2011). Social exchange: Empirical examination of form and focus. *Journal of Business Research, 64*(5), 460–466.

Van Dierendonck, D., & Jacobs, G. (2012). Survivors and victims, a meta-analytical review of fairness and organizational commitment after downsizing. *British Journal of Management, 23*(1), 96–109.

Van Maanen, J., & Schein, E. H. (1979). Toward a theory of organizational socialization. *Research in Organizational Behavior, 1*, 209–264.

Wasti, A. S. (2003). The influence of cultural values on antecedents of organizational commitment: An individual-level analysis. *Applied Psychology: An International Review, 52*(4), 533–554.

Wong, Y.-T., Wong, C.-S., Ngo, H.-Y., & Lui, H.-K. (2005). Different responses of job insecurity of Chinese workers in joint ventures and state-owned enterprises. *Human Relations, 58*(11), 1391–1418.

Yalabik, Z. Y. (2013). Mergers and acquisitions: Does organizational socialization matter? *Human Resource Development International, 16*(5), 519–537.

Yukl, G., O'Donnell, M., & Taber, T. (2009). Influence of leader behaviors on the leader-member exchange relationship. *Journal of Managerial Psychology, 24*(4), 289–299.

10

Interpersonal Communication

10.1 Introduction

As we have encountered in previous chapters, during periods of significant change those engaged with the process often experience increased levels of uncertainty, which leads to a sense of heightened awareness of fair treatment (Rodell & Colquitt, 2009). With this increased vigilance comes a closer scrutiny of others in the workplace as the distribution of fairness among peers and superiors is evaluated. As part of this process, relationships that are deemed to be important to individuals, such as those with team colleagues and the dyadic relationships with superiors, become more relevant in relation to the core principles of justice and an evaluation of how fairly the change will be handled. The focus of this chapter is to investigate the process of communication on a more personal basis within a social exchange framework, which in the realms of justice theory is captured within the auspices of interactional justice and its key components.

The importance of communication in relation to human behavior is discussed in Chap. 2 and more intensively in relation to the organizational justice framework in Chap. 3, where the concept of interactional

N. Jackson, *Organizational Justice in Mergers and Acquisitions*,
https://doi.org/10.1007/978-3-319-92636-0_10

justice is introduced in detail. I remind the reader about the role of communication within the justice framework before taking a more nuanced approach to its various manifestations in organizational life.

10.2 An Exchange Relationship

First, a distinction needs to be drawn between relationships founded on the bases of either a social exchange or an economic exchange. A social exchange relationship is generally more long-term focused, and obligations of each party are likely to be less specific and dependent on short-term reciprocal acts. Obligations are often unspecified, and methods of measurement are not necessarily made explicit between parties entering the exchange. The reciprocal expectations arise and develop through a series of mutual (not necessarily simultaneous) exchanges that form a pattern of reciprocal obligations to each of the committed parties (Blau, 1964). The relationship is developed and maintained on the principle that each party receives something of value that then forms the obligation through the practice of reciprocation. Leader-member exchange (LMX) depicts the exchange relationship formed in a dyadic relationship between two individuals in a hierarchic chain within the workplace (normally represented by the employee-supervisor relationship). This is measurable on the strength or quality of the LMX relationship (e.g. Graen & Scandura, 1987) with strong relationships encouraging positive behaviors, such as in-role behavior and organizational citizenship behaviors (OCBs) (Settoon, Bennett, & Liden, 1996; Wayne, Shore, & Liden, 1997). Graen and Scandura (1987) acknowledge the importance of perceived fairness built into this exchange relationship if it is to be maintained and flourish, as they state, "each party in an LMX must offer something the other sees as valuable and each must see the exchange as reasonably equitable and fair" (p. 182). As we will see, another configuration of the social exchange relationship can be recognized between the employee and the organization itself.

However, studies in this field have also moved on to acknowledge a relationship between outcomes of how employees evaluate the dyadic relationship with their supervisor and broader connotations relating to perceptions of how well supported they are within the more general context of the organization. The relationship between employees and their supervisor is critical and will form perceptions that are likely to have a major impact on the behaviors they demonstrate at work. Acknowledged as perceived supervisor support (PSS), the reciprocal exchange relationship discussed earlier is a highly pertinent aspect of the successful management of change because of its meaningful relationship with positive attitudes, such as commitment, job satisfaction, and perceived organizational support (POS). Subsequently, these attitudes inspire positive workplace behaviors, such as OCB and in-role behavior, besides discouraging withdrawal behaviors (e.g. intention to leave) at a time when employee engagement is crucial. These assertions are supported in work that has focused on the impact of relational conflict (such as that between supervisor and employee) drawing a relationship with more general negative affect-laden feelings toward the organization, which have then manifested in lower organizational commitment (Eisenberger, Huntington, Hutchison, & Sowa, 1986).

The social exchange relationship developed by PSS is particularly important because it demonstrates an agent of the organization cares about well-being, behavior that is expected to increase the emotional bond with both an employee's supervisor and the employing organization (Rhoades, Eisenberger, & Armeli, 2001; Stinglhamber & Vandenberghe, 2003). Therefore, it is feasible that the positive outcome also includes reciprocation in a more general sense toward the organization rather than to just the supervisor (Eisenberger, Stinglhamber, Vandenberghe, Sucharski, & Rhoades, 2002), opening the route for a positive orientation toward the program of change being pursued. When employees feel they are being supported, they are more willing to accept and embrace conditions that are of significance to organizational outcomes and have an increased tendency to embrace a certain element of risk (e.g. a program of organizational change). This obligation to the change that is generated through feelings of support may not only have ties to affective commitment but also stimulate acceptance of the change via the principles of normative commitment (an obligation to help the organization) as detailed in Chap. 9.

10.3 Interactional Justice

Interactional justice is recognized in Chap. 3 for its integral manifestations within the frameworks of procedural justice, particularly through the enactment and communication of procedures that are developed to determine distributions or outcomes. Therefore, its influence on how recipients perceive the communication of distributions, both from an informational and interpersonal aspect, is paramount.

Early studies into the effect of perceived justice and its different constructs indicated there was a distinct pattern between employee outcomes from interactional justice and those from procedural justice. There is evidence that employees' interactional justice perceptions will predict outcomes relating to interpersonal relationships (e.g. supervisor), which has connotations with LMX theory. Whereas procedural justice-related outcomes will predict organizational-level outcomes, such as organizational commitment, perceived organizational support, and intentions to leave (Moorman, 1991). While both distributive and procedural justice are evaluated within the context of the organization, interactional justice reflects the social exchange within the superior-subordinate relationship. Within this context, empirical research supports the proposition that whereas procedural justice is related to trust in upper management, interactional justice is related to the manager with whom the individual has been directly involved (e.g. see Cropanzano, Prehar, & Chen, 2002). In most circumstances it is fair to assume that this relationship will be represented by the employee's supervisor or line manager and interpreted as the LMX. It has been described as a predictor of reactions to supervisors and an employee's immediate work environment (Masterson, Lewis, Goldman, & Taylor, 2000).

10.3.1 Interpersonal Justice

It is worth investigating in greater depth the factors that will impede and enhance the quality of the employee-supervisor relationship, which is so critical in helping to develop the levels of perceived interactional justice. One of the strengths prevalent within the more effective forms of this dyadic relationship is that the levels of social interaction tend to mature beyond the more formal channels that are commonly established within other less-developed formats. Interpersonal justice (a component of interactional justice) demands the presence of dignity and respect if it is to be enacted, and where this is present (i.e. a supervisor is perceived to treat the employee with dignity and respect), ambiguity and anxiety may be mitigated (Bies & Moag, 1986; Colquitt, 2001). Schein (1996) recognized that if individuals feel they are not being treated with dignity and respect in situations of organizational change, then they have a lower tendency to support it because they are more likely to perceive it as harming their self-concept of well-being. These factors are all important if psychological safety (e.g. the feeling of being protected and valued) is to be developed by the employee and a relationship between low levels of interpersonal justice and an undermining of psychological safety has been experienced (Kahn, 1990).

There are indications that even where the two parties are not in complete agreement with the outcomes, if the employee experiences interpersonal justice this will increase the chance of the change being accepted because it helps to ward off some of the negative emotions it will cause. In contrast, there is evidence that where relational strains are experienced via their interactions with supervisors, low levels of perceived interpersonal justice will exacerbate perceptions of the change process and encourage negative emotions. According to Lazarus and Folkman (1984), where this is the case there is also an increased risk that such negative emotions will similarly impact employees' cognitive abilities to cope with the resulting stress and ambiguity. It was suggested by Pelled (1996) that in such experiences where there is relational conflict, this may affect employees' ability to deal objectively with information about the change. Alternatively, it has been recognized that where an enhanced level of social interaction within a supervisor-employee dyad exists, this may improve each party's ability to understand the causes of complex situations (Uzzi, 1997).

10.4 Relationship Interactions

Bouckenooghe, De Clercq, and Deprez (2014) recognize that organizational change processes are socially constructed. This is exemplified by the way an individual's response to, and commitment to, the change is influenced by others within their environment and the way these relationships are perceived. A relational context is key to understanding the individual's commitment to change, which should also encompass the wider social unit along with the relationship with the employee's supervisor (Basu & Green, 1997). However, we need to consider that this may have both positive and negative consequences as these relational forces can be developed as either facilitators or inhibitors (Armenakis & Bedeian, 1999; Bouckenooghe, 2012; Cunningham et al., 2002). A strong employee-supervisor relationship that is perceived as supportive to the employee is more likely to generate positive facilitating influences. Such high-quality relationships can reduce anxiety about the forthcoming change, whereas absence of these positive forces may develop negative attitudes in the employee, which, conversely, will inhibit acceptance of change (Choi, 2011; Tierney, 1999). Where change has been invoked without effective consultation, employee ambiguity will typically arise leading to an increase in levels of anxiety within the context of an individual's daily working life (Bouckenooghe, 2012).

Subsequently, there is a need to acknowledge how decisive the quality of LMX relationships can be in their capacity to help facilitate successful change. Relational conflict and other interpersonal issues are likely to reduce employees' energy, impact their coping mechanisms for dealing with the change, and therefore interfere with effective implementation of the change (Amason, 1996; Jehn, 1995, 1997). Interpersonal conflict is typically associated with forms of radical change as those involved disagree about the process of change and achieving goals and targets. This becomes a problem when employees and their supervisors endure such disagreements, which is why it is important to develop and maintain high-quality supervisor-employee relationships and help to avoid the likelihood of these emotional clashes (Pondy, 1967; Roscigno & Hodson, 2004). Situations of organizational change will typically induce high levels of employee stress and anxiety, which, in turn, will reduce their positive energy. Relational resources, such as those experienced in a strong supervisor-employee dyad, will help reduce anxiety and uncertainty (Turner Parish, Cadwallader, & Busch, 2008), rather than the alternate situation which will encourage employees to focus their energies on protecting well-being as opposed to supporting the change (Bouckenooghe, 2010). In situations where low relational conflict is experienced, energy can be devoted to coping with the change as opposed to expending copious amounts on restoring the cohesive relationship with supervisors (Jehn & Mannix, 2001).

An interesting phenomenon within this dyadic relationship is the interface between the intensity of social interaction and levels of interpersonal justice experienced by the employee. Studies have previously found this relationship to exist, and when high levels of interpersonal justice are an outcome, this will have the influence of reducing relational conflict (Heide & Miner, 1992; Uzzi, 1997) and fuel positive energy that is channeled to overcome the challenges. In turn, there is more of an inclination for this positive energy, which is generated in the absence of relational conflict, to be channeled toward a stronger commitment to the change (Leana & van Buren, 1999). Strong forms of social interaction can heighten the levels of communication quality in dyads of this nature and the enhanced interpersonal fairness that this may encourage will help employees understand and appreciate fair treatment by their supervisors (Leana & Van Buren, 1999). Enhanced social interaction in these cases can increase the impact of positive energy produced as an outcome of high interpersonal justice levels, enabling these exchanges to be channeled into further reducing any potential levels of conflict as opposed to situations where the parties have weak social ties (Nahapiet & Ghoshal, 1998).

Even so, we need to take into account that intense interactions in dyadic relationships can also spawn an awareness between conflicting parties of their personal differences. This becomes a problem where interactors within this dyadic realtionship focus on their conflict rather than on productive activities (De Clercq, Thongpapanl, & Dimov, 2009), thereby escalating and reinforcing employees' negative emotions (Murnighan & Conlon, 1991). In these cases, social interaction can emphasize the negative elements of the dyadic relationship, which may be difficult to resolve if they are founded on issues concerning personalities and life-long experiences (De Dreu & van Vianen, 2001). In such instances, any negative strain that is enhanced or activated will detract from focusing individuals' energies on supporting and implementing the change but will be guided toward the energy depleting role of absorbing the conflict that has developed.

10.4.1 Communication as Social Action

Besides communication being influenced by its immediate environment, it also becomes a critical component of informing and influencing those operating within it (Goldhaber, 1999). In this form, communication is viewed as an important practice of social interaction that can contribute toward overcoming threats emerging from the change to interpersonal relationships. Lack of close interaction at this stage helps to create rumors and subsequent feelings of anxiety because of the unknown (Ford & Ford, 2009; Waddell, Cummings, & Worley, 2007). These psychological insecurities can be avoided if high-quality information is disseminated during the critical phases of change. In turn, action such as this is likely to increase commitment to the change or reorganizations due to the reduction in anxiety levels being experienced by employees.

An example of how central effective use of communication can be in developing employee behavior is using social interaction as a form of employee influence. In a scenario where the planning and organizing of change is advanced without the involvement of employees, it is quite likely this action will encourage resistance to change because of the distance between them and the decision-making process. If this course of action is extended to involve those influenced by the change in the planning and organizing stages, then communication can become a form of social interaction enabling employees an element of influence over events that will impact both them and their environment. Employee contribution to the process of planning and implementing change has been found to help negate resistance (Argyris & Schön, 1996). To some extent we should also include third party involvement (e.g. trade unions), although it has been found not to have the same level of impact experienced in firsthand exchanges. For example, Christensen (2014) found that union assistance had a weaker association with organizational communication than was expected. Even so, third-party involvement such as union assistance can, in certain circumstances, be recognized for its contribution toward enhancing relations at this critical stage in the planning and implementation of change.

In the study developed by Christensen (2014) it was found that communication played an important role in linking people together in the organization, and so would perform a critical function during a change program. Specifically, there were several elements identified as being crucial to a well-functioning communication system during the change program, including contact among employees and between employees and their leadership. Conversely, this emphasizes the point that disruptive relations between these groups can have catastrophic consequences toward the success of change in this arena. These forms of social contact are essentially important during periods of radical change, and none more so than the disruptive and potentially divisive circumstances to evolve from a merger situation. Tukiainen (2001) cites the significance of effective and efficient communication processes within such scenarios and goes on to emphasize the need for more personal contact from management involving face-to-face communication. Here we can relate to the body of research resulting from interactional justice, how significant fairness is perceived regarding the "personal touch" and how this can help to encourage the acceptance of change. The connections that are built between leadership and their workforce can determine the success or failure of change when commitment to those changes is required. The strength of social relationships is fundamental in this process.

Social Interaction and Decision-Making

As depicted in Fig. 10.1, the promotion of an authority's self-interest during integration decision-making gives rise to a further potential ambiguity in the conflict of interests that may follow (Hambrick & Cannella, 1993). Also, as confrontation increases between actors, issues become politicized as they grow to be "increasingly aware of the political actions of the other actors and feel a need to act accordingly" (Vaara, 2003, p. 866). Because of ambiguities and politicking in the decision-making process, hypocrisy may also become an issue when integration ideas are not met with subsequent action during change implementation and become empty rhetoric. Perceptions of decision-making irrationality creep into the workforce, which may impinge on future perceptions regarding the fairness surrounding these aspects of the process. Lipponen, Olkkonen, and Moilanen (2004) refer to mergers often raising "issues of fair decision-making procedures in reallocation of rewards, space, status, and resources between the merger partners" (p. 392).

Internal communication and discussion forums will help individuals affected by the change process to better understand the differences in their views and will also make meaningful advances toward them committing to joint action in the postintegration process. In addition, Lipponen et al. (2004) maintain, "It seems likely that if the merger is implemented in a fair manner using fair decision-making processes, many negative outcomes often associated with mergers could be mitigated" (p. 410).

A four-factor typology of impediments to post-acquisition integration based around irrational decision-making characteristics is presented in Fig. 10.1.

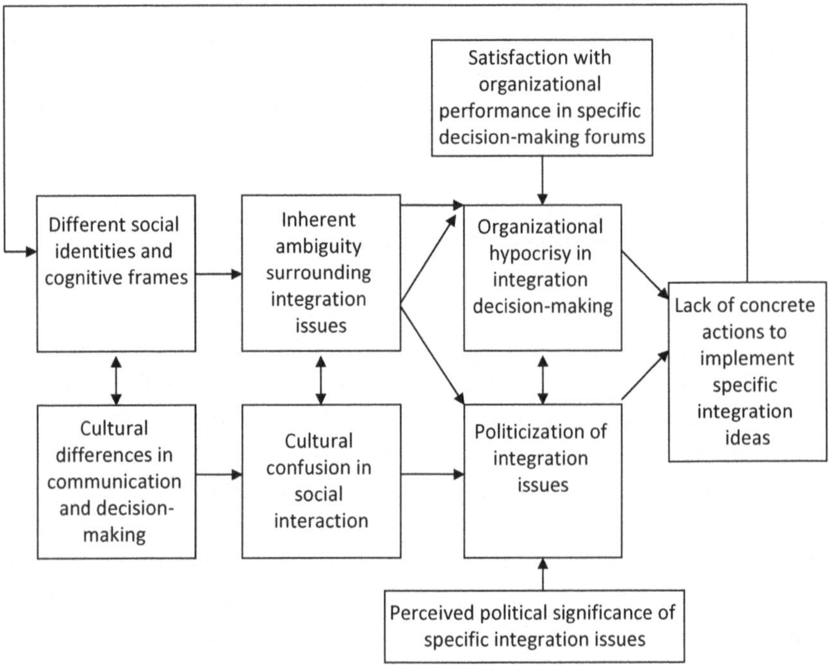

Fig. 10.1 Inherent ambiguity, cultural confusion, organizational hypocrisy, and issue politicization as impediments to postacquisition integration. (Note: Based on Vaara, 2003)

10.4.2 Social Accounts

Social accounts are part of the communication process recommended to motivate employees toward acceptance of the change and form part of the social interaction process. *Information cues* have been identified as an integral part of the process for developing a justice frame, and the use of social accounts to justify an action and manage impressions of fairness is an important factor in this activity (Folger & Cropanzano, 1998). When an individual is presented with a different point of comparison, this may alter their own frame of reference used to evaluate their perception of justice. Similarly, when the details of a change program are communicated effectively, this can also influence an individual's level of uncertainty toward the event and any affect this may have upon them. A study by Schweiger and DeNisi (1991) supports the notion that when an individual is provided with a sincere and adequate explanation of the reasons for the change, this will have a positive impact on their ability to cope with the changes. Their findings provided further support that an individual will be less dissatisfied with an outcome they are unhappy with if they experience perceptions of interactional justice in their relationship with the agents of that change. At such times when an employee experiences unfavorable treatment, the effect of social accounts has been recognized as a method of mitigating a potential reduction in perceived organizational support.

Organizations can either attempt to legitimize their actions using *exonerating accounts* or try to alter employees' perceptions of their unfavorable action using *reframing accounts*. Using *reframing accounts* involves persuading employees to accept a new standard of comparison with an aim of altering perceptions toward the favorableness of their treatment. Sitkin and Bies (1993) confirm:

> A social account is an explanation attempting to influence a person's perception of: (a) responsibility for an incident or action, (b) motives for an action, or (c) the unfavourability of an incident or action. Whether conflict occurs, and, if so, its dynamic, depends on the use and effectiveness of social accounts by the parties involved (p. 351).

Exonerating accounts may take the form of persuading individuals to accept unintended consequences of well-meant actions through sincere regret and by use of an apology. Exonerating accounts should provide a weakening of the reduction effect on POS due to its very nature of providing an explanation of unintended consequences and therefore eliminating the intent of unfavorable action (Eisenberger, Jones, Aselage, & Sucharski, 2004).

Cobb, Wooten, and Folger (1995) recommend that communication during change is imperative and maintain four types of social account should be engaged by management. New frames of reference and standards for defining success (*referential accounts*), sufficient explanation of the reasons for the change (*causal accounts*), protracting the vision for the changed organization (*ideological accounts*), and, with consideration of potential retaliation by employees, an express of regret for any adverse effects experienced from the change (*penitentiary accounts*).

However, it is emphasized that the effect of using social accounts may be impacted by several moderating factors (Folger & Cropanzano, 1998). Examples of these are as follows:

- The *medium* by which the account is communicated (oral communication is favored)
- The *honesty* and *sincerity* of the account
- *Adequacy* of the account (sufficient and credible)
- *Thoroughness* of the account (level of detail provided)
- The *sensitivity* with which the account is communicated
- The *outcome severity* of the event (impact of the event necessitating the account)

Role of Actors in the Process

Preacquisition planning involves only a relatively small group of people, and these tend to be members of corporate management from the acquiring organization, but considerably more (including both change agents and change subjects) become involved in the postacquisition change process. At this point the ambiguity of the decision-making process becomes dependent on several factors. These include organizational identity (Cartwright & Cooper, 1993; Fried, Tiegs, Naughton, & Ashford, 1996; Greenwood, Hinings, & Brown, 1994), national identities in cross-border mergers and acquisitions (M&A) (Calori, Lubatkin, & Very, 1994; Olie, 1994; Very, Lubatkin, Calori, & Veiga, 1997), and communication barriers (Gertsen & Soderberg, 1998). In addition, role identities can lead to ambiguity in the decision-making relationship, particularly in the case where the size of integrating organizations is disparate and distinctions need to be drawn between owners and corporate managers (Chandler, 1977; Williamson, 1996), and corporate managers and business unit managers (Floyd & Woolridge, 1994). As Vaara (2003) points out, "These dramatic events bring together people of various backgrounds and social identities who are likely to interpret specific issues in different ways" (p. 873).

Based on their closeness to decision-making and opportunity to influence the outcomes of those decisions, Hubbard and Purcell (2001) recognized three categories of employee within the process as *negotiators*, *enactors*, and *recipients* (Hubbard & Purcell, 2001). The three subject categories and their roles in the decision-making process can be described as follows:

- Negotiators: senior managers that are most likely to be involved in the preimplementation planning stage. These individuals will normally possess a high degree of discretion in managing the acquisition process and will have the most accurate expectations of future events. Typically, they will be near the top of their career paths so of primary concern will be job title or board membership rather than future role development.
- Enactors: form management tiers below the negotiators and will have responsibility for implementation, although little input into its design. They will also act as the chief communicators as lower-level employees will look to them for information and guidance. Potentially a difficult role because information flows from negotiators may be restricted due to secrecy or commercial confidentiality. Future role development will be of importance.
- Recipients: usually nonmanagerial and typically will have little or no input in decision-making during integration, being reliant upon enactors for news and information when it is available.

Partly due to their low involvement in the process, there is an expectation for recipients to emphasise transitional fears, such as "will I have a job?" These will typically extend to group worries about what will happen to them and how they will fit in to the new firm. These concerns and anxieties are examples of the antecedents of resistance and reinforce the benefits of process involvement for employees throughout the structure.

10.5 Relationship Transgressions

10.5.1 Exchange

Galpin and Whittington (2010) identify the need for "merger repair" following any perceived management transgressions that have had a negative impact on workforce attitudes. A key area of scrutiny that is often in need of repair following a perceived merger transgression is the exchange relationship between two or more parties involved in the transaction. As will be recalled, the exchange relationship is governed by the norms of reciprocity (Gouldner, 1960; Blau, 1964), which have characteristics dependent on the type of exchange (i.e. whether this is social or economic in nature). The norms of reciprocity may be affected in such situations due to the perceived mistreatment in the relationship by the other party where any positive exchange may be suspended. As an outcome, it can be expected that cooperative behaviors, such as OCB, and positive interaction in the workplace (e.g. teamworking) will be negatively impacted. Cooperation may not only be affected but may reduce to the extent that it no longer exists (Bottom, Gibson, Daniels, & Murningham, 2002). In addition to a withholding of effort, other findings in this area of research have experienced quite extreme behaviors including revenge and reprisals (Bottom et al., 2002; Nakayachi & Watabe, 2005; Ren & Gray, 2009; Schweitzer, Hershey, & Bradlow, 2006; Tomlinson, Dineen, & Lewicki, 2004).

The significance of the supervisor in this role of perceived support is exemplified through the account of organizational support theory. The theory claims that employees will develop feelings of support more broadly within the organization if they have formed a strong relationship with an organizational agent who is perceived as supportive toward the day-to-day needs of their role (Rhoades & Eisenberger, 2002). It is suggested that employees will evaluate their immediate supervisor in his or her role based on the supervisor's behavior and perceived characteristics and competence in certain actions, such as planning, directing, observing, and evaluating subordinates' work and performance (Dowell & Wexley, 1978; Eisenberger et al., 2002). Consequently, how supervisors communicate with others within their dyadic subordinate relationships will bear outcomes for the employee that are instrumental not only in the reciprocation of attitude and behavior toward the supervisor, but also concerning the organization and its support for programs of change, such as M&A.

Broken promises by management are normally the root of these transgressions, which may be exemplified by general statements of no reductions in the workforce or promises of enhanced benefits that never materialize. If these statements are not followed through, then any newly-formed relationships between the new management team and organizational members will soon be compromised. Communication of this type is tantamount to destroying any goodwill that may have been developed thus far and trust of the workforce will take some winning back. As we have seen in Chap. 7, regular communication bulletins from the organization with reliable information are crucial throughout this period. As mentioned, they set expectations, a topic that has its scholarly foundations rooted in the psychological contract literature, and although this will be discussed in more detail in Chap. 11, it is worth considering the core principles of this framework within the context of the current discussion.

The psychological contract between the employee and the organization is fundamentally a relationship that is formed on a set of implicit expectations that are inextricably bound to the norms of reciprocity, and, from an employee perspective, based on what they have heard and understood. If these expectations fail to materialize, there is an impact on levels of future trust. It is easy to see why expectations that are forged in the first instance need to be sourced from reliable information and need to be achievable if they have maximum opportunity of being followed through. Of course, member expectations that are not fulfilled may not be due to transgressions of a sinister nature, but merely because of actions that are not within the immediate remit of the management team, such as a change in circumstances or prevailing conditions that are unfavorable for delivering on expectations at that point in time.

10.5.2 The Impact on Trust

One of the key outcomes of any perceived transgression is the damage to trust within the relationship between management and organization members. Trust is an attitude already discussed at length in Chap. 8, and we have seen how critical this can be in helping to bind those relationships that are so crucial to merger success. One of the key constructs of trust is integrity, which is defined by Bews and Rossouw (2002) as "the application of a set of moral and ethical principles, acceptable to both trustor and trustee, which are predictable and reliable" (p. 382). There is an indication in this definition that organizational members will scrutinize managers throughout the M&A process for their ability to offer a set of predictable and reliable moral and ethical principles that are acceptable to both parties. The integrity of the manager is, in part, determined by how this is perceived, which will then become a highly important ingredient in the ability to develop trust within the employee-employer relationship.

Dirks, Lewicki, and Zaheer (2009) recognize trust as one of the three most prominent factors that are damaged and therefore in need of repair following any merger transgressions that impact relationships between employees and the organization(s). This is because expectations begin to be formed about future behavior and the nature of these experiences are likely to set the trend of how they may continue (i.e. negative experience perceived as replacing any hopes of positive expectations going forward), resulting in a reduced tendency to be exposed in vulnerable situations. Transgressions may relate to specific incidences and events and therefore be limited to that activity in future, or they may be perceived as being of a more general nature. For example, in a situation where overall integration efforts have been observed as having been poorly conducted, there may be little faith in the newly-integrated organization, leading to a diminution of trust in more general terms (Maguire & Phillips, 2008; Searle & Ball, 2004).

Integrity and Competence

Damage to the development of trust within those employment relationships will be compounded where transgressions involve a compromise to integrity rather than perceived incompetence. An association between integrity and competence of the individual or entity (e.g. senior management board) through the eyes of the transgressed has also been established (see Sitkin & Roth, 1993). Where integrity is questioned in relation to the transgression, this will have a more serious impact on the creation of negative emotions for the transgressed. For example (rightly or wrongly), if the integrity of an individual comes under scrutiny, then this may also influence how others perceive their levels of competence to manage or lead (i.e. competent management would not consider violating integrity). Agents of change management need to avoid matters that could compromise integrity (such as the breaking of promises made earlier) at all costs. If there is a transgression relating to a serious issue of integrity, then the only solution may be to replace those seen as the cause of the transgression if damage to the reputations of those involved is not to become embedded, irreversible, and permanent.

Accordingly, it is established that the perceived competence of management can be a leading factor affecting the circumstances where trust is to be developed or maintained within the employer-employee relationship. The role of competence in building trust has been studied by several scholars and, in this situation, has been defined as "the trustor's perception that the trustee possesses the technical and interpersonal skills required for a job" (Kim, Ferrin, Cooper, & Dirks, 2004, p. 106). An emphasis on the technical and interpersonal skills raises the competence in the technical abilities of the manager, but also the interpersonal skills that are a vital element of successfully communicating both the technical and social aspects of the merger with confidence and reliability. While both integrity and competence have been found to be critical elements of forging trust within interpersonal relationships during the M&A process, integrity tends to come under the spotlight and the impact that this will have on the abilities to either increase or diminish trust when compared to concerns about managerial competence. While examples of incompetence, such as lacking the necessary skills to introduce change, may be unintentional and not necessarily the fault of the transgressor, where integrity is lacking it is more likely to be intentional.

Competence in leadership has also been related to a potential to influence others, particularly within a specific domain (e.g. change and M&A). If a leader is seen as unable to possess the ability to perform a task because of a certain lack of knowledge or skill set, then it is unlikely that they will be able to influence potential followers to perform in their shadow within that situation (Mayer, Davis, & Schoorman, 1995). Therefore, the role of trust in one's supervisor is, in part, dependent on their competence to operate effectively within a given context, a necessary presence to form positive and stable relationships with subordinates in their charge. Indeed, prior research links the strength of competence being demonstrated in this relationship to compliance with supervisor decisions (Price & Garland, 1981) and the role of modelling by supervisors (Weiss, 1977). Furthermore, perceived competence in a supervisor is more likely to attract positive attitudes within subordinates (Andersson, 1996) and reduce the potential for supervisors themselves to feel they are in a situation where they are challenged by their subordinates due to their own incompetence (Neves, 2011).

10.5.3 Affective State

Another prominent factor identified by Dirks et al. (2009) as often in need of reparation following a merger transgression is affect, or one's emotional state, which may manifest itself negatively in a number of forms including disappointment, frustration, or anger (Barclay, Skarlicki, & Pugh, 2005; Conway & Briner, 2002). This negative state of affect may encourage behavioral reactions from any of the parties involved (employee, supervisor, or organization), which, in extremity, will lead to a termination of the relationship to eliminate the consequential emotion being experienced. Therefore, it has important connotations toward the ongoing viability of the relationship. Previous studies have implicated mergers that are poorly conducted as being a cause of employee negative affect (Klendauer & Deller, 2009), leading to an unexpected turnover of key staff and, subsequently, talented individuals leaving the organization at a crucial point in time (Kiessling, Harvey, & Thompson Heames, 2008; Kummer, 2008).

The communication of quality, timely, and unambiguous information will make an important contribution toward avoiding situations arising where negative emotion is invoked. Change agents need to avoid potential contradictions in communication if messages are to remain consistent, even if these messages are not always popular with staff. Similarly, negative emotion could also be encouraged by the length of time taken by management to form decision outcomes at critical stages of the merger process, thereby leaving staff waiting in anticipation of the result (Galpin & Whittington, 2010). A general lack of information can be included in these scenarios.

Alternatively, trust will begin to strengthen again when both parties in the exchange relationship are able to respond consistently and productively to any of these problems (Pervan, Bove, & Johnson, 2009). Accordingly, if each of these attitudes and behaviors are given consideration and recognized for their significance, then attaining harmony and avoiding conflictual instances leading to uncertainty and resistance will be a more likely outcome. According to Galpin and Whittington (2010), addressing each after transgressions that lead to merger repair will not only provide temporary short-term relief in the employee-employer relationship but will provide a solid base for the longer-term mechanisms upon which the integration process will be dependent.

10.6 Case in Question: The Role of Social Exchange in Fairness

Effective communication was one of the most divisive issues in the business school merger. The problems of inadequate justification and an ineffective mechanism for process control are each bound within the subsequent breakdown in the social exchange relationship between the leadership of the new business school and its employees. The outcome for the employees was further uncertainty because an incomplete understanding of the decision-making process resulted in ambiguity. In a search to make sense of this knowledge gap, employees used their own social cues drawing information from their personal realm of social exchange relationships (*grapevine interaction*). This had an impact on their evaluations and judgments of the situation which were now being informed from a more subjective position.

The survey distributed to both business school and NHS Trust staff in Phases 3 and 4 of the research offered the opportunity to develop new insights into the study, but it also provided support for the findings from

Phase 2 in a triangulation of data. Although all relationships in both surveys had highly significant correlations, those with the most significant correlations were between the three dimensions of justice.

When a deeper analysis of the results was conducted, it became evident that at the NHS Trust interactional justice was the dimension of organizational justice most highly correlated with each of the four outcome variables, psychological contract breach, organizational commitment, OCB, and intention to leave. At the business school, both procedural and interactional justice were equally important to the behavior of intention to leave, and procedural justice was most important to OCB. In relation to the variable psychological contract breach interactional justice was again the most highly correlated of the three justice dimensions and was approximately equal in significance with procedural justice to the attitude affective commitment. It should be recalled that the dynamics of interactional justice include communication, justification, respect, and trust, and these were among the most prominent outcomes from the Phase 2 discussions.

It has been determined that problems with the quality of communication at the business school were a primary reason for the levels of anxiety experienced by staff and a root cause of uncertainty that led to a further erosion of trust in the leadership. It has been identified that involving the individual in the process of change by offering voice can provide many positive behavioral outcomes. However, further to this it has been recognized in this study that a successful communications strategy can only be developed if it includes a structured plan for justification of the decisions made and the actions taken. Ineffective use of social accounts by authorities led to confusion and increased uncertainty about the future direction of the organization, the current policies and practices of the organization, and even the reason the merger was initiated.

In Chap. 7, a framework offered by Larsson, Brousseau, Driver, and Sweet (2004) was discussed, capturing what they deemed to be the three important characteristics of communication during an M&A. The three characteristics were identified as voice, involvement, and precision; hence, they entitled their framework the VIP model. The findings from the current study confirm the three characteristics proposed by Larsson et al. However, a proposition is that results from the current study extend

Table 10.1 The extended VIP model

Characteristic	Interpretation
Voice	Timely, honest communication that reduces employee uncertainty, active listening to their thoughts, and feelings to learn how to best integrate the combining companies
Involvement	Involvement in the integration process by retaining as much of the acquired corporate values as possible and by seeking ideas and suggestions from employees about their integration and improvement solutions
Precision	Precision in two-way communication and integration because people process information in different ways, have different career motives, experience threats in different ways, and therefore need different information and solutions
Social accounts	In support of an honest voice mechanism, the use of justification of managerial actions, providing reasoning and the grounds upon which this was based by presenting alternative courses of action that were considered but eliminated

Note: Adapted from Larsson, Brousseau, Driver, and Sweet (2004)

their three-component model. The use of social accounts to support this communication strategy and the act of justifying managerial decision-making during merger implementation should also be taken into account, resulting in the model being extended.

The three characteristics presented by Larsson et al. are discussed in more detail in Chap. 7, but are presented in Table 10.1, which, in line with findings from the current study, extends the existing model to recognize the contribution of social accounts. It may also be recalled from the discussion on social accounts presented earlier in this chapter that justification of managerial actions had been identified as a required function in the implementation of a change program. Subsequently, this had been recognized as an *a priori* Level 1 theme in the current research as an antecedent of justice. Following the qualitative interviews in Phase 2 this was confirmed as a major function of the postmerger Level 1 theme of *social exchange relationships* and therefore is considered a vital element of a successful integration program.

Findings from the current research propose that the most complete explanation of managerial actions will have two desired outcomes:

1. It will present the context in which the decisions were made, raising any dependent factors that were important in the making of that decision of which the employee was not aware. It will also allow the opportunity for authorities to present all possible considered outcomes of both the decision made and the alternative options and, in doing so, present the case for why that particular option was chosen.
2. A comprehensive justification of their actions by authorities to include employees at all levels across the organization will present a case of consideration at a time of increased anxiety for the individual. This action will promote employee feelings that they have been treated with dignity and respect and therefore reduce any perceptions that their psychological contract with the organization has been breached.

Further support for the implications of not using justification of the communicated message has been emphasized in Phases 3 and 4 of the study where a significant relationship with perceived psychological contract breach was identified, along with negative attitudinal and behavioral outcomes.

While the framework offered by Larsson et al. recognizes the need for timely and honest communication as part of an effective strategy, this does not necessarily involve the justification of managerial decisions and actions. It can be recalled that within the current study employees at the business school indicated that they received sufficient information from their leadership regarding progress with the merger implementation and, as a result, changes to policy and practice. Even so, there were two deficiencies in the quality of this communication that had a major influence on its effectiveness among employees: (i) trust in the communicated message and (ii) justification of the communicated message. The first of these two factors is considered by Larsson et al. when they refer to "honest communication that reduces employee uncertainty." Equally, ineffective justification is a primary cause of employee uncertainty and this is not alluded to in their framework.

Interactional justice was the dominant form of experienced injustice which can be mainly attributed to issues of trust and communication between employees and authorities. This can be related to a breakdown in the social exchange and a perceived reneging of the relational aspect of the psychological contract. Therefore, from the findings of this research, during a merger the exchange of interpersonal relationships between employee and authorities is the most obvious protagonist of perceived injustice.

References

Amason, A. C. (1996). Distinguishing the effects of functional and dysfunctional conflict on strategic decision making: Resolving a paradox for top management teams. *Academy of Management Journal, 39*(1), 123–148.

Andersson, L. M. (1996). Employee cynicism: An examination using a contract violation framework. *Human Relations, 49*(11), 1395–1418.

Argyris, C., & Schön, D. (1996). *Organizational learning II: Theory, method and practice.* Reading, MA: Addison-Wesley.

Armenakis, A. A., & Bedeian, A. G. (1999). Organizational change: A review of theory and research in the 1990s. *Journal of Management, 25*(3), 293–315.

Barclay, L. J., Skarlicki, D. P., & Pugh, S. D. (2005). Exploring the role of emotions in injustice perceptions and retaliation. *Journal of Applied Psychology, 90*(4), 629–643.

Basu, R., & Green, S. G. (1997). Leader-member exchange and transformational leadership: An empirical examination of innovative behaviors in leader-member dyads. *Journal of Applied Psychology, 27*(6), 477–499.

Bews, N. F., & Rossouw, G. J. (2002). A role for business ethics in facilitating trustworthiness. *Journal of Business Ethics, 39*(4), 377–390.

Bies, R. J., & Moag, J. F. (1986). Interactional justice: Communication criteria of fairness. In R. J. Lewicki, B. H. Sheppard, & M. H. Bazerman (Eds.), *Research on negotiations in organizations* (Vol. 1, pp. 43–55). Greenwich, CT: JAI Press.

Blau, P. (1964). *Exchange and power in social life.* New York: Wiley.

Bottom, W. P., Gibson, K., Daniels, S. E., & Murnighan, J. K. (2002). When talk is not cheap: Substantive penance and expressions of intent in rebuilding cooperation. *Organization Science, 13*(5), 497–513.

Bouckenooghe, D. (2010). Positioning change recipients' attitudes toward change in the organizational change literature. *Journal of Applied Behavioral Science, 46*(4), 500–531.

Bouckenooghe, D. (2012). The role of organizational politics, contextual resources, and formal communication on change recipients' commitment to change: A multilevel study. *European Journal of Work & Organizational Psychology, 21*(4), 575–602.

Bouckenooghe, D., De Clercq, D., & Deprez, J. (2014). Interpersonal justice, relational conflict, and commitment to change: The moderating role of social interaction. *Applied Psychology: An International Review, 63*(3), 509–540.

Calori, R., Lubatkin, M., & Very, P. (1994). Control mechanisms in cross-border acquisitions: An international comparison. *Organization Studies, 15*, 361–379.

Cartwright, S., & Cooper, C. L. (1993). The psychological impact of merger and acquisition on the individual: A study of building society managers. *Human Relations, 46*, 327–347.

Chandler, A. (1977). *The visible hand: The managerial revolution in American business*. Cambridge, MA: Harvard University Press.

Choi, M. (2011). Employees' attitudes toward organizational change: A literature review. *Human Resource Management, 50*(4), 479–500.

Christensen, M. (2014). Communication as a strategic tool in change processes. *International Journal of Business Communication, 51*(4), 359–385.

Cobb, A. T., Wooten, K. C., & Folger, R. (1995). Justice in the making: Toward understanding the theory and practice of justice in organizational change and development. *Research in Organizational Change and Development, 8*, 243–295.

Colquitt, J. A. (2001). On the dimensionality of organizational justice: A construct validation of a measure. *Journal of Applied Psychology, 86*, 368–400.

Conway, N., & Briner, R. B. (2002). A daily diary study of affective responses to psychological contract breach and exceeded promises. *Journal of Organizational Behavior, 23*(3), 287–302.

Cropanzano, R., Prehar, C. A., & Chen, P. Y. (2002). Using social exchange theory to distinguish procedural justice from interactional justice. *Group and Organizational Management, 27*, 324–351.

Cunningham, C. E., Woodward, C. A., Shannon, H. S., Macintosh, J., Lendrum, B., Rosenbloom, D., et al. (2002). Readiness for organizational change: A longitudinal study of workplace, psychological and behavioural correlates. *Journal of Occupational & Organizational Psychology, 75*(4), 377–392.

De Clercq, D., Thongpapanl, N., & Dimov, D. (2009). When good conflict gets better and bad conflict becomes worse: The role of social capital in the conflict-innovation relationship. *Journal of the Academy of Marketing Science, 37*(3), 283–297.

De Dreu, C. K. W., & Van Vianen, A. E. M. (2001). Managing relationship conflict and the effectiveness of organizational teams. *Journal of Organizational Behavior, 22*(3), 309–328.

Dirks, K. T., Lewicki, R. J., & Zaheer, A. (2009). Repairing relationships within and between organizations: Building a conceptual foundation. *Academy of Management Review, 34*(1), 68–84.

Dowell, B. E., & Wexley, K. N. (1978). Development of a work behavior taxonomy for first-line supervisors. *Journal of Applied Psychology, 63*(5), 563–572.

Eisenberger, R., Huntington, R., Hutchison, S., & Sowa, D. (1986). Perceived organizational support. *Journal of Applied Psychology, 71*, 500–507.

Eisenberger, R., Jones, J. R., Aselage, J., & Sucharski, I. L. (2004). Perceived organizational support. In J. A. M. Coyle-Shapiro, L. M. Shore, M. S. Taylor, & L. E. Tetrick (Eds.), *The employment relationship: Examining psychological and contextual perspectives* (pp. 206–225). New York: Oxford University Press.

Eisenberger, R., Stinglhamber, F., Vandenberghe, C., Sucharski, I. L., & Rhoades, L. (2002). Perceived supervisor support: Contributions to perceived organizational support and employee retention. *Journal of Applied Psychology, 87*(3), 565–573.

Floyd, S. W., & Woolridge, B. (1994). Dinosaurs or dynamos? Recognizing middle management's strategic role. *Academy of Management Executive, 8*, 47–57.

Folger, R., & Cropanzano, R. (1998). *Organizational justice and human resource management*. Thousand Oaks, CA: Sage.

Ford, J., & Ford, L. (2009). Resistance to change: A reexamination and extension. *Research in Organizational Change and Management, 17*, 211–239.

Fried, Y., Tiegs, R. B., Naughton, T. J., & Ashford, B. E. (1996). Managers' reactions to a corporate acquisition: A test of an integrative model. *Journal of Organization Behavior, 17*, 401–427.

Galpin, T., & Whittington, J. L. (2010). Merger repair: A conceptual framework for restoring employer/employee relationships. *Journal of Behavioral and Applied Management, 12*(1), 48–68.

Gertsen, M. C., & Soderberg, A.-M. (1998). Foreign acquisitions in Denmark: Cultural and communicative dimensions. In M. C. Gertsen, A.-M. Sederberg, & J. E. Torp (Eds.), *Cultural dimensions of international mergers and acquisitions*. Berlin, Germany: Walter de Gruyter.

Goldhaber, G. M. (1999). Organizational communication in 1976: Present domain and future directions. In P. Salem (Ed.), *Organizational communication and change* (pp. 4–30). Cresskill, NJ: Hampton Press.

Gouldner, A. W. (1960). The norm of reciprocity: A preliminary statement. *American Sociological Review, 25*, 161–178.

Graen, G. B., & Scandura, T. A. (1987). Toward a psychology of dyadic organizing. *Research in Organizational Behavior, 9*, 175–209.

Greenwood, R., Hinings, C. R., & Brown, J. (1994). Merging professional service firms. *Organization Science, 5*, 239–257.

Hambrick, D., & Cannella, A. (1993). Relative standing: A framework for understanding departures of acquired executives. *Academy of Management Journal, 36*, 733–762.

Heide, J. B., & Miner, A. S. (1992). The shadow of the future: Effects of anticipated interaction and frequency of contact on buy-seller cooperation. *Academy of Management Journal, 35*(2), 265–291.

Hubbard, N., & Purcell, J. (2001). Managing employee expectations during acquisitions. *Human Resource Management Journal, 11*(2), 17–33.

Jehn, K. A. (1995). A multimethod examination of the benefits and detriments of intragroup conflict. *Administrative Science Quarterly, 40*(2), 256–282.

Jehn, K. A. (1997). A qualitative analysis of conflict types and dimensions in organizational groups. *Administrative Science Quarterly, 42*(3), 530–557.

Jehn, K. A., & Mannix, E. A. (2001). The dynamic nature of conflict: A longitudinal study of intragroup conflict and group performance. *Academy of Management Journal, 44*(2), 238–251.

Kahn, W. A. (1990). Psychological conditions of personal engagement and disengagement at work. *Academy of Management Journal, 33*(4), 692–724.

Kiessling, T., Harvey, M., & Thompson Heames, J. (2008). Acquisition issues: Operational changes to the acquired firm's top management team and subsequent organizational performance. *Journal of Leadership & Organizational Studies, 14*(4), 287–302.

Kim, P. H., Ferrin, D. L., Cooper, C. D., & Dirks, K. T. (2004). Removing the shadow of suspicion: The effects of apology versus denial for repairing competence- versus integrity-based trust violations. *Journal of Applied Psychology, 89*(1), 104–118.

Klendauer, R., & Deller, J. (2009). Organizational justice and managerial commitment in corporate mergers. *Journal of Managerial Psychology, 24*(1), 29–45.

Kummer, C. (2008). Motivation and retention of key people in mergers and acquisitions. *Strategic HR Review, 7*(6), 5–10.

Larsson, R., Brousseau, K. R., Driver, M. J., & Sweet, P. L. (2004). The secrets of merger and acquisition success: A co-competence and motivational approach to synergy realization. In A. L. Pablo & M. Javidan (Eds.), *Mergers and acquisitions: Creating integrative knowledge*. Oxford, UK: Blackwell.

Lazarus, R. S., & Folkman, S. (1984). *Stress, appraisal, and coping*. New York: Springer.

Leana, C. R., & Van Buren, H. J., III. (1999). Organizational social capital and employment practices. *Academy of Management Review, 24*(3), 538–555.

Lipponen, J., Olkkonen, M. E., & Moilanen, M. (2004). Perceived procedural justice and employee responses to an organizational merger. *European Journal of Work and Organizational Psychology, 13*, 391–413.

Maguire, S., & Phillips, N. (2008). 'Citibankers' at Citigroup: A study of the loss of institutional trust after a merger. *Journal of Management Studies, 45*(2), 372–401.

Masterson, S. S., Lewis, K., Goldman, B. M., & Taylor, M. S. (2000). Integrating justice and social exchange: The differing effects of fair procedures and treatment on work relationships. *Academy of Management Journal, 43*, 738–748.

Mayer, R. C., Davis, J. H., & Schoorman, F. D. (1995). An integrative model of organizational trust. *Academy of Management Review, 20*(3), 709–734.

Moorman, R. H. (1991). Relationship between organizational justice and organizational citizenship behaviors: Do fairness perceptions influence employee citizenship? *Journal of Applied Psychology, 76*, 845–855.

Murnighan, J. K., & Conlon, D. E. (1991). The dynamics of intense work groups: A study of British string quartets. *Administrative Science Quarterly, 36*(2), 165–186.

Nahapiet, J., & Ghoshal, S. (1998). Social capital, intellectual capital, and the organizational advantage. *Academy of Management Review, 23*(2), 242–266.

Nakayachi, K., & Watabe, M. (2005). Restoring trustworthiness after adverse events: The signalling effects of voluntary "hostage posting" on trust. *Organizational Behavior and Human Decision Processes, 97*(1), 1–17.

Neves, P. (2011). Building commitment to change: The role of perceived supervisor support and competence. *European Journal of Work & Organizational Psychology, 20*(4), 437–450.

Olie, R. (1994). Shades of culture and institutions in international mergers. *Organization Studies, 15*, 381–405.

Pelled, L. H. (1996). Demographic diversity, conflict, and work group outcomes: An intervening process theory. *Organization Science, 7*(6), 615–631.

Pervan, S. J., Bove, L. L., & Johnson, L. W. (2009). Reciprocity as a key stabilizing norm of interpersonal marketing relationships: Scale development and validation. *Industrial Marketing Management, 38*(1), 60–70.

Pondy, L. R. (1967). Organizational conflict: Concepts and models. *Administrative Science Quarterly, 12*(2), 296–320.

Price, K. H., & Garland, H. (1981). Compliance with a leader's suggestions as a function of perceived leader/member competence and potential reciprocity. *Journal of Applied Psychology, 66*(3), 329–336.

Ren, H., & Gray, B. (2009). Repairing relationship conflict: How violation types and culture influence the effectiveness of restoration. *Academy of Management Review, 34*(1), 105–126.

Rhoades, L., & Eisenberger, R. (2002). Perceived organizational support: A review of the literature. *Journal of Applied Psychology, 87*, 698–714.

Rhoades, L., Eisenberger, R., & Armeli, S. (2001). Affective commitment to the organization: The contribution of perceived organizational support. *Journal of Applied Psychology, 86*, 825–836.

Rodell, J. B., & Colquitt, J. A. (2009). Looking ahead in times of uncertainty: The role of anticipatory justice in an organizational change context. *Journal of Applied Psychology, 94*(4), 989–1002.

Roscigno, V. J., & Hodson, R. (2004). The organizational and social foundations of worker resistance. *American Sociological Review, 69*(1), 14–39.

Schein, E. H. (1996). Three cultures of management: The key to organizational learning. *Sloan Management Review, 38*(1), 9–20.

Schweiger, D., & Denisi, A. (1991). Communication with employees following a merger: A longitudinal field experiment. *Academy of Management Journal, 34*(1), 110–135.

Schweitzer, M. E., Hershey, J. C., & Bradlow, E. T. (2006). Promises and lies: Restoring violated trust. *Organizational Behavior & Human Decision Processes, 101*(1), 1–19.

Searle, R. H., & Ball, K. S. (2004). The development of trust and distrust in a merger. *Journal of Managerial Psychology, 19*(7), 708–721.

Settoon, R. P., Bennett, N., & Liden, R. C. (1996). Social exchange in organizations: Perceived organizational support, leader-member exchange, and employee reciprocity. *Journal of Applied Psychology, 81*(3), 219–227.

Sitkin, S. B., & Bies, R. J. (1993). Social accounts in conflict situations: Using explanations to manage conflict. *Human Relations, 46*, 349–370.

Sitkin, S. B., & Roth, N. L. (1993). Explaining the limited effectiveness of legalistic "remedies" for trust/distrust. *Organization Science, 4*(3), 367–392.

Stinglhamber, F., & Vandenberghe, C. (2003). Organizations and supervisors as sources of support and targets of commitment: A longitudinal study. *Journal of Organizational Behavior, 24*(3), 251–270.

Tierney, T. (1999). Work relations as a precursor to a psychological climate for change. *Journal of Organizational Change Management, 12*(2), 120–134.

Tomlinson, E. C., Dineen, B. R., & Lewicki, R. J. (2004). The road to reconciliation: Antecedents of victim willingness to reconcile following a broken promise. *Journal of Management, 30*(2), 165–187.

Tukiainen, T. (2001). An agenda model of organizational communication. *Corporate Communications: An International Journal, 6*(1), 47–52.

Turner Parish, J., Cadwallader, S., & Busch, P. (2008). Wat to, need to, ought to: Employee commitment to organizational change. *Journal of Organizational Change Management, 21*(1), 32–52.

Uzzi, B. (1997). Social structure and competition in interfirm networks: The paradox of embeddedness. *Administrative Science Quarterly, 42*(1), 35–67.

Vaara, E. (2003). Post-acquisition integration as sensemaking: Glimpses of ambiguity, confusion, hypocrisy, and politicization. *Journal of Management Studies, 40*, 859–894.

Very, P., Lubatkin, M., Calori, R., & Veiga, J. (1997). Relative standing and the performance of recently acquired European firms. *Strategic Management Journal, 18*, 593–614.

Waddell, D., Cummings, T., & Worley, C. (2007). *Organization development and change*. Pyrmont, Australia: Nelson ITP.

Wayne, S. J., Shore, L. M., & Liden, R. C. (1997). Perceived organizational support and leader-member exchange: A social exchange perspective. *Academy of Management Journal, 40*(1), 82–111.

Weiss, H. M. (1977). Subordinate imitation of supervisor behavior: The role of modelling in organizational socialization. *Organizational Behavior & Human Performance, 19*(1), 89–105.

Williamson, O. (1996). *The mechanisms of governance*. New York: Oxford University Press.

11

Psychological Contract

11.1 Introduction

The psychological contract (PC) is a framework that is central to understanding the employment relationship in both its relational and transactional forms. Of more recent times, Rousseau has made a significant contribution to its development within the working environment following earlier contributions by Argyris (1960), Levinson, Price, Munden, and Solley (1962) and Schein (1965). Furthermore, the perceived obligation that an organization must fulfill employee expectations of their PC is an important predictor of key workplace attitudes and behaviors, such as job satisfaction (Turnley & Feldman, 2000), organizational citizenship behavior (Hui, Lee, & Rousseau, 2004), employee performance (Conway & Coyle-Shapiro, 2012), and in-role performance (Dabos & Rousseau, 2004). Hence, in addition to forming an inherent part of the employment relationship it is also recognized for its contribution toward the quality of that relationship.

N. Jackson, *Organizational Justice in Mergers and Acquisitions*,
https://doi.org/10.1007/978-3-319-92636-0_11

11.2 Characteristics of the Psychological Contract

The nature of change is often determined by the depth of merger integration, and where this is intense, the change and upheaval experienced by those going through it may be considerable. In extreme cases there are similarities with those entering a new employment arrangement in which the employee needs to enter a period of organizational socialization. For those undergoing a new start, it has been recognized that the PC is shaped within a process that will unfold gradually throughout different stages of the employment (De Vos, Buyens, &, Schalk, 2003; Rousseau & McLean Parks, 1992; Shore & Tetrick, 1994). The dynamic nature of the early stages of employment is usually where new starters will encounter a phase of getting to know the habits and needs of others in the worker pool. Changes to the perceived obligations and expectations of early PC formation are believed to be particularly likely during this period.

Throughout this period of socialization, employees will need to become familiar with the new environment, its principles, and values, adjusting their attitudes and behaviors accordingly to fit the scene (Chao, O'Leary-Kelly, Wolf, Klein, & Gardner, 1994; Major, Kozlowski, Chao, & Gardner, 1995). This period of adjustment can be unsettling and very stressful for those enchained within as there are many potential opportunities for uncertainty and the insecurities that follow. To mitigate some or all of this uncertainty, Morrison (1993a, 1993b) has proposed that individuals will need to learn quickly about their new surroundings and how to function effectively within them.

In situations of new recruits entering the workplace, it has been suggested that organizations are inclined to overemphasize the positive aspects of employment they offer and tend to underemphasize those aspects that are deemed to be negative. Socialization literatures are well versed in these phenomena (e.g. see Boswell, Shipp, Payne, & Culbertson, 2009; Dugoni & Ilgen, 1981; Wanous, 1977). As Conway and Briner (2005) have stated, there is often a case where line managers will mislead during the recruitment and early employment process and are disposed to "exaggerate the extent of provision and quality of human resource practices during communications… leading to inflated employee expectations which are not met" (p. 50). However, in situations of new encounters for those employees transitioning through the process of integration, the reality may be antithetical. Instead of an overemphasis of the benefits, there is likely to be rumor and speculation generating images of negativity. As discussed in Chap. 7, this would resemble a common feature of change from mergers and acquisitions (M&A) in an environment of poor organizational communication mechanisms where the voids are filled with falsehoods and speculative gossip.

In situations akin to those referred to earlier, employee expectations may be far worse than they experience, and therefore the PC will be forged on lower than expected outcomes formed on potential inaccuracies and false accusation. New starters tend to adjust rapidly to their roles in the first few months of taking on the job and may find that this includes a period during which attitudes and behavior are conditioned accordingly as they transit through the socialization period. This period of socialization adjustment is aided by information sharing with coworkers and feedback mechanisms triggered through coworkers and other stakeholders. In addition, there will be tangible experiences developed from social interaction within their environment, which will present the employees with greater accuracy of what organizational life will be like henceforth (Lester, Kickul, & Bergmann, 2007). This reality check may have positive or negative connotations depending on premerger expectations and how individuals perceived these.

Through this period of readjustment, the PC will be reassessed and reevaluated based on any changes to the employee's perceived obligations of the organization. Perceived contract obligations in comparison to actual expectations will have important implications toward the potential of an apparent breach in the PC. Changes that take place as the merger process begins to develop, such as the revelation of new information, additional support for the employee to help with coping with the change, or any other matters that become known to reduce their uncertainty and anxiety will have an impact on the employee's reckoning of the contract obligations of the employer. Subsequently, this will have an impact on expectations, by either changing the nature of events, or managing expectations for a softer landing than first considered.

Reflecting on this process, we can see that the characteristics of the PC are dynamic and any assessment and understanding of the situation should be expected to remain fluid. To illustrate this, let us consider a case where an individual assesses their current situation and concludes that they have exaggerated the obligations of their employer, perhaps through misinterpreting their word or via rumor and hearsay communicated along the grapevine. In circumstances where employees take partial or complete ownership for the misunderstanding, they will acknowledge a requirement to reduce their employer's obligations within that given situation. This reevaluation and correction in-line with more up-to-date information can be compared to the principles upon which Adams' equity theory of distributive justice is based. A rebalancing of the scales to consider a fair assessment of the situation is necessary. Therefore, witnessing a change in contract obligations may be very different to an understanding that one's PC has been breached. A change in circumstances may bear new light on the situation and a reevaluation that eliminates any concern of PC breach. Inevitably, this can also work the other way and if one's expectations are changed for the worse through the revelation of new information, lack of progress, or weak communication processes, there is a greater prospect of PC breach occurring. Moreover, this represents a contract change and moves expectations by either increasing or decreasing what is expected of the employer. In contrast, a contract breach arises where there is a discrepancy between what is expected within the confines of the PC as perceived by the individual and what has been delivered (Rousseau, 1995).

Evidence suggests that there is a temporal element that intervenes in this relationship, indicating that there are greater expectations of employers over time. Based on the tenets of social exchange theory (Blau, 1964) and the reciprocal principle, through the lens of an employee, employer-based obligations increase as time progresses (i.e. De Vos, 2005; De Vos et al., 2003; Robinson, Kraatz, & Rousseau, 1994; Thomas & Anderson, 1998). As explicated by Robinson et al. (1994), length of tenure increases the expected obligations where a "continued receipt and payment over time tends to increase both the number and diversity of obligations between parties in an exchange relationship" (p. 139). This also indicates increased expectations from the employee by the employer in this workplace relationship as the connections of that relationship become more deeply intertwined and embedded. This prediction is dependent on the assumption that employees will perceive their length of tenure as an investment in the organization, which subsequently will increase their felt obligations from the organization itself, acting as the return element of the social exchange relationship.

11.2.1 The Role of Trust

Although we have considered trust in a much deeper context in Chap. 8, its mutual inclusivity and interconnections with the PC denotes that any meaningful discussion of the PC would be incomplete without considering the relationship and its implications. So, the attitude of trust appears once again as it has in other chapters within this text. It is evident how integral this is to all aspects of the employment relationship in its many forms, including organizational justice and how the individual perceives the psychological contract. Employees will be increasingly aware of the organization's perceived obligations to them at a time of change and the ensuing uncertainty which will be a test of any problems arising with trust in the employment relationship. Evidence points toward employees being more vigilant when they have experienced negative consequences from previous change initiatives, such as downsizing, either within their current employing organization or elsewhere. Whether justified or not, within these circumstances it is expected that employees will demonstrate less trust to their new employing organization (Rousseau & McLean Parks, 1992).

Where more dramatic forms of action, including redundancy and reduction in working hours, are a result of the integration, one would expect that this will be a sensitive time that will aggravate negativity from both the financial loss and emotional cost for those leaving the organization. However, we must also consider the impact for those members of the organization who will remain, often referred to as the survivor syndrome. For those employees, there may be consequences to manage, such as increased workload and additional responsibilities to bear at a time when any reduction in trust within the employment relationship will have negative connotations for attitudes and behaviors at work (Cascio, 1993; Hopkins & Weathington, 2006). The knowledge impact is also a downside that is often experienced when there is an exodus of talent, as vital domain-specific knowledge and skills are lost to the organization (Mellahi & Wilkinson, 2010). Typically, within M&A this may be due to downsizing, but also because of migration from the organization by those who are unable to accept the working practices of their new environment.

From an individual's perspective, it is the existence of these complex relationships that will determine the impact of change associated with M&A, and if positivity for both sides of the social exchange relationship is to be retained, then it is crucial that the act of reciprocity is maintained. If this is to occur, trust needs to exist. Trust has been identified as an essential ingredient if obligations are to be discharged through this act of reciprocation on an ongoing basis (Blau, 1964). Conversely, where the reciprocation is challenged and there is discontinuity, the relationship dissipates, and each party will terminate future obligations whether these are expected or not (Robinson, 1996). In this context, trust has been found to be an important mediator between contract breach and work outcomes, such as future contributions to the workplace and withdrawal behaviors (e.g. turnover intentions) as well as positive outcomes including OCB.

11.2.2 Psychological Contract Breach and Violation

In their influential conceptual paper, Morrison and Robinson (1997) developed a model of PC breach and violation. Their offering opens the cognitive process of breach development, presenting the stages from outset through to a point of comparison where the individual will determine whether a breach of contract has taken place. The model moves on to consider a potential step of interpretation that may result in an emotional reaction to the breach, which, if established, is deemed to be a perceived violation of contract. It must be recognized that not all cases of perceived contract breach will progress to the stage where it is believed there has been a violation. The development of psychological contract breach is germane to both transactional and relational contracts and is dependent on each party's perception of the balance of benefits provided and promised compared to the level of their own contributions. From the employee's perspective, this is contingent on how well they perceive that the organization has fulfilled their promises and, importantly, any potential misunderstanding in what exactly the organization is expected to deliver.

The framework provides an opportunity to investigate the expectations of the individual in terms of their PC with the organization. Up to and including the point of perceived contract breach, the model breaks down the activity into three stages, and these are portrayed in Fig. 11.1. It suggests that each of the three stages is critical if the perceived breach of contract is to be managed and perhaps even mitigated altogether. The factors recognized as being contingent to a perceived unmet promise being developed are highlighted in stage 1. It is then at stage 2 where the employee will enter into a period of comparison to reflect on whether the unmet promise is identified as a perceived breach of contract. The strength of this relationship will be moderated by other factors that affect the salience of the transgression and how vigilant the employee is in identifying it. It is therefore worthwhile to spend some time considering how these stages can be managed.

The model tells us from the outset that if the individual perceives a misalignment between some expectation and the actual experience, then they will enter a period of consideration and interpretation. This cognitive process begins with reflection on whether the disagreement entails an actual reneging of a promise or a misunderstanding or misinterpretation of events. The distinction between the two can be considered critical because a reneging may involve a conflict with the promissory element of the contract, whereas a simple misunderstanding would be classed as nonpromissory and therefore removes any intentional act of breach.

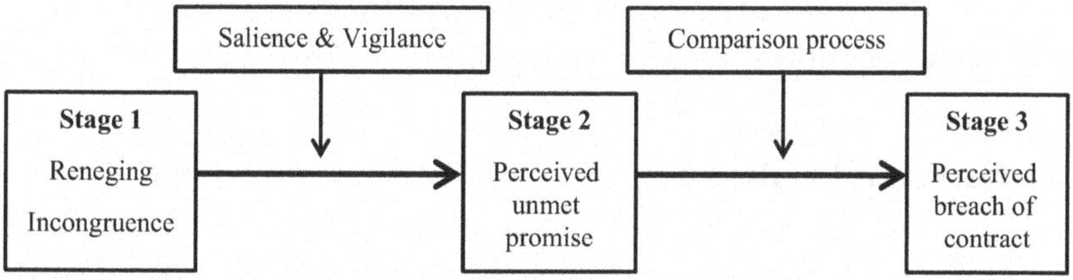

Fig. 11.1 Based on: *The Development of Contract Breach* (Note: From Morrison & Robinson 1997. Adapted with permission)

Morrison and Robinson (1997) go on to expand on these two elements and identify a range of influential factors that exemplify the incidence of both perceived reneging and incongruence by the employee. We need to recognize that while this model and its antecedents of a perceived unmet promise are relevant to all employees of varying lengths of tenure, they will be particularly pertinent to those who are just entering their period of employment and at a stage where their understanding of the new workplace environment will be tested. This should be considered representative and inclusive of those within the workforce who are entering a new environment even if they have been part of the fixtures and fittings for some time. In extreme circumstances and perhaps more representative of employees from an organization that has been acquired, this change may be more radical. In which case, one would consider those employees to be more susceptible to a realignment of their PC with the newly-formed entity.

The idea of reneging on earlier promises is seen as either an inability to fulfill obligations or even unwillingness to do so. Organizations often put themselves under enormous pressure with the offerings promised at the outset of the integration, where it is easier to try and bring existing employees onboard with plans for change by making promises that they will find difficult to fulfill at a later stage. Where industry competition is fierce, early marketization of any new offering may mean promises are made to retain not only the clients and customers, but also vital elements of the workforce that are highly skilled and valued by the organization. There needs to be a realization that these stakeholders may also be highly valued by others. These early promises could be difficult to fulfill and this inability to deliver will be left in the hands of those on the front line (frontline managers, or FLMs), who often find themselves in a situation where they must answer for the perceived reneging on earlier promises by the organization. Developing excessive expectations of employee support is partly dependent on the actual delivery and therefore their behavior is going to be crucial here.

The Nature of PC Breach

The influence of integrity and fairness are also recognized for their contribution in the relationship. Robinson and Morrison (2000) go on to maintain that if an employee feels that they have been treated dishonestly by the organization this will be particularly detrimental to feelings of contract breach and their subsequent reactions to that perceived breach. Evidence of authorities demonstrating either dishonesty or disrespect in communication has been recognized for its important contribution to perceptions of interactional justice (Bies & Moag, 1986) and, in turn, has been identified for its implications toward development of PC breach (Bies & Shapiro, 1988).

Turnley and Feldman (1999) discuss the relationship and consequences of employee voice and the psychological contract. They provide support for the proposition that when some individual feels aggrieved at not receiving genuine voice in the decision-making process, they may also experience a greater intensity of PC breach and assert that voice is "a constructive effort aimed at repairing the employment relationship" (p. 900). Identified as a primary mechanism through which employees can stimulate positive change (Hirschman, 1970), voice can be used to correct perceived injustices in situations where, due to changes in their psychological contracts, employees would normally show resistance to an expected loss of valued rewards (Rousseau, 1995).

Reneging and Incongruence

Morrison and Robinson's (1997, 2000) model of PC breach and violation highlights the individual's evaluation of contract breach and factors that will determine whether this will lead to an emotional reaction of perceived contract violation. An important factor within this cognitive process is whether the employee perceives a breach of their contract is due to either reneging (the conscious breaking of a promise) or incongruence of the perpetrator(s) (a divergence in understanding by the two parties in the employment relationship that have formed the PC).

As Morrison and Robinson recognize in their conceptual approach to the PC, an individual first needs to be aware that their PC has been breached and for this to happen a high level of vigilance will need to be maintained. There are two main conditions forming the antecedents of vigilance as defined in relation to the PC, consisting of the amount of trust that characterizes the employment relationship and the levels of uncertainty surrounding the same relationship. Uncertainty and trust have been discussed in many guises throughout this text in relationship to both organizational change and organizational justice, so we are already aware of their significance. I have also related uncertainty to situations of unpredictability inspired by organizational change and with reference to transformational change and/or frequent change. Therefore, under these conditions individuals will become more vigilant about whether the obligations of their PC with the organization are being met, or indeed whether there is a case for accusations of reneging.

I have also discussed the accepted change in obligations that would not result in perceived PC breach but become much more acceptable to employees in these situations. Obligations that are not entirely aligned due to an incongruence of understanding between the two parties may also become more evident during a time of increased vigilance by the employee, such as during the time of transformational change pertaining to a merger or acquisition. Uncertainty caused by previous bad experiences of change implemented by the organization, or even instigated by an individual's recollection of incidences detached from the current organization, may increase the atmosphere of uncertainty within the present environment. On this basis, we can assume that past experiences will either create or negate uncertainty and make employees either more or less vigilant about the obligations of their PC, resulting in them being better placed to detect any issues of contract breach (Tomprou, Nikolaou, & Vakola, 2012).

Individual Differences

There has been acceptance among those that have made the PC their area of study that it is highly subjective and idiosyncratic in nature (i.e. Rousseau, 1989; Robinson & Morrison, 2000; Shore & Tetrick, 1994). This is confirmed by Sparrow and Cooper (1998), who state that "contracts are portrayed as an individual level phenomenon" (p. 360). While research in this area has been in its infancy (Bellou, 2007), a few studies have investigated the relationship between personality characteristics and perceptual differences in contract breach and violation (see Ho, Weingart, & Rousseau, 2004; Raja, Johns, & Ntalianis, 2004). Other studies have acknowledged the contribution of individuality when considering the impact of the PC in change and personal interpretation and its influence on the variation of how employees perceive and understand the change that is unfolding (e.g. Coyle-Shapiro & Neuman, 2004; Hallier & James, 1997). This is likely to be particularly apt in the circumstances of relational contracts due to these being more open-ended (as opposed to implying a defined term-date of expected reciprocation) and susceptible to individual interpretation (Conway & Briner, 2005; Rousseau 1995; Rousseau & McLean Parks, 1992).

Individual differences that will need to be considered include the smoothness of transition into their new surroundings. This will be affected by their propensity to cope with stress, fear of the unknown, uncertainty of the situation, and the insecurities these will bring (Panchal & Cartwright, 2001). Of course, organizations also need to take into consideration the nature of the change and how it will impact the individual (i.e. differences in perception among those individuals affected by the change). For example, some will be predisposed to exaggerate negative outcomes of the changes from M&A and there will be others who will perceive them as challenges to be embraced because of the potential benefits at both individual and organizational levels (Buono & Bowditch, 1989). There will be a tendency for this characteristic to be dependent on the individual's personality traits.

A factor of significance here that will have a bearing on the evaluation process is how the change outcomes will relate to the individual's values and both short- and long-term goals (Folkman, Lazarus, Dunkel-Schetter, Delongis, & Gruen, 1986). For example, one influence when evaluating whether the change is perceived as a benefit or harm will be the individual's future long-term plans and whether the change will be beneficial or detrimental toward their desired career goals. If the change is perceived as extensive, then it is more likely that those individuals will see challenges in embracing the change and adapting as necessary (Caldwell, Herold, & Fedor, 2004). Those who perceive the change through this lens will be more inclined to see it as introducing new obligations or a lower fulfillment of expected obligations by the organization, which, as a consequence, may trigger thoughts of contract breach and violation (Freese, 2007). So, we can see that the impact of change on individuals is indeed multifaceted and complex to understand because it will depend on personal circumstances, perception, and patterns of reaction to the change.

As individual behavior is informed by experience, so their reaction to change within the organizational context will, to some extent, have a dependency on their previous understanding of past changes or change history. A dependency on the successfulness of past change is discussed by Oreg, Vakola, and Armekanis (2011), who noted that the variability of this within a given group of employees will have some impact, which may be considerable, on their acceptance of new change programs in their working environment. If their previous experiences were negative, this may have undesirable connotations for their current perceptions, particularly if the current change event resembles the previous situation of change. Where this is the case, those who have received exposure to either negative or positive experiences will be influenced in forming important attitudes such as trust of those concerned in implementing the change. Experience will set those individuals in a very different place to their colleagues in relation to evaluating their openness to the change event. Inevitably, this will also bear serious consequences toward either acceptance or some form of resistance to the current change. This can have important reverberations within a team environment where those individuals with previous experience can help to influence the climate of the team and whether they are likely to be persuaded to buy into the change.

The significance of career dedication or focus (i.e. careerism) is also worth considering for its impact on the employment relationship. "Careerism" is a term applied to those who see their current employing organization as a stepping stone to further development along the journey of their wider career trajectory (Rousseau, 1990). The primary focus therefore is not the organization, but their broader career path, which has connotations for the focus of their commitment (i.e. career commitment vs. organizational commitment). From this perspective, individuals in the workplace may have a very different view of change and how this will impact their short- and long-term interests. Change will need to be considered in the round of their overall career plan instead of how this is going to affect their interest within the social context of the organization. For the individual, change may open different opportunities, and, if so, it will be more graciously received. This will be particularly so if the change is perceived as developmental. Rather than being viewed as an obstacle to maintaining predictability and certainty within a routinized work schedule, change may have much wider implications that lead to a much broader and holistic evaluation. It is probable that a careerist will have forged a less relational form of PC with the employing organization, and this is more likely to resemble a contract that is transactional in nature (i.e. based on short-term benefits with little concern of the longer-term implications of that relationship and less dependent on the reciprocation within a social exchange interaction). This also indicates that lower levels of trust will develop with the employment relationship they have formed (Rousseau, 1990). There is supporting evidence pointing toward a more moderate negative impact on the relationship between breach and trust where there are high levels of careerism (Rousseau, 1990). If we are to assume that this will also reduce the tendency for violation of contract to occur and, consequently, any negative emotional responses, then important attitudes such as organizational commitment and job satisfaction are also less likely to be negatively affected (Tomprou et al., 2012).

11.3 Impact on the Employment Relationship

Considering the PC as an element of the employment relationship helps us place this concept within the employee-organization framework. This framework is dynamic and, in addition to being dependent on individual characteristics, will also be contingent on the impact of contextual factors (Rousseau, 1995). Such contextual factors will set the terms and conditions of the employment relationship and help to shape what it becomes and how it is perceived through the lens of those at the center of it. An organization does not operate in a vacuum and will need to be adaptable to its immediate and more long-term environmental factors, and these will include considerations of the economic climate that the organization finds itself in. During a merger, the role for decision-makers will be to identify and account for these factors. Whether the economic climate has changed because of the integration or whether it is a reaction to changing circumstances outside the organization's control, it is expected that tough decisions will mean a reevaluation of priorities. If tough decisions, including reorganization or, more drastically, downsizing, are involved, this may mean a temporary or even permanent suspension of the terms upon which the employment relationship was originally set. This need for flexibility and fluidity is not necessarily agreeable for the employee, and, subsequently, the quality of the employee-organization relationship may suffer (Somaya & Williamson, 2008). This will have important connotations toward employee outcomes, such as employee engagement, job satisfaction, and, from a behavioral perspective, retention of staff (Shore, Tetrick, Taylor, & Coyle-Shapiro, 2004). There is evidence that where economic conditions prevail, these become the immediate focus of organization strategy even though a price to be paid may be the quality of the employee-organization relationship (the employment relationship) (Metz, Kulik, Brown, & Cregan, 2012).

Of course, situational factors pertaining to the organization are not the only consideration in this scenario. For the individual there will be contextual factors to account for, and these will challenge the common assumption that a breach of an individual's PC will automatically lead to reduced employee contributions. As an example, let us consider a period of difficulty, where change may instigate insecurities about the continuation of future employment for individuals involved. A reduction in job security may have a converse affect and encourage those at the center to increase their contribution as those in work begin to see a more competitive and hostile environment beginning to emerge between themselves and their colleagues. The battle for survival may result in fostering a climate where common core instincts are on display and withdrawal behaviors are contained for the time being until more definite plans of the newly-formed organization's future are revealed. With their employment prospects already under scrutiny, individuals may want to reduce further possibilities of jeopardizing these even more. This theory is substantiated by existing research that suggests a positive relationship exists between those who have a feeling of job insecurity and their tendency to demonstrate citizenship behaviors toward the organization (Staufenbiel & König, 2010;

Ye, Cardon, & Rivera, 2012). Inevitably, these senses will be stimulated when those involved feel that their perceived value toward the organization will be diminished when there is no presence or visibility of their OCBs, particularly where colleagues are able to demonstrate their contribution. Where OCB or discretionary behavior is withdrawn, this may influence managers' reward allocation as employees who demonstrate these behaviors are more likely to be rewarded by their line managers (MacKenzie, Podsakoff, & Paine, 1999). Consequently, allocation of rewards will then impact perceptions of perceived fairness.

These feelings are particularly relevant during the period of integration change and how employees react to a perceived breach of PC will be moderated (enabled or disabled) by contextual factors (Johns, 2006). This process of sense-making is impacted by several moderating factors, including how employees perceive their employer has behaved toward them and their colleagues, the perceived justice of the situation, how negatively they view the losses, and, of course, alternative prospects for employment elsewhere (Conway & Briner, 2002, 2009; Robinson & Morrison, 2000).

If we consider the PC in these terms, there becomes an inherent concern about what happens during a period of radical change, such as that inspired by a merger or acquisition. We know that psychological contracts are more prone to a perceived violation during a period of change (Freese, 2007), in part because there is greater difficulty for organizations to continue fulfilling employee expectations to the same level, and perceived obligations are often left unmet. The notion that organizational change often impacts the fulfillment of expected obligations has been substantiated in various studies, particularly where this involves negative and threatening change that comprises downsizing and outsourcing of jobs (see for example Beaumont & Harris, 2002; Ghoshal & Bartlett, 2000). In addition to problems honoring commitments within the realms of job security, other commonly situated examples of reneging on obligations during the process of merger include career opportunities, organizational rewards, communication, and the general social atmosphere within the working environment (Pate, Martin, & Staines, 2000; Turnley & Feldman, 1998). Often, the usual HR practices which bind a number of these expectations together will become no-go areas as structures and systems enter a process of change and, in extremity, are completely removed. Work performed by Freese, Schalk, and Croon (2008) demonstrates that there is not only an increase in perceived contract breach but also an increase in the emotive events of PC violation (identified as the next stage after a perceived breach) during these times of organizational transformation.

11.4 The Nature of Change

Individual circumstances have a significant bearing on the way change is perceived and will predicate a disruption of the psychological contract. I have discussed human differences and how they exacerbate the complexity of understanding employee behavior in relation to their PC at work. However, situational factors and the context of the change are also highly influential factors in these equations and form an important element of the relationship between employee perceptions of change and their current understanding of the PC and the wider employment relationship with the organization. Organizational change has already been discussed in some detail in Chap. 4, but when trying to assess the importance of the PC on employee perceptions of justice, it is necessary to contextualize situational factors (e.g. the scale and type of change) that will also influence perceptions of breach and perhaps violation. For instance, can we identify a scale of change that is typical before attitudes and behaviors begin to be established (e.g. a perceived breach of obligations that leads to feelings of injustice)?

11.4.1 Minor and Major Change

We have considered various forms of change, but with reference to the PC it is helpful to understand how Rousseau (1995) defines this in relation to specific forms of change, such as accommodation and transformational change. Accommodation change is better understood as adjustments that can occur to the current framework through an evolutionary process of change. This form of change is much more gradual and seamless to everyday social processes within the workplace and includes more isolated incidences of change, such as adjustments to performance criteria, benefit packages, working hours, and so on (van der Smissen, Schalk, & Freese, 2013). This type of change will generally be more readily acceptable to most employees than a more transformational form of change, which, typically, is radical in its execution and includes major systemic reorganizations in the working environment, such as downsizing or the introduction of major new HR policies and procedures. A transformational form of change is more likely to have a radical impact on the employee over a short period of time and is more akin to that experienced in some forms of M&A.

It is helpful to distinguish between the features of accommodation change and more transformational forms through the lens of frameworks proposing planned and emergent models of change. Transformational change is described as likely to impact the social systems through organizational structure and culture, which will be much more fundamental to daily routines than the more sedate pace of incremental (or planned) change. Planned forms will normally be implemented over longer timescales and have less chance of being noticeable to operational functioning. While this form of change program may result in similar levels of change within the organization overall, it is at a much slower pace and is often perceived as continuous rather than perceived as a single episode of change (episodic change). Dahl (2011) has also attempted to add another dimension to these definitions, which may help to further illuminate the nuances involved by referring to them as broad and extensive (transformational and episodic) versus narrow and small (planned and incremental).

11.4.2 Frequency of the Change

As referred to earlier, transformational change is less likely to happen on a frequent basis, whereas incremental, or stepped, change may take place over a period either with pauses in between or at a more continuous pace. The frequency of change is an important factor that can be influential in the evaluation process and subsequent outcomes that lead to either acceptance or resistance. Several studies have argued the case that at an individual level employees are more prone to influence and concern about change that happens on a frequent basis (even if the changes being imposed are small) rather than sporadic events of change (e.g. see Smollan, Sayers, & Matheny, 2010; Rafferty & Griffin, 2006). These studies found that people grow tired of continual change and being confronted by it, resulting in a disposition of feeling overwhelmed and, subsequently, leading to greater levels of anxiety being experienced by those recipients.

This feeling of being overwhelmed by continuous change can also raise detrimental consequences for their PC with the organization. As Freese (2007) purports, if change is able to raise serious questions about the nature of the PC and its disposition in the relationships between individuals and their employing organization, then it seems logical that the more often they are faced with a period of change, the more it is expected to impact the PC and any consequential behavioral tendencies of those employees. This relationship can only develop more harmful atmospheres where unpredictability, uncertainty, and resulting employee anxiety are a constant threat in the working environment because of those frequent and impactful changes (Rafferty & Griffin, 2006).

Earlier, we considered how the employee's previous experiences of transformed personal circumstances (even relating to a different time and place) affect how they perceive change within their current time period. This encounter may relate to similar circumstances (e.g. another merger at a different organization) or just the impression left from having been through a period of transformational change that had tendencies similar to the one currently being experienced. However, in addition to the individual's past experiences there will be intense interest in any similar situational experiences that the current employing organization(s) have engaged with in the past. For example, it is commonplace for an organization entering a period of merger to have a previous record of integration(s) (or even a serial record of multiple mergers). In which case, individuals will seek information about how the change was handled on previous occasions and resulting outcomes and impact for stakeholders of the merging entities (e.g. what were the priorities of merger strategy). For example, how did they treat the employees in the merging organizations? Did they demonstrate leadership in the negotiations with their merger partner and, importantly here, did they have to renege on their obligations to their own employees, and was this understandable due to the circumstances, or was it willful neglect of those obligations? If previous examples of the process were deemed successful, then this may act as a key moderator in the relationship of how change is assessed and its likely impact on the psychological contract. Consequently, if stories of previous change events raise concerns or doubts, this may be liable to impact the motivation of current employees, encouraging negative behaviors toward any current or future change (Reichers, Wanous, & Austin, 1997; Wanous, Reichers, & Austin, 2000).

This demonstrates that where the frequency of change is high, it is even more important that previous examples of change are positive and point employees toward a perception that, once again, this is more likely to lead to positive outcomes for them, reducing uncertainty and potential anxiety, and have less chance of negatively encroaching on their PC (Akhtar, Bal, & Long, 2016). Of course, we need to also bear in mind that reporting of bad experiences will need to be managed for their negative connotations to avoid provoking forces of resistance to change developing.

11.5 Case in Question

11.5.1 Relationships with Psychological Contract Breach

Commonalities emerged from the interviews conducted in Phase 2 that were crucial to the outcomes of the current study. Five aspects of organizational justice were recognized as having a major influence on employees' opinions of the merger process, and each was identified for its relationship with the individual's perception of PC breach. These propositions were formulated to provide hypotheses 1 to 5. It may be worth noting that the following were the independent variables in each case: (i) *justification of the communicated message*, (ii) *voice* (process control), (iii) *distribution of outcomes*, (iv) *honest treatment*, and (v) *respectful and dignified treatment*. Each proposition stated that employees' experience of these five organizational justice variables would be significantly related to their experience of PC breach as an outcome of the merger.

Rousseau (1989) defines PC breach as one party providing a contribution for a promise of future returns, and there is then a belief that an obligation to provide those future returns has been created. For those at the premerger business school, the change in strategic focus that impacted publishing strategy was an act of PC breach, but, as asserted by Bellou (2007), in the event of a merger the initial contract formation ceases to exist. This proposition is supported by Baruch and Hind (1999) that in organizational restructuring the old contract is simply replaced, supported by the notion that employees will enter into a risk analysis and self-appraisal where they will then decide whether to form a new contract with their employer (Cartwright & Cooper, 1992). This period of reflection was detected in many of the conversations conducted during the Phase 2 interviews where, as a sign of their resistance to change, several staff stated they were considering their options with some signifying an intention to leave the organization.

Following a merger or acquisition, for a new contract to be formed the employee will need to enter into a process resembling socialization where trust and communication become two crucial factors in the binding relationship of the new contract (Hubbard, 2001). Conversely, the trust that employees held in their leadership from the premerger business school had been affected because of the changing nature of their organization's identity and strategy, and therefore this emphasizes some of the difficulties they were experiencing with the socialization process and considerations of whether to form a new PC with the merged business school. These factors were also extremely important to employees from the premerger management college, but their perception differed considerably. Although matters of PC breach were even more considerable for these employees, this was related to issues with the merger process and interactional issues with the current leadership. Because these factors were based on the principles of social exchange, they affected their relational contract with the organization and went to the heart of their commitment in that exchange contract.

Interestingly, an outcome from those employees who had experienced a history of PC violations was that they were more likely to switch to a transactional form of contract rather than pursuing a relational form of contract. The loss of trust meant that the relationship was reduced from one that was dependent on an interaction based on social exchange toward a more formal contract based on economic exchange, or a focus on the extrinsic benefits of continuing in the role. The employment relationship had been devalued to a more formal and mechanistic format that was dependent on transactions rather than a more interactive social form of relationship.

11.5.2 Organizational Justice and the Employment Relationship

For any organization embarking on a merger or acquisition strategy, this study has demonstrated that the concept of fairness as perceived by the employee is of considerable importance to the judgments they will make. These judments are not confined to the distributions they will receive from change but also the judgments they will make of the change agents responsible for those decisions and how effectively they have been implemented. While fairness of distributions are a primary concern, fairness in the process that determines those distributions and the communication strategy through which the employee will be informed are also a key determinant of this process. These are important considerations for the organization because of the affect perceived fairness will have on employee attitudes and behaviors, and the subsequent impact this will have on the organization itself and those working within. The significant relationship supported between organizational justice and PC breach is of concern for the organization. It has been demonstrated that the PC is based on a reciprocal relationship forming a common bond between an employee and the organization, and that breach is also related to negative workplace attitudes and behaviors (e.g. see Robinson & Morrison, 1995; Turnley, Bolino, Lester, & Bloodgood, 2003).

References

Akhtar, M. N., Bal, M., & Long, L. (2016). Exit, voice, loyalty, and neglect reactions to frequency of change, and impact of change. *Employee Relations, 38*(4), 536–562.

Argyris, C. (1960). Organizational effectiveness under stress. *Harvard Business Review, 38*(3), 137–146.

Baruch, Y., & Hind, P. (1999). Perpetual motions in organizations: Effective management and the impact of the new psychological contracts on survivor syndrome. *European Journal of Work and Organizational Psychology, 8*(2), 295–306.

Beaumont, P. B., & Harris, R. I. (2002). Examining white-collar downsizing as a cause of change in the psychological contract: Some UK evidence. *Employee Relations, 24*(4), 378–388.

Bellou, V. (2007). Psychological contract assessment after a major organizational change: The case of mergers and acquisitions. *Employee Relations, 29*(1), 68–88.

Bies, R. J., & Moag, J. F. (1986). Interactional justice: Communication criteria of fairness. In R. J. Lewicki, B. H. Sheppard, & M. H. Bazerman (Eds.), *Research on negotiations in organizations* (Vol. 1, pp. 43–55). Greenwich, CT: JAI Press.

Bies, R. J., & Shapiro, D. L. (1988). Voice and justification: Their influence on procedural fairness judgments. *Academy of Management Journal, 31*(3), 676–685.

Blau, P. (1964). *Exchange and power in social life*. New York: Wiley.

Boswell, W. R., Shipp, A. J., Payne, S. C., & Culbertson, S. S. (2009). Changes in newcomer job satisfaction over time: Examining the pattern of honeymoons and hangovers. *Journal of Applied Psychology, 94*, 844–858.

Buono, A. F., & Bowditch, J. L. (1989). *The human side of mergers and acquisitions*. San Francisco: Jossey-Bass.

Caldwell, S. D., Herold, D. M., & Fedor, D. B. (2004). Toward an understanding of the relationships among organizational change, individual differences, and changes in person-environment fit: A cross level study. *Journal of Applied Psychology, 89*(5), 868–882.

Cartwright, S., & Cooper, C. L. (1992). *Mergers and acquisitions: The human factor*. Oxford, UK: Butterworth-Heinmann.

Cascio, W. F. (1993). Downsizing. *Academy of Management Executive, 7*, 95–104.

Chao, G. T., O'Leary-Kelly, A. M., Wolf, S., Klein, H. J., & Gardner, P. (1994). Organizational socialization: Its content and consequences. *Journal of Applied Psychology, 79*, 730–743.

Conway, N., & Briner, R. B. (2002). A daily diary study of affective responses to psychological contract breach and exceeded promises. *Journal of Organizational Behavior, 23*, 287–302.

Conway, N., & Briner, R. B. (2005). *Understanding psychological contracts at work: A critical evaluation of theory and research*. Oxford: University Press.

Conway, N., & Briner, R. B. (2009). Fifty years of psychological contract research: What do we know and what are the main challenges? *International Review of Industrial and Organizational Psychology, 21*, 71–131.

Conway, N., & Coyle-Shapiro, J. A. M. (2012). The reciprocal relationship between psychological contract fulfillment and employee performance and the moderating role of perceived organizational support and tenure. *Journal of Occupational and Organizational Psychology, 85*(2), 277–299.

Coyle-Shapiro, J. A.-M., & Neuman, J. H. (2004). The psychological contract and individual differences: The role of exchange and creditor ideologies. *Journal of Vocational Behavior, 64*, 150–164.

Dabos, G. E., & Rousseau, D. M. (2004). Mutuality and reciprocity in the psychological contracts of employees and employers. *Journal of Applied Psychology, 89*(1), 52–72.

Dahl, M. S. (2011). Organizational change and employee stress. *Management Science, 57*(2), 240–256.

De Vos, A. (2005). The psychological contract of organizational newcomers: An investigation of antecedents and changes over time. *International Journal of Human Resources Development and Management, 5*, 371–388.

De Vos, A., Buyens, D., & Schalk, R. (2003). Psychological contract development during organizational socialization: adaptation to reality and the role of reciprocity. *Journal of Organizational Behavior, 24*(5), 537–559.

Dugoni, B. L., & Ilgen, D. R. (1981). Realistic job previews and the adjustment of new employees. *Academy of Management Journal, 24*, 579–591.

Folkman, S., Lazarus, R., Dunkel-Schetter, C., Delongis, A., & Gruen, R. (1986). The dynamics of a stressful encounter: Cognitive appraisal, coping, and encounter outcomes. *Journal of Personality and Social Psychology, 50*, 992–1003.

Freese, C. (2007). *Organizational change and the dynamics of psychological contracts: A longitudinal study*. PhD thesis, Tilburg University, Tilburg.

Freese, C., Schalk, R., & Croon, M. A. (2008). Schending van het psychologisch contract tijdens organisatieveranderingen. *Tijdschrift voor HRM, 4*, 49–66.

Ghoshal, S., & Bartlett, S. (2000). Rebuilding behavioral context: A blueprint for corporate renewal. In M. Beer & N. Nohria (Eds.), *Breaking the code of change*. Boston: Harvard Business School Press.

Hallier, J., & James, P. (1997). Management enforced job change and employee perceptions of the psychological contract. *Employee Relations, 19*(3), 222–247.

Hirschman, A. O. (1970). *Exit, voice, and loyalty: Responses to decline in firms, organizations, and states*. Cambridge, MA: Harvard University Press.

Ho, V. T., Weingart, L. R., & Rousseau, D. M. (2004). Responses to broken promises: Does personality matter? *Journal of Vocational Behavior, 65*(2), 276–293.

Hopkins, S. M., & Weathington, B. L. (2006). The relationship between justice perceptions, trust, and employee attitudes in a downsized organization. *The Journal of Psychology, 140*, 477–498.

Hubbard, N. (2001). *Acquisition strategy and implementation.* Basingstoke, England: Palgrave.

Hui, C., Lee, C., & Rousseau, D. M. (2004). Psychological contract and organizational citizenship behavior in China: Investigating generalizability and instrumentality. *Journal of Applied Psychology, 89*(2), 311–321.

Johns, G. (2006). The essential impact of context on organizational behavior. *Academy of Management Review, 31*, 386–402.

Lester, S. W., Kickul, J. R., & Bergmann, T. J. (2007). Managing employee perceptions of the psychological contract over time: The role of employer social accounts and contract fulfilment. *Journal of Organizational Behavior, 28*, 191–208.

Levinson, H., Price, C. R., Munden, K. J., & Solley, C. M. (1962). *Men, management, and mental health.* Cambridge, MA: Harvard University Press.

MacKenzie, S. B., Podsakoff, P. M., & Paine, J. B. (1999). Do citizenship behaviors matter more for managers than for salespeople? *Journal of the Academy of Marketing Science, 27*, 396–410.

Major, D. A., Kozlowski, S. W. J., Chao, G. T., & Gardner, P. D. (1995). A longitudinal investigation of newcomer expectations, early socialization outcomes, and the moderating effects of role development factors. *Journal of Applied Psychology, 80*(3), 418–431.

Mellahi, K., & Wilkinson, A. (2010). Slash and burn or nip and tuck? *The International Journal of Human Resource Management, 21*, 2291–2305.

Metz, I., Kulik, C. T., Brown, M., & Cregan, C. (2012). Changes in psychological contracts during the global financial crisis. *International Journal of Human Resource Management, 23*(20), 4359–4379.

Morrison, E. (1993a). Longitudinal study of the effects of information seeking on newcomer socialization. *Journal of Applied Psychology, 78*(2), 173–183.

Morrison, E. (1993b). Newcomer information seeking: Exploring types, modes, sources, and outcomes. *Academy of Management Journal, 36*(3), 557–589.

Morrison, E. W., & Robinson, S. L. (1997). When employees feel betrayed: A model of how psychological contract violation develops. *The Academy of Management Review, 22*(1), 226–256.

Oreg, S., Vakola, M., & Armekanis, A. (2011). Change recipients' reactions to organizational change: A 60 year review of quantitative studies. *Journal of Applied Behavioral Science, 47*(4), 461–521.

Panchal, S., & Cartwright, S. (2001). Group differences in post-merger stress. *Journal of Managerial Psychology, 16*(6), 424–433.

Pate, J., Martin, G., & Staines, H. (2000). Exploring the relationship between psychological contracts and organizational change: A process model and case study evidence. *Strategic Change, 9*(8), 481–493.

Rafferty, A. E., & Griffin, M. A. (2006). Perception of organizational change: A stress and coping perspective. *Journal of Applied Psychology, 91*(5), 1154–1162.

Raja, U., Johns, G., & Ntalianis, F. (2004). The impact of personality on psychological contracts. *Academy of Management Journal, 47*, 350–367.

Reichers, A., Wanous, J., & Austin, J. (1997). Understanding and managing cynicism about organizational change. *The Academy of Management Executive, 11*(1), 48–59.

Robinson, S. L. (1996). Trust and the breach of the psychological contract. *Administrative Science Quarterly, 41*, 574–599.

Robinson, S. L., Kraatz, M., & Rousseau, D. M. (1994). Changing obligations and the psychological contract: A longitudinal study. *Academy of Management Journal, 37*, 137–152.

Robinson, S. L., & Morrison, E. W. (1995). Psychological contracts and OCB: The effect of unfulfilled obligations on civic virtue behavior. *Journal of Organizational Behavior, 16*, 289–298.

Robinson, S. L., & Morrison, E. W. (2000). The development of psychological contract breach and violation: A longitudinal study. *Journal of Organizational Behavior, 21*(5), 525–546.

Rousseau, D. M. (1989). Psychological and implied contracts in organizations. *Employee Responsibilities and Rights Journal, 2*(2), 121–139.

Rousseau, D. M. (1990). New hire perceptions of their own and their employer's obligations: A study of psychological contracts. *Journal of Organizational Behavior, 11*, 389–400.

Rousseau, D. M. (1995). *Psychological contracts in organizations: Understanding written and unwritten agreements*. Newbury Park, CA: Sage.

Rousseau, D. M., & McLean Parks, J. (1992). The contracts of individuals and organizations. *Research in Organizational Behavior, 15*, 1–47.

Schein, E. H. (1965). *Organizational psychology*. Englewood Cliffs, NJ: Prentice Hall.

Shore, L. M., & Tetrick, L. E. (1994). The psychological contract as an explanatory framework in the employment relationship. In C. L. Cooper & D. M. Rousseau (Eds.), *Trends in organizational behavior* (pp. 91–109). New York: Wiley.

Shore, L. M., Tetrick, L. E., Taylor, M. S., & Coyle-Shapiro, J. A. M. (2004). The employee–Organization relationship: A timely concept in a period of transition. *Research in Personnel and Human Resources Management, 23*, 291–370.

Smollan, R. K., Sayers, J. G., & Matheny, J. A. (2010). Emotional responses to the speed, frequency and timing of organizational change. *Time Society, 19*(1), 28–53.

Somaya, D., & Williamson, I. (2008). Rethinking the 'war for talent'. *MIT Sloan Management Review, 49*, 29–34.

Sparrow, P., & Cooper, L. (1998). New organizational forms: The strategic relevance of future psychological contracts scenarios. *Canadian Journal of Administrative Sciences, 15*(4), 356–371.

Staufenbiel, T., & König, C. J. (2010). A model for the effects of job insecurity on performance, turnover intention, and absenteeism. *Journal of Occupational and Organizational Psychology, 83*, 101–117.

Thomas, H. D. C., & Anderson, N. (1998). Changes in newcomers' psychological contracts during organizational socialization: A study of recruits entering the British Army. *Journal of Organizational Behavior, 19*, 745–767.

Tomprou, M., Nikolaou, I., & Vakola, M. (2012). Experiencing organizational change in Greece: The framework of psychological contract. *The International Journal of Human Resource Management, 23*(2), 385–405.

Turnley, W. H., Bolino, M. C., Lester, S. W., & Bloodgood, J. (2003). The impact of psychological contract fulfilment on the performance of in-role and organizational citizenship behaviors. *Journal of Management, 29*(2), 187–206.

Turnley, W. H., & Feldman, D. C. (1998). Psychological contract violations during corporate restructuring. *Human Resource Management, 37*, 71–83.

Turnley, W. H., & Feldman, D. C. (1999). The impact of psychological contract violations on exit, voice, loyalty, and neglect. *Human Relations, 52*, 895–922.

Turnley, W. H., & Feldman, D. C. (2000). Re-examining the effects of psychological contract violations: Unmet expectations and job dissatisfaction as mediators. *Journal of Organizational Behavior, 21*(1), 25–42.

Van der Smissen, S., Schalk, R., & Freese, C. (2013). Contemporary psychological contracts: How both employer and employee are changing the employment relationship. *Management Revue, 24*(4), 309–327.

Wanous, J. P. (1977). Organizational entry: Newcomers moving from outside to inside. *Psychological Bulletin, 84*, 601–661.

Wanous, J. P., Reichers, A. E., & Austin, J. T. (2000). Cynicism about organizational change: Measurements, antecedents and correlates. *Group & Organization Management, 25*, 132–153.

Ye, J., Cardon, M. S., & Rivera, E. (2012). A mutuality perspective of psychological contracts regarding career development and job security. *Journal of Business Research, 65*, 294–301.

12

Conclusion

12.1 Introduction

A significant rise in the completions of merger and acquisition (M&A) over the past 25 years has also meant that organizations have had to encounter several substantive barriers while embracing this often-radical form of change. These are the issues that have laid the foundations for this text and the study of organizational justice within a climate of M&A. Through both the academic and practitioner lens it is important to ascertain and understand the origins of these barriers. In doing so, the psychological concept of perceived organizational justice has been identified as having a central role in shaping employee attitudes and behaviors within this context. Although there is a body of existing literature that has studied the psychological concept of justice and its influential presence in alternative situations of change, the concept of perceived fairness and its implications for employees are less well known within the specific change context of a merger or acquisition. The study presented in this text, investigating the psychological processes of fairness, will raise awareness for the practicing manager of their significance and influence in the evaluation of change and any subsequent implications for the organization while in pursuit of integration objectives. The academic contribution

N. Jackson, *Organizational Justice in Mergers and Acquisitions*,
https://doi.org/10.1007/978-3-319-92636-0_12

improves current knowledge about the important psychological concept of perceived fairness by identifying and exploring its dynamic relationships and considering their impact on employee attitudes and behaviors during the change processes encountered through M&A.

The study was designed to start addressing a need to develop our understanding of fairness and its role in the practice of M&A. In this concluding chapter, consideration is given to outcomes from the study in light of their inferences for current theory, followed by an account of the practical implications of the research. First, there is an overview of the study findings.

12.2 Overview of Findings

12.2.1 A Summary of the Main Findings

I begin by briefly setting out and illustrating the main findings to emerge from the study:

1. Three aspects of the business school merger were influential in developing employee opinion, and how this was interpreted happened to be dependent upon which premerger organization the employees originated from. This shaping of opinion was responsible for a great deal of the divisive atmosphere upon which employee perceptions of fairness were based. The three aspects were as follows:
   (i) The relative power and status of the organizations
   (ii) The strength of cultural cohesiveness and organizational identity
   (iii) An incompatible implementation strategy (i.e. hard/controlling for processes, soft/avoiding for human integration)
2. Interactional justice was the dominant form of experienced injustice which can be mainly attributed to issues of trust and communication between employees and authorities. The felt injustice can be related to a breakdown in the social exchange and a perceived reneging of the relational aspect of the psychological contract. From the findings of this research, the exchange of interpersonal

relationships between employee and authorities during a merger is a primary cause of perceived injustice.

3. Evidence from this study demonstrates that during M&A it is common for employees to form feelings of injustice simultaneously with a perception of psychological contract breach. It is likely that the exceptional circumstances created by a merger, where it is perceived that a new contract is formed along with the development of the new organization, is responsible for the prominence and proximity of this relationship.

These important findings have been identified in this study and are considered more specifically throughout the remainder of this chapter.

The results from the Phase 1 survey were emphatic in their portrayal of a workforce that recognizes all three dimensions of fairness as a critical factor in its judgment: outcomes from the merger, the decision-making process upon which those outcomes were determined, and the methods of their communication. In the contextual setting of this survey, organizational justice was compared to two other critical factors (culture and identity) for which there is already substantial and conclusive evidence supporting their influence on employee behavior within a merger context. In both cases, perceived justice was found to be of greater importance to the individual, a finding that is central to the outcomes of this study. These findings were substantiated in the Phase 2 interview conversations.

Once the significance level of fairness had been established, the next series of questions related to how the individual perceives this concept, what is the role of each of its three dimensions, and how do they interact with each other and their antecedents? At the business school the most significant dimension of fairness was procedural justice, and this was stimulated by major concerns over the process used to implement the merger. Unfair distributions were the main concern at both campuses but in each case these perceived inequities could have been partly mitigated by the procedures and interactions employed in the implementation and distribution of these outcomes. However, the leadership fell far short of requirements and exacerbated a situation in the methods that they used. It was quite evident that any preimplementation planning had not considered several factors elementary to any general change program, but also some specific to the dynamics of a merger or acquisition.

These factors, identified in this study as the five main pillars of influence in the development of perceived organizational justice, consisted of the following: (i) expectation, (ii) control, (iii) social exchange, (iv) trust, and (v) values. Findings from the study identified that the effect of a diminution in any of these five pillars resulted in psychological contract breach for the employee. Change instigated a level of uncertainty, which led to a need for control and efforts from employees to maintain a status quo in their daily routines. The withdrawal of benefits led to a perceived decrease in their levels of control (compounding uncertainty) and to a radical change in the social setting at the premerger management college. This also impacted cultural values and an attachment to the organizational identity and, in some cases, its relationship with personal identity.

12.2.2 A Model of Justice and Its Antecedents

At this stage it is useful to draw together the conclusions of the research and form an impression of the broad findings from the study. This is demonstrated in Fig. 12.1.

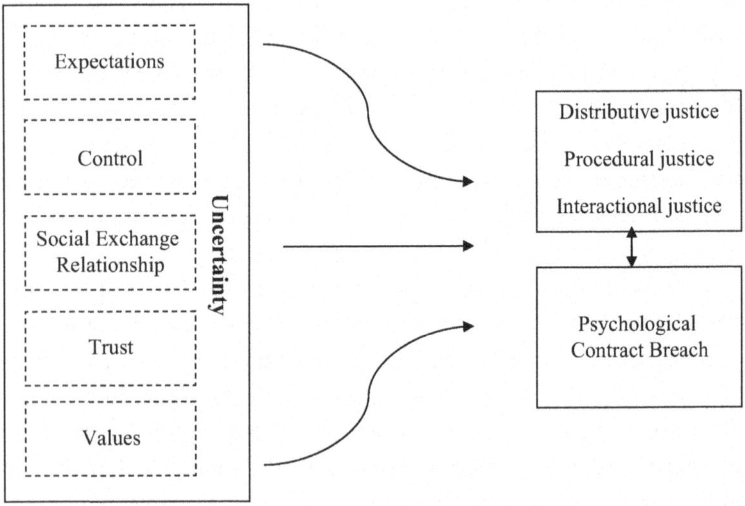

Fig. 12.1 The five antecedents of perceived justice during a merger

The model demonstrates that each of the five Level 1 antecedents is depicted with dashed boundaries, which represent the fact that they do not act independently in their influence of organizational justice but are interrelated and often unified in their actions. This is exhibited in the final template of themes to emerge from the study, which demonstrates 'distrust' as a subtheme of expectations, control, and social exchange relationships, and 'voice', which becomes a subtheme of both Level 1 themes, expectations, and control. When considering the model, it is important to understand that each of the five Level 1 themes is a representation of the many complex relationships underpinning it. Equally, their level in the hierarchy does not necessarily indicate a degree of greater importance in the relationship with organizational justice. Each theme and its hierarchy of subthemes are therefore highly interdependent and the dynamics of their relationships remain multifaceted.

The level of uncertainty that is affected by the presence of each of the five antecedents also has a dynamic influence in their relationship with organizational justice, and this is acknowledged in the model. Finally, the multidirectional relationship between organizational justice and psychological contract breach was identified in the Phase 2 interviews, and its significance was supported in the Phase 3 and 4 surveys.

12.3 Implications of the Findings for Current Theory

One of the main findings to emerge from this study was that although there were many commonalities among employees from both parties about the principal factors of fairness, organization-specific attributes of the merger were responsible for very different perspectives taken toward forming those perceptions. After reviewing the current literature, it can be observed that there has been a tendency to overlook this more nuanced approach. It is evident that in relation to organizational justice a more idiosyncratic approach that recognizes the complex relationships attached to previous experience from culture, identity, and support within the organization needs to be taken. While the formation of culture and identity is complex, how one forms a perception of justice needs to be recognized as exceptional and for its capacity to be inimitable. It is proposed that findings from the current study in relation to organization and integration specific attributes and the dynamics of perceived fairness within this context are entering a new field and should be considered as an important contribution of the research.

Three specific elements of the business school merger can be identified for producing differentiating contextual features that were central to shaping employee perceptions of the change. Each is considered for their contribution to forging a better understanding of organizational justice during organizational integration.

1. The size of each organization in its premerger capacity had implications for the perceived balance of power, which appeared to have influence on the recognition of control and, subsequently, the effect of employee voice. Although status has previously been identified as an important contributing factor toward the development of identity in a merger or acquisition, it has also been recognized in this study as a principal factor in forming perceptions of procedural justice.
2. Recalling Larsson's (1990) three approaches to integration (see Chap. 5), the two-dimensional strategy that was adopted for the integration of processes and people at the business school had the effect of provoking incoherency and confusion. A hard/controlling strategy for the integration of processes and terms and conditions was more akin to the deeper integration of a horizontal or vertical merger model, whereas the stand-off approach for the integration of people emulated a soft/controlling strategy, more suitable for a concentric integration. Birkinshaw, Bresman, and Hakanson's (2000) model stresses the importance of a simultaneous task and human integration strategy if acquisition success is to be achieved. This inconsistency of approach, due to difficulties in identifying a single model of integration, created barriers, raised issues of trust, and, subsequently, affected employee perceptions of both procedural justice and interactional justice. Findings from this research testify that in either an acquisition or merger it is particularly distressing for the organization with lower status or power because they are more likely to be affected by a hard/controlling strategy than the organization that holds the balance of power.

3. A third element of the study that emerges as a differentiating factor between the premerger organizations, and upon which employee perceptions of justice were contingent, was the extent of cohesiveness experienced in their time before the integration. A particularly high level of cohesiveness was demonstrated by employees from the premerger management college, and this was recognized in their significantly higher levels of identity and commitment. It is evident from this study that when higher levels of organizational commitment and identity are associated with feelings of powerlessness or a loss of control, then this is perceived as a threat to their cohesive state and increases their feelings of injustice.

These three differentiating aspects of research conducted at the business school (relative size of organizations, incoherent integration strategy, and level of cohesiveness among employees) provided a contextual basis from which employee perceptions of fair practice during the merger were developed.

As discussed at greater length in Chap. 11, expectations have a pivotal role in the formation of workplace attitudes and behaviors and were one of the principal factors in determining employee perceptions of fairness in the current study. These are now discussed along with the presentation of a theoretical framework capturing the interactions of *a priori* and future expectations.

12.3.1 The Role of Expectation in Fairness

A finding that developed from the Phase 2 interviews was an individual's perception of fairness can be influenced by expectations that have either been established from the past or anticipated from future events. These attitudes and opinions were encouraged by personal beliefs and preferences, and there is evidence that the individual's affective state influenced perception of expectation. Examples of this came from employees who expected new opportunities to develop from the merger and, consequently, were more likely to express feelings of fairness toward the process in general. It is also influenced by experience, and

Table 12.1 Expectation and its role in forming attitudes to fairness

Temporal mode of expectation	Characteristics	Object of expectation
A priori	Built on past experience	Leadership (characteristics, for example style and character) Level of respect Level of trust (see model of trust)
A priori *expectations will also influence affective state, which will affect future expectations*		
Future	May be influenced by past experience and built on desirability of expectations	Opportunities to improve job satisfaction Uncertainty (e.g. job security and safety of environment) Conformity of values (incongruence between personal and organizational values relating to culture and identity)

those familiar with the autocratic leadership of the premerger management college were guided by expectations very different from the democratic leadership style encountered by those employees from the premerger business school.

A framework of expectation depicted by the two dimensions of experience and future predictions is presented in Table 12.1. The framework differentiates between *a priori* expectations, developed from experience, and future expectations, which may also be influenced by experience, but are developed primarily on how the employee perceives his or her pathway to future progress. Experience will also bear consequences for the affective state of the individual and, therefore, within a deductive process, contribute to how they determine projections of the future. With regard to *a priori* expectations, three dimensions were particularly manifest among business school employees, identified in the model as leadership, respect, and trust. The influence of their leadership's past behavior was important to all business school employees, but because the leadership team guiding the process through the merger implementation period originated from the premerger management college, it was these employees who were most likely to harbor preconceived expectations of their leaders' behavior. This is also very true for the dimensions of respect and trust, which have both been discussed, and the model of trust in Chap. 8, Table 8.1, should be referred to. One of the conclusions that can be drawn here is that while an increase in the level of knowledge about leadership and its expected behaviors may increase or reduce levels of uncertainty, it can also influence the affective state of the individual in any projection of future expectations. Whether this will have a positive or negative affect will depend on how the individual perceives the leadership characteristics, which will include both level of respect and level of trust in their reciprocal relationship of social exchange.

As depicted in the framework, it should be added that although future expectations will also be dependent on these perceptions, there are a further three dimensions that were portrayed as important by business school employees in their projections. These were opportunities to improve job satisfaction, and uncertainty, which were, conversely, influenced by knowledge of previous states (e.g. leadership) and the unknown environment that change will bring for the individual. Also, a conformity of values (acknowledged in more detail in Chap. 5) relates to the tensions raised between shifting personal and organizational cultures and identities. As a direct consequence, this had resulted in several staff proposing an intention to leave the new organization.

12.4 Practical Implications of the Study

An aim of the current study was to raise awareness for the practicing manager about the implications of fairness in an M&A climate by recognizing the factors used in its evaluation and any subsequent effect in the workplace. Because of the consistencies found between employee attitudes within both the business school merger and NHS Trust merger, it is feasible that these commonalities can also be considered within the broader remit of the M&A population. With reference to the survey findings, and support from the results of the Phase 2 interviews, a summary of the practical implications of the study is provided.

12.4.1 The Effect on Employee Attitudes and Behavior

The complexity of leading an organization through the transitional change of a merger or acquisition and at the same time remaining focused on the core strategic objectives of the premerger environment has undoubtedly been accountable for some of the concerns raised by employees in relation to their unfair experiences. What often appears as the best path for the survival or sustainability of the organization does not necessarily conform to the interests of the employee, and, subsequently, these disparities often influence negative attitudes and barriers to change. The findings from this study emphasized that while employees from both organizations raised concerns with the fairness of outcomes from the merger (distributive justice), the issues that related most strongly to their attitudes and behaviors were those concerning unfair process (procedural justice) and unfair communication of outcomes (interactional justice).

The quality of leadership and the strategies they design for procedures and communication will influence the attitude and behaviors of their employees, which, as a consequence, will have an impact on organizational outcomes of the integration. The facets of justice causing most anxiety for employees in this study formed damaging relationships with psychological contract breach. There is also support in this research that, in addition to a perception of breach in psychological contract, outcomes of perceived unfair treatment will result in a lowering of affective commitment, an increase in intentions to leave the organization and less of an inclination to work beyond what is required. The inverse of what is required during a period of radical organization change.

Recommendations

Several policy areas identified as influencing these relationships should be considered by practicing managers in the organization's preimplementation merger plan. The three factors outlined below will each have the effect of increasing an employee's perceived level of organizational justice and reducing the negative attitudes and behaviors referred to earlier. It is therefore recommended that all three factors are given careful consideration and mechanisms are provided to develop each as an integral part of the pre- and postmerger implementation plan.

1. Process control (involvement): Allowing employees a voice in the process of determining policies that will affect their role in the merged organization will improve their perception of fair treatment, and, as a consequence, they will be more accepting of any outcomes they receive. It is also an acknowledgment of respect for their knowledge, skills, and abilities, which has been found to improve their levels of self-efficacy at a time when this may be challenged.
2. Justification: Forming part of an effective communications strategy, justification of the decisions made due to the integration provides clarity of reason and purpose. An account of the decision-making process reduces opportunities developing for employee speculation and grapevine activity and, subsequently, reduces subjectivity in their evaluation of fairness. Justification also reduces employee uncertainty by increasing the flow of knowledge about the merger process.
3. Trust in leadership: Sustaining or developing trust in the leadership team should be considered as a further strand of an effective communications strategy. This course of action will be particularly important where

    (a) there is reason to believe that employees' experience will influence a negative judgment about the leadership's abilities or integrity.
    (b) employees are unfamiliar with the leadership, or the leadership remains detached from employees.

In addition to these three policy areas, there is also a need to ensure that the strategy for depth and speed of the merger is consistent for integration of policy and process and the combining of people across both organizations. A situation where many of the operational functions of the two organizations have been integrated and yet there has been little contact between the employees should be avoided because this provides barriers to shaping culture and an entrenchment of their personal and organizational identities with the premerger organizations. There is evidence in this study that it could lead to issues of resentment and noncooperation between staff, which may impede the integration of operational functions.

12.5 Summary

In meeting the research objectives, there have been several important findings to emerge from this research, and it is hoped that it will inspire future discussion about the practices of those agents responsible for designing and implementing M&A activity. It is also hoped that this research begins to fill the large gap in knowledge left unexplored by a distinct lack of empirical research into the behavior of individuals affected by the change processes of a merger or acquisition. In addition, practical implications were discussed, and policy recommendations have also been considered. Recommendations for future research include further work on the effect of communication and trust in leadership on perceived fairness, in addition to further exploring the dynamics of the tripartite relationship between culture, identity, and organizational justice. Because there is an expectation that different situational factors will encourage a variation in the findings, there is also a need to conduct this research within divergent M&A typologies.

References

Birkinshaw, J., Bresman, H., & Hakanson, L. (2000). Managing the post-acquisition integration process: How the human integration and task integration processes interact to foster value creation. *Journal of Management Studies, 37*, 395–425.

Larsson, R. (1990). *Coordination of action in mergers and acquisitions: Interpretive and systems approaches towards synergy*. Lund, Sweden: Lund University Press.

Index

N. Jackson, *Organizational Justice in Mergers and Acquisitions*,
https://doi.org/10.1007/978-3-319-92636-0

The manufacturer's authorised representative in the EU is Springer Nature Customer Service Centre GmbH, Europaplatz 3, 69115 Heidelberg, Germany. If you have any concerns regarding our products, please contact ProductSafety@springernature.com

Printed and bound by CPI Group (UK) Ltd, Croydon, CR0 4YY
05/10/2026
02228128-0012